The Internet, Social Networks and Civic Engagement in Chinese Societies

The Internet in China reflects many contradictions and complexities of the society in which it is embedded. Despite the growing significance of digital media and communication technologies, research on their contingent, non-linear, and sometimes paradoxical impact on civic engagement remains theoretically underdeveloped and empirically understudied. As importantly, many studies on the Internet's implications in Chinese societies have focused on China. This book draws on a variety of theoretical and methodological approaches to advance a balanced and context-rich understanding of the effects of digital media and communication technologies, especially social media, for state legitimacy, the rise of issue-based networks, the growth of the public sphere, and various forms of civic engagement in China, Taiwan, and the global Chinese diaspora. Using ethnography, interview, experiment, survey, and big data, scholars from North America, Europe, and Asia show that the culture and impacts of digital activism depend on issue and context.

This book was originally published as a special issue of *Information, Communication & Society*.

Wenhong Chen is an Assistant Professor in the Department of Radio-TV-Film at the University of Texas Austin, USA. Before joining the faculty she earned her PhD in Sociology from the University of Toronto, Canada, and was a SSHRC postdoctoral fellow at Duke University, USA. Her research has been focused on the social implications of digital media and communication technologies. She has published more than 20 articles, including publications in *Human Communication Research, Journal of the Association for Information Science and Technology, New Media and Society, Journal of Computer-Mediated Communication, The Information Society, Management and Organization Review*, and *Entrepreneurship Theory & Practice*.

Citation Information

The chapters in this book were originally published in the *Information, Communication & Society*, volume 17, issue 1 (February 2014). When citing this material, please use the original page numbering for each article, as follows:

Chapter 7

Expanding civic engagement in China: Super Girl *and entertainment-based online community*
Jingsi Christina Wu
Information, Communication & Society, volume 17, issue 1 (February 2014) pp. 105–120

Chapter 8

Regional variation in Chinese internet filtering
Joss Wright
Information, Communication & Society, volume 17, issue 1 (February 2014) pp. 121–141

Notes on Contributors

Maria Bondes is a Research Fellow at the GIGA Institute of Asian Studies in Hamburg, Germany. Her research centres on popular contention and social movements in contemporary China with a special focus on environmental activism and social media. She is currently writing her PhD thesis in Chinese Studies at Hamburg University on local environmental activism in urban and rural China.

Boris H.J.M. Brummans is Associate Professor at the Département de Communication, Université de Montréal, Canada. He obtained his PhD from Texas A&M University, USA. His research looks at Buddhist organizing in various parts of Asia.

Wenhong Chen is an Assistant Professor in the Department of Radio-TV-Film, College of Communication, at the University of Texas at Austin, USA. She obtained her PhD in Sociology from the University of Toronto, Canada. Before joining the faculty, she was a SSHRC Postdoctoral Research Fellow at Duke University. Her research has focused on the implications of new media and communication technologies in entrepreneurial, organizational, and multi-ethnic settings. Her research has been funded by the Pew Internet and American Life Project, the Social Sciences and Humanities Research Council of Canada, Asia Pacific Foundation of Canada, Advanced Micro Devices, and Bell Canada. Dr Chen's work has appeared in leading journals such as *Human Communication Research, Journal of Association of Information Science and Technology, New Media and Society, Journal of Computer-Mediated Communication, Information, Communication & Society, The Information Society, Computers in Human Behavior, Cyberpsychology, Behavior and Social Networking, Information, Communication & Society, Journal of Broadcast and Electronic Media, Management and Organization Review, Entrepreneurship Theory & Practice, Journal of Small Business Management*, and others.

Pauline Hope Cheong is Associate Professor at the Hugh Downs School of Human Communication, Arizona State University, USA. She obtained her PhD from the Annenberg School for Communication, University of Southern California, USA. Her research focuses on the social and cultural implications of communication technologies, including the examination of religious authority and community.

Yuli Patrick Hsieh is a survey methodologist and digital sociologist in the Program on Digital Technology and Society in the Survey Research Division at the RTI International. His research interests concern the implications of information and communication technologies (ICTs) for social interaction and social relationship, as well as their implications for inequalities regarding social, psychological, and economic well-being. Patrick earned his PhD in Media, Technology, and Society at Northwestern University's School of Communication. He also received a MA in Sociology from the University of Illinois at Chicago and another MA in Social Informatics from Yuan-Ze University in Taiwan.

Ronggui Huang is an Assistant Professor in the Department of Sociology, Fudan University, China. His research interests include Internet and contentious politics, neighborhood governance in China, social capital and social networks.

Jennie M. Hwang is an invited researcher at the Département de Communication, Université de Montréal, Canada. She obtained her PhD from the State University of New York at Buffalo, USA. Her research focuses on the effects of new technologies on individual well-being and learning, as well as children and media.

Meng-Hao Li is currently participating in a doctoral program in the Department of Public Administration at the University of Ilinois, Chicago, USA. Digital inequality, e-government, innovation theory, science policy and social network analysis are among his areas of interest. His research focus aims to understand how technologies are invented and diffused and therefore, influence citizens' political life.

Günter Schucher is a Senior Research Fellow at the GIGA Institute of Asian Studies. He earned his PhD from the University of Hamburg, Department of Chinese Language and Culture, Germany. His research interests include the Chinese labour market, vocational education, social security, industrial relations, and collective action.

Xiaoyi Sun is a postdoctoral fellow in the Department of Public Policy, City University of Hong Kong. She is also a beneficiary of the AXA Research Fund Postdoctoral Grant. Her research interests include urban studies, neighbourhood governance, and environmental activism in China.

Jingrong Tong is a Lecturer in Media and Communication at the University of Leicester, UK. Her research is on the relationship between news/new media and society, with a current focus on online communication analysis, environmental investigative journalism, and how new media technologies shape news media and journalism. Her recent publications include articles on the transformation of journalism and newspapers, investigative journalism, self-censorship, and the media-government relationship in China. She is the author of *Investigative Journalism in China: Journalism, Power, and Society* (2011 and 2012).

Joss Wright is a Research Fellow at the Oxford Internet Institute, University of Oxford, where his research focuses on the themes of privacy enhancing technologies and online censorship, both in the design and analysis of techniques and in their broader societal implications. He obtained his PhD in Computer Science from the University of York in 2008, where his work focused on the design and analysis of anonymous communication systems.

Jingsi Christina Wu is an Assistant Professor of Media Studies at Hofstra University, USA. She received her PhD from the joint programme of Sociology and Communication at SUNY Albany, where her dissertation won the University Distinguished Doctoral Dissertation Award. Her primary research areas include popular culture and politics, human interactions in new media environments, and global media. She teaches and publishes about both the Western media and Chinese media.

Landong Zuo is an IT Consultant and Data Scientist specializing in data mining and Nature Language Processing. His research interests include data integration, analysis, and visualization in the fields of Semantic Web, Linked Data, and Big Data.

Taking stock, moving forward: the Internet, social networks and civic engagement in Chinese societies

Wenhong Chen

Department of Radio-TV-Film, University of Texas Austin, Austin TX, USA

The Internet in China reflects many contradictions and complexities of the society in which it is embedded. Despite the growing significance of digital media and technologies, research on their contingent, nonlinear, and sometimes paradoxical impact on Chinese citizens' civic engagement remains theoretically underdeveloped and empirically understudied. As importantly, many studies on the Internet implications in the Chinese societies have centered on China. This essay introduces seven articles that draw on a variety of theoretical and methodological approaches to advance a balanced and context-rich understanding of the implications of digital media and technologies in China, Taiwan, and the global Chinese diaspora. It further discusses venues for future research, especially studies that take into account the evolving Chinese media landscape and the rise of the mobile Internet, civic and political participation across multiple platforms and their interactions, as well as organizational and interpersonal networks as the state and an emerging civil society inform, empower, and engage one another via digital media.

Taking stock

Almost 600 million of Chinese are connected via a variety of digital media and communication technologies, facilitating self-representation, creative expression, and social and cultural participation. The prevalent political control and aggressive commercialization notwithstanding, a vast, ephemeral, online communicative space has been formed where users comment and discuss public and private affairs, greatly enhancing the individualization of civic engagement while making censorship difficult.

Digital media and technologies increase transparency and enhance the visibility of oppressed groups, in particular in comparison with print and broadcast media under tighter government control (Norris, 2001). A growing number of so-called online mass incidents has been facilitated by social media, especially Sina Weibo – a Chinese micro-blogging service started in 2009. The literature has offered rich account of the esthetics, genres, and strategies of online activism in China (Yang, 2009).

While early studies may have drawn on a simplistic dystopian or utopian framework and pundits have primarily celebrated technological affordance in the forms of Facebook or Twitter revolution, other scholars doubt whether technology *per se* would achieve any genuine political

1

or social changes. Morozov (2011) uses China as a prime counter-example of 'the Dictator's Dilemma'. The lack of Chinese response to the Arab Spring seems to reinforce the notation that China has been successful in harnessing the power of the Internet without significant political changes. On the one hand, the hope that the Internet will automatically bring democracy to authoritarian regimes is slim. On the other hand, despite the prevalent political control, rapid commercialization, and digital divides, digital media provided millions of Chinese opportunities for civic participation (Hassid, 2012).

In this sense, China offers an interesting case to understand the potentials and limitations of digital media and technologies. After all, the extent to which technologies live up to their potential is contingent on the social and institutional contexts as well as how people use them and what they use them for. Despite the growing significance of digital media, research on their contingent, non-linear, and sometimes paradoxical impact on Chinese citizens' civic engagement remains theoretically underdeveloped and empirically understudied. Given its growing significance in the global economy and an inherent tension between the Internet and an authoritarian regime, many studies on the Internet implications in the Chinese societies have focused on China. Addressing these knowledge gaps, this special issue presents seven articles that draw on diverse theoretical and methodological approaches to understand the implications of digital media and technologies in China, Taiwan, and the global Chinese diaspora.

Combining interview and social media data on Tzu Chi Foundation, a large Taiwan-based transnational Buddhist organization active in and beyond the Chinese diaspora, Cheong, Huang, and Brummans demonstrate that information and communication technologies (ICTs) play a critical role in the communicative coproduction and reinforcement of the organization's meaning, value, and mission. Internal and external stakeholders such as organizational leaders, members, and non-members appropriate digital media for both strategic and mundane autocommunicative practices such as archiving and broadcasting the organization's aspiration and accomplishment embedded in its founder's teaching or posting messages and interacting on social media. Cheong, Huang, and Brummans conclude that the ongoing mediated communicative action has become profoundly co-constitutive, giving the organization symbolic meaning and logic to develop a coherent 'virtual self' that helps it stand out in the global spiritual marketplace and contributing to the formation of transnational spiritual ties for global humanitarian work.

The concept of media multiplexity has often been used in research on interpersonal networks or media use (Haythornthwaite & Wellman, 1998). Drawing on data from the Taiwan Social Change Survey, Hsieh and Li evaluate the extent to which online media multiplexity – regularly using multiple types of online media for social interaction – as well as civic talk online with friends in the interpersonal space are related with online expressive political participation such as contacting politicians or expressing political opinions online. Hsieh and Li's findings resonate with existing empirical studies on a positive relationship between Internet use and civic participation in democratic societies (Xenos & Moy, 2007). More importantly, their work expands the existing literature focusing on the relationship between media multiplexity and interpersonal networks to its civic implications by highlighting media multiplexity as a critical link between interpersonal communication in the private space and political participation in the public sphere.

Advancing an emerging literature on Sina Weibo and other Chinese micro-blogging services, three articles in this special issue draw on data collected on Weibo to examine its civic and political implications. Based on a content analysis of more than 4600 Weibo posts, Bondes and Schucher investigate the discourse, composition, and transformation of Sina Weibo discussion on the high-speed train crash near Wenzhou in July 2011. Analyzing 278,980 Weibo posts collected via computational methods on two mass online incidents in 2011, the Wukan case and the Haimen case, respectively, Tong and Zuo assess the effect of Weibo communication on state legitimacy. Huang and Sun examine an issue-based network on Weibo, namely the network between and among the 1840 followers of an activist who uses the Weibo handle – Homeowner Association Communication.

On the one hand, Weibo rapidly expands the alternative public sphere, promotes expression of personal emotion, concerns, and opinion on public affairs, and pushes the government for transparency and accountability. Bondes and Schucher report that the intensive Weibo discussion on the derailed high-speed train triggered broader debates on national issues such as product safety, official corruption, and government transparency. In a similar vein, Tong and Zuo reveal that Weibo discussion on the Wukan case – where villagers protested local corruption, land seizure, and police power abuse – facilitated a rapid diffusion of information and opinions on a politically sensitive event, bypassing the agenda setting and censorship in the mainstream media.

However, both studies caution against celebrating digital media for enabling a self-organized networked form of contentious politics, simply by aggregating and scaling up millions of micro actions from ordinary citizens without conventional organization or a coherent collective identity. In tandem with the existing studies, Bondes and Schucher carefully point out that the lack of organization hindered the transformation of reactive defense such as calling for consumer boycotts to normative political agenda. Without organization, Weibo discussion fades as quickly as it emerges. Interestingly, Bondes and Schucher note that it was Sina Weibo staff who played a role of organizing agent by setting up a page devoted to the train crash.

Adding more cold water, Tong and Zuo's unique two-case comparison reveals that the contour, trajectory and eventual impact of online mass incidents are highly contingent on issue and context. The extent to which local protestors were able to attract attention from national elites and media is crucial for the length and intensity of Weibo discussion, the composition of the participants, as well as the type of claims and demands made. The Wukan case trigged by land seizure quickly gained national attention and thus became more sustainable, led by local and national elites and eventually generated discussions on the political system and development policy. In comparison, the not-in-my-backyard type Haimen case on keeping a polluter out of the city was more transient, led by local elites, and focused on specific local demands.

Rather than the event-based approach adopted by Bondes and Schucher as well as by Tong and Zuo, Huang and Sun use an issue-based approach and analyze the structure of an issue network among homeowner associations and activists. They identify widespread cross-province follower relations in this issue network on Weibo, in stark contrast to the extremely local nature of homeowner associations offline. That is, Weibo facilitates glocalized networks with local embeddedness and global outreach (Chen & Wellman, 2009), allowing homeowner associations and activists to extend their geographic outreach while remaining embedded in local contexts. They further reveal that retweet is related to the number of followers within rather than outside of the issue network. On the one hand, it shows that issue relevance remains important to information diffusion and potential consensus building. On the other hand, it indicates a lack of networks of civic organizations and activists that span both geographic and issue boundaries. The issue network developed and maintained by one individual activist is large, geographically diverse, and active in information diffusion but has a long way to go if compared with Tzu Chi Foundation's mastery of ICTs for organizational communication. Nonetheless, Huang and Sun convincingly demonstrate that digital media allows local actors to form glocalized networks, which may contribute to long-term collective action and activism through organization building and mobilization.

Civic engagement can come from unexpected places and actors. Wu directs attention to the fascinating yet often downplayed relation between entertainment media and civic engagement. She provides a valuable insight on how online discourse centered on entertainment can contribute to an alternative, participatory form of civic engagement. Drawing on content analysis of discussion threads, Wu examines how seemingly apolitical yet public discourse in an online fan community based on *The Super Girl*, one of the most popular reality TV shows developed by Hunan

TV in China, offered opportunities for fans to not only discuss the esthetics of the show but also express concerns and opinions on broader social issues, develop civic values, and practice civic engagement. Most interestingly, when comparing fans' online discussion and the discourse in mainstream newspaper about the show, Wu detects a new journalistic space as professional reporters carved out new freedom – limited and precarious – in their coverage by tacitly citing controversial information or opinion from anonymous 'net pals' that may challenge the authority while protecting themselves from being held directly accountable.

However, both traditional media and the Internet in China were designed to enhance the Party rule and have been under state control. The state has built the 'Great Firewall' – a massive maze of laws, regulations, and administrative practices to monitor and censor Internet service providers and individual users. Many studies have examined the extent to which the government filters or blocks foreign news sites, social media sites, and sites carrying politically sensitive topics. Joss Wright significantly advances this literature through a layered analysis of the policy and technological architecture of the Chinese national-level filtering system and its regional variations by targets, applications, and effects. Conducting innovative experiments that represent a nation-wide remote survey of the filtering experienced by Chinese Internet users, Wright makes visible a 'centrally coordinated, local implemented' censorship mechanism, in which censors prefer misdirection rather than blocking, trying to make users perceive outright censorship as network error.

Moving forward

The Internet in China reflects the many contradictions and complexities of the society in which it is embedded: rapid economic growth accompanied by glaring social inequalities, relative economic freedom parallel to strict political control. The seven articles have made significant contribution to a balanced and context-rich understanding of the implications of digital media and technologies in Chinese societies. They open up promising venues for future research on the contingent and sometimes paradoxical impacts of digital and social media in Chinese societies.

Since China began its ongoing transformation from a command to a market economy in 1978, the state has built its legitimacy on economic growth and political stability. Although upward mobility has become less attainable than it was in the early years of the reform, many citizens, especially members of the new middle class, have benefited from the recent prosperity. Few people see a regime change would be a viable or desirable solution. However, the distribution of the prosperity gained through more than three decades of economic reform has become increasingly uneven. While most protest cases have been driven by narrowly defined socioeconomic or environmental injustice rather than normative political claims and protest participants seek for solutions within the current Chinese political system (Lu, Li, & Chen, 2012), many participants in more recent protests are not necessarily direct victims of injustice or deprivation.

The state has tried to curtail the rising tide of collective action through surveillance, prevention, and intervention. Although collective action challenging the legitimacy of the political power would be harshly suppressed, environmental, livelihood, and civil rights issues have become increasingly tolerated (Hassid, 2012; Yang, 2009). The Chinese government has invested enormous computational and human resources for censorship as well as for influencing public opinion. On the one hand, government censorship has grown more pervasive and aggressive. For instance, starting from late 2012, Weibo service providers have been required to verify the identities of users. While identity verification signals trustworthiness and increases the likelihood of being followed and retweeted, it makes surveillance more convenient. One study of more than two million Weibo posts showed that 4.5% were deleted by the system and about 30% of deletion occurred within 5–30 minutes (Zhu, Phipps, Pridgen, Crandall, & Wallach, 2013). On the other hand, aiming to understand and 'guide' public opinions online, the government hires more than two million people to analyze online public opinions (BBC, 2013) and had opened 176,700 Weibo accounts as of 2012 (Li, 2013).

Technologies are used for surveillance and crackdown as well as mobilization and resistance. A better understanding has to take into account forces at multiple levels including the state, civic organizations and issue networks, and interpersonal ties that affect networked actions by structuring the flow of information and resources. More attention needs to be paid to the evolving Chinese media landscape, the multiple forms and venues of civic and political participation, and individuals' network position in the larger social structure.

A booming economy and an emerging middle class with an unfettered appetite for information and entertainment have enabled the rapid growth and commercialization of the Chinese media industries both online and offline. With growing repertoires of channels, platforms, media multiplexity as well as multidirectional interaction between online and offline media, more studies are needed to examine the implications of digital, social, and mobile media in a Chinese media landscape operating under the double logic of political propaganda and corporate profitmaking. Future research needs to take into account individuals' media use via multiple platforms: digital, traditional, and mobile. Given that 70% of Chinese Internet users use mobile Internet, it is important to study how the personal, pervasive, portable, and perpetual communication accommodated by mobile devices allows users to easily switch between the most private and the most public spaces and helps to give members of disadvantaged social groups a more accessible tool for civic engagement.

As importantly, most studies have examined digital activism rather than civic engagement both online and offline. In particular, it is crucial to investigate the differential manifestation of civic and political participation online and offline and their dynamic interactions with one another, as a joint product of technological empowerment and institutional constraints. A thorny question is slacktivism (Morozov, 2011). Future research needs to explore the underlying institutional, social, and psychological mechanisms that link multi-platform civic engagement and when the Internet serves as a 'safety valve' that allows people to vent anger and reduce their drive for real changes and when it works as a 'pressure cooker' that trigger and intensify action on the ground (Hassid, 2012).

More studies need to look at the glaring gaps and subtle variations in the access, use, and especially the unintended consequences of digital media. Although the digital divides – gaps in Internet access and use – have narrowed in many aspects, more than half of Chinese citizens still do not use the Internet. On top of an online population dominated by better educated and more affluent urbanites, about 5% of Weibo users generated more than 80% of the original posts (Fu & Chau, 2013).

Big data have generated great expectation as well as many concerns on reliability and validity. Big data are not necessarily representative or inclusive, which indeed often have limited information on users' sociodemographic or psychological attributes. Yet such attributes can have great impacts on the circulation and content of Weibo post. As importantly, how individuals interpret their digital appropriations may not be easily accessible via big data. Thus, mixed methods that combine online data with surveys or interviews as well as comparative analysis across multiple cases, media platforms, or societies may help to present a more comprehensive picture with greater depth and granularity.

Combined, the seven articles in this special issue refresh and enrich the existing literature on the transformative power and limitations of the Internet and other media and communication technologies. The research on the Internet in Chinese societies will benefit from and contribute to fundamental debates on social networks, social movement, and social changes that have been central in political science, sociology, and communication and media studies. As Castells (2009) argues, the power relationships embedded in the existing communication networks among media, politics, and businesses are 'programmed' to favor the status quo rather than social change. How the Chinese

Internet paradox evolves will depend on the negotiation between the state and an emerging civil society inform, empower, and engage one another through media and especially digital media.

Acknowledgements

The author deeply appreciates the insight and wisdom shared by Barry Wellman, Stephen Reese, Joseph Straubhaar, and Heidi Campbell in the process of editing this special issue. Without the hard work from the authors and the reviewers, this special issue would not be possible. Special thanks go to Brian Loader and Sarah Shrive-Morrison for their guidance and assistance.

References

BBC. (2013). *China employs two million microblog monitors state media say*. Retrieved from http://www.bbc.co.uk/news/world-asia-china-24396957

Castells, M. (2009). *Communication power*. Oxford: Oxford University Press.

Chen, W., & Wellman, B. (2009). Net and jet: The internet use, travel and social networks of Chinese Canadian entrepreneurs. *Information Communication & Society, 12*(4), 525–547. doi: 10.1080/13691180902858080

Fu, K.-w. & Chau, M. (2013). Reality check for the Chinese microblog space: A random sampling approach. *PloS One, 8*(3), e58356.

Hassid, J. (2012). Safety valve or pressure cooker? Blogs in Chinese political life. *Journal of Communication, 62*(2), 212–230. doi: 10.1111/j.1460-2466.2012.01634.x

Haythornthwaite, C., & Wellman, B. (1998). Work, friendship and media use for information exchange in a networked organization. *Journal of the American Society for Information Science, 49*(12), 1101–1114.

Li, Y. (2013). Number of Gov't Weibo Accounts Soars: Huge growth in official microblogging accounts in 2012 as government seeks better communication with public. Retrieved from http://english.caixin.com/2013-03-28/100507640.html

Lu, X., Li, P., & Chen, G. (Eds.). (2012). *The blue book of China's society: Society of China analysis and forecast (2013)*. Beijing: Social Sciences Academic Press.

Morozov, E. (2011). *The net delusion: The dark side of internet freedom*. New York, NY: PublicAffairs.

Norris, P. (2001). *Digital divide: Civic engagement, information poverty, and the internet worldwide*. Cambridge: Cambridge University Press.

Xenos, M., & Moy, P. (2007). Direct and differential effects of the Internet on political and civic engagement. *Journal of Communication, 57*(4), 704–718. doi: 10.1111/j.1460-2466.2007.00364.x

Yang, G. (2009). *The power of the internet in China: Citizen activism online*. New York: Columbia University Press.

Zhu, T., Phipps, D., Pridgen, A., Crandall, J. R., & Wallach, D. S. (2013). *The velocity of censorship: High-fidelity detection of microblog post deletions*. Ithaca, NY: Cornell University Library. Retrieved from http://arxiv.org/

Transnational immanence: the autopoietic co-constitution of a Chinese spiritual organization through mediated communication

Pauline Hope Cheong[a], Jennie M. Hwang[b] and Boris H.J.M. Brummans[b]

[a]Hugh Downs School of Human Communication, Arizona State University; [b]Département de Communication, Université de Montréal

Information and communication technologies are often cited as one major source, if not the causal vector, for the rising intensity of transnational practices. Yet, extant literature has not examined critically how digital media appropriation affects the constitution of transnational organizations, particularly Chinese spiritual ones. To address the lack of theoretically grounded, empirical research on this question, this study investigates how the Buddhist Compassion Relief Tzu Chi Foundation (Tzu Chi), one of the largest Taiwan-based civil and spiritual nonprofit organizations among the Chinese diaspora, is co-constituted by various social actors as an operationally closed system through their mediated communication. Based on an innovative theoretical framework that combines Maturana and Varela's notion of 'autopoiesis' with Cooren's ideas of 'incarnation' and 'presentification', we provide a rich analysis of Tzu Chi's co-constitution through organizational leaders' appropriation of digital and social media, as well as through mediated interactions between Tzu Chi's internal and external stakeholders. In so doing, our research expands upon the catalogue of common economic and relational behaviors by overseas Chinese, advances our understanding of Chinese spiritual organizing, and reveals the contingent role of digital and social media in engendering transnational spiritual ties to accomplish global humanitarian work.

This article aims to address several prominent gaps in the literature on transnationalism and, in particular, Chinese spiritual transnationalism, by examining the mediated co-constitution of the Buddhist Compassion Relief Tzu Chi Foundation (Tzu Chi), one of the largest Taiwan-based spiritual nonprofit organizations among the Chinese diaspora. With the quickening cadence of globalization, transnational spiritual organizations are growing in significance as they shape the identities and daily practices of migrants around the world. Concomitantly, information and communication technologies (ICTs) play a cardinal role in creating and sustaining the networks of interconnected communities of practice that co-constitute these organizations (Khagram & Levitt, 2008; Levitt, 2003). However, due to a common focus on technological artifacts, extant research tends to overlook the role of mediated communication in this co-constitution.

This knowledge gap is strikingly apparent in Chinese transnational studies, which have privileged the economic and political dimensions of globalization at the expense of analyzing social and spiritual dimensions. Traditionally, these studies have highlighted the interplay between the financial imperatives to migrate and family obligations, suggesting that *guanxi* is valued for cross-border relations, transnational business enterprises (Ong & Nonini, 1997), and entrepreneurial networks (Chen & Wellman, 2009). On the other hand, as Cadge, Levitt, and Smilde's (2011) review showed, research on non-Abrahamic religions in non-US locales remains scant. That is, studies on media and religion published in the last decade have over-emphasized Western religions and concentrated on Judeo-Christianity (Chen, 2007; see also Tracey, 2012), which not only limits our awareness of the great variety of spiritual organizations, but also overlooks the changing spiritual practices of immigrant populations.

Particularly noteworthy is that research on Chinese transnational religious practices has paid comparatively little attention to the role of the internet, although globally dispersed Chinese populations rely on digital media to enable the exchange of various resources and sustain ties to their physical church, *jia,* or spiritual home, thus transcending national borders (see Cheong & Poon, 2009). Most important with regard to the current article is that publications on the renowned Tzu Chi Foundation have primarily attributed the organization's stellar growth to the extraordinary charisma of its founder and leader, Master Cheng Yen. As Huang's (2009) treatise on Tzu Chi's 'transnationalization' suggests, the Master's philosophy of 'humanistic (or engaged) Buddhism' is communicated through various media, including the Tzu Chi website. However, the author did not examine the role of the internet in the organization's overall humanitarian outreach, let alone its role in defining the organization's identity. Chen (2007), on the other hand, showed that Tzu Chi has been resourceful in its media use and adopted a 'macrolevel approach within cultural studies' (p. 187), providing a broad sweep of Tzu Chi's media outlets and content instead of a systemic analysis of its digitally mediated communication. The author drew upon a single interview with the editor-in-chief of Tzu Chi's English quarterly to illustrate how the organization creates its cultural discourse at home and abroad. More recently, Liao (2012) discussed how Tzu Chi's 'multimedia' approach enables Master Cheng Yen's leadership, primarily based on a textual analysis of Tzu Chi's television dramas.

While these studies invite us to think more deeply about the ways a Chinese transnational spiritual organization, such as Tzu Chi, extends its influence through media across borders, they do not theorize or empirically investigate the mediated communication practices that enable the co-constitution of this kind of organization. To address this limitation, this article explores how ICTs are appropriated in Tzu Chi's transnational co-constitution. Digital appropriation includes discursive *reinterpretation*, which implies changes in language associated with the technological artifact, as well as *adaptation*, entailing the modification of both the discourse and use based on the flexibility of the technology to be modified by discovering a latent function or using it in a different way from the one originally conceived (Eglash, 2004). Specifically, the current study examines how Tzu Chi is co-constituted or 'coproduced' as a socio-technical network by different social actors through the appropriation of digital media and mediated communication, including Facebook.

To construct an innovative conceptual basis for this research, we develop a theoretical framework that draws upon Maturana and Varela's (1987) concept of 'autopoiesis', which refers to the idea that living beings are 'continually self-producing' (p. 43; see also Luisi, 2003). That is, within a dynamic network of ongoing interactions, an autopoietic unity emerges, characterized by operational closure in that it reproduces itself through the creation of boundaries with its environment. Accordingly, autopoietic unities are continuously focused on sustaining their own 'sense of self' or 'being', which means that their 'being and doing … are inseparable, and this is their specific mode of organization' (p. 49). The notion of autopoiesis allows us to investigate how the appropriation of digital and social media enables Tzu Chi's enactment within and across Taiwan's borders as a collective 'self' with symbolic and material characteristics, such as a coherent discourse expounding a specific philosophy and recognizable artifacts. Hence, drawing upon a systematic analysis of interview and social media data, we illustrate how mediated interactions enable Tzu Chi's transnational co-constitution by making Master Cheng Yen's humanistic Buddhism present, which provides Tzu Chi members around the world with an inspirational and legitimate basis for their activities.

Tzu Chi offers a compelling case study for our investigation of organized Chinese spirituality in a transnational context, as it is 'simultaneously an intrinsically Taiwanese phenomenon and a cultural deterritorialization' (Huang, 2009, p. 6). While its headquarters are located in Taiwan, Tzu Chi operates in many countries in the Americas, Africa, Europe, and Asia (including Hong Kong, Mainland China, Singapore, Malaysia, Indonesia, Thailand, Japan, and the Philippines). As O'Neill (2010) noted, it is 'the largest non-government organization in the Chinese-speaking world, with 10 million members in more than 30 countries'. 'It is [also] the richest charity in Taiwan, with annual donations of $300 million and an endowment of more than NT $26 billion ($780 million)' (p. 2). Tzu Chi's rapid growth makes its 'concept of universal love and a worldwide program that acts on it ... unprecedented in the Chinese experience' (p. 2).

The organization's humanitarian programs primarily consist of Chinese migrants, middle-class overseas Taiwanese volunteers who gradually develop branches in accordance with 'local culture and social needs and in conformity with the Tzu Chi spirit' (Ho, 2009, p. 140). It defines itself as a volunteer-based, spiritual and welfare organization (Tzu Chi Foundation, 2010a) and was founded as a grassroots women's group in 1966. Inspired by the humanistic Buddhism of her own Master, Cheng Yen established Tzu Chi believing that Buddhism should alleviate spiritual poverty and material deprivation. Organizationally, this belief is translated into the implementation of four missions: charity; medical care; education; and 'humanitarianism', that is, promoting kindness and love through community voluntarism and media (including self-produced publications, radio, TV and internet programs). More recently, Tzu Chi has also started to focus on environmental conservation. As described on its website, the Mandarin word *ciji* ('compassion relief') captures the organization's overall mantra: 'to cultivate sincerity, integrity, faith, and honesty within while exercising kindness, compassion, joy, and selflessness to humanity through concrete actions', to 'promote the universal value of "Great Love"', and to 'fully employ the humanitarian spirit of Chinese culture to its utmost' (see Tzu Chi Foundation, 2011a, para. 2).

By studying the central role of media appropriation in Tzu Chi's worldwide enactment, this article provides valuable insights into the communicative dynamics of a prominent Chinese transnational spiritual organization. While ICTs are usually understood as being rather revolutionary in that they destabilize spatio-temporal orders and hierarchy, our study shows that digital and social media can also afford the sustenance and reinforcement of a spiritual organization by enabling its internal and external stakeholders to coproduce it communicatively as an operationally closed social system in a competitive global environment. Before detailing our study, we develop our theoretical framework in the next section.

Autopoiesis and the communicative co-constitution of transnational spiritual organizations

United in their conviction that communication does not merely happen *in* organizations, but plays an integral role in their continuous making, a number of researchers have studied the communicative constitution of nonprofit organizations (e.g. see Chaput, Brummans, & Cooren, 2011; McPhee & Iverson, 2009). These organizations are often run by employees and volunteers, governed in non-traditional ways, and 'face significant challenges to their existence, let alone success' (Lewis, Hamel, & Richardson, 2001, p. 7). This is especially true for transnational spiritual nonprofit organizations, which need to be sensitive to fulfilling the expectations of external stakeholders and ensure the continued identification and commitment of internal organizational members. Given these challenges, it is important that we examine the emergent ontologies or 'modes of being' (Cooren, Brummans, & Charrieras, 2008) of these organizations, as they are communicatively co-constituted by various social actors via contemporary digital and social media.

To study this phenomenon, we draw on Maturana and Varela's (1987) idea of autopoiesis, which presumes that 'an autopoietic unit is a system that is capable of self-sustaining owing to an inner network of reactions that re-generate all the system's components' (Luisi, 2003, p. 51). Maturana and Varela's (1987) way of looking at the world is useful for our purposes because their perspective focuses on explaining how 'the organization of living things' (p. 33) emerges in ongoing interactions between 'beings' who exist on different levels of aggregation, such as biological cells or human beings, and, by extension, social collectivities, such as groups or organizations.

Looking at a cell's interaction with molecule X, Maturana and Varela (1987) observed that what takes place is 'determined not by the properties of molecule X but by the way in which that molecule is "seen" or taken by the cell as it incorporates the molecule in its autopoietic dynamics'. In other words, the 'changes that occur therein as a result of this interaction will be those changes caused by the cell's own structure as a unity' (p. 52). Moreover, the authors noted that the interactions between autopoietic unities can become recurrent or more or less stable (p. 75). For a given autopoietic unity, the activities of other unities that constitute its environment are thus perturbations that may trigger interior structural changes. Unity and environment are operationally distinct, yet structurally coupled through continuous interactions. Similarly, the autopoietic unity is 'a source of perturbations' for its environment, meaning that it does not instruct the environment (p. 96); rather, the outcomes of these interactions are determined by the environment's structure. In turn, living beings are autopoietic systems, caught up in a 'natural drift' (p. 109) of ongoing interactions with their environment, bringing forth their own worlds by, metaphorically speaking, 'laying down [their] path in walking' (Varela, 1987, p. 48).

While Maturana and Varela (1987) suggested that through structural coupling, autopoietic unities can form higher-order unities like groups, James Taylor (1995, 2001) introduced autopoiesis to conceptualize the communicative constitution of organizations – although his writings on this subject have not been taken up to conduct empirical research. Taylor (2001) proposed that Maturana and Varela present a constitutive view of social life that is inherently communicative: Higher-order unities' structural coupling is of a social kind and this coupling is made possible through communicative practices. Although human social systems follow the same 'laws' of autopoiesis, their distinctive feature is that they 'exist also as unities for their components in the realm of language'. Therefore, 'the identity of human social systems depends on the conservation of adaptation of human beings not only as organisms but also as components of their linguistic domains' (p. 198). These domains are characterized by operationally closed ways of interacting involving the recurrent use of similar language, artifacts, etc. Thus, collections of human beings who engage in regular interaction bring forth or enact (Varela, Thompson, & Rosch, 1991) their own, more or less autonomous, universes of meaning through their consistent and coherent 'languaging' (Maturana & Varela, 1987, p. 210). Languaging is essential because it enables human actors to refer to themselves vis-à-vis others and to the collectivity they coproduce through their interactions vis-à-vis other social collectivities. In other words, self-referentiality is important for the communicative co-constitution of organizations, as it enables the coproduction of their identities through the management of ongoing tensions between autonomy and adaptation (or independence and interdependence) vis-à-vis their larger environments, and prolonged incongruence may result in deterioration or extinction.

Laying down the path of a Chinese transnational spiritual organization through mediated communication

Internal and external stakeholders of contemporary transnational spiritual organizations are enmeshed in exactly these kinds of communicative struggles for identity: Through recurring interactions, these organizations emerge as autopoietic unities with more or less distinct identities as they bring forth their own universes of meaning within which others (individuals, organizations) figure as potential perturbations. But what role do digital and social media play in the autopoietic processes of these organizations, engaged in distinguishing themselves in a global religious 'marketplace' replete with organizations that challenge their existential legitimacy or *raison d'être* because they are vying to occupy similar symbolic and material spaces through the use of limited resources?

Although prior organizational communication research by Taylor, Cooren, and colleagues has not looked at mediated communication per se, their studies suggest that an organization's self-constitution occurs through the interplay between the linguistic and the material. For example, their analyses show the central role of an organization's name (e.g. 'Apple Macintosh') because it enables the creation of a semantic point of reference that both unites and divides (e.g. see Brummans, Cooren, & Chaput, 2009). Hence, the name 'incarnates' the organization (incarnation literally meaning 'in-flesh-ment') and makes it present as a 'macro actor' that is constituted by other 'micro actors' (human beings, texts, artifacts, etc.), authorizes members to do things on its behalf, and provides people with a source of identification (or dis-identification). An organization is thus 'presentified' (Cooren et al., 2008) through all the human and nonhuman actors who incarnate it, suggesting that names, pronouns, logos, media, discourses, etc. all contribute to the incarnation and presentification that make the autopoietic co-constitution of an organization possible (see also Brummans, Hwang, & Cheong, 2013).

To extend this research, we propose that the appropriation of digital and social media is central to the self-production of transnational spiritual organizations, as it enables them to be incarnated in such a way that they are perceived and experienced as identifiable unities around the world. What is particular about these organizations is that their operational systems are grounded in specific spiritual philosophies, be they Christian, Muslim, Buddhist, or other, as well as cultural values. These systems can therefore be seen as institutional incarnations or manifestations of such philosophies and values. In this article, we aim to understand how the appropriations of ICTs enable a collectivity of individual Chinese actors to engage in communicative practices that coproduce this kind of organization transnationally as an autopoietic unity. Thus, we explore how these human agents appropriate various technologies (nonhuman agents) to speak or act on the organization's behalf (Cooren & Taylor, 1997) and, in turn, contribute to its presentification. These social actors may be clerics, lay leaders, members, or even people who are not officially affiliated with the organization, such as interactants posting on its social media sites. Each of these actors' ICT appropriation practices have different degrees of import, for they contribute in different ways to the coproduction of its presence by giving it a voice and appearance that sets it apart from its environment.

As we suggested, conducting this study is important because relatively little is known about the role of digital media appropriation in the autopoietic co-constitution of Chinese transnational spiritual organizations, even though prior studies have discussed the historical ubiquity of other transnational faith-based organizations and their use of 'new' media, in particular early organizational incarnations of Christianity and Islam. For instance, Stamatov (2010) highlighted how 'long-distance advocacy' was initiated and enacted by Catholic and Protestant organizations in Europe in the sixteenth century and Turner (2007) discussed how information technologies have helped create a 'diaspora democracy' for global Islam. More closely related to our inquiry is recent research that highlights the appropriation of ICTs by Buddhists in Asian contexts to build community and gain influence. Lee (2009), for example, showed how Korean Won priests have created blogs for self-cultivation, empowerment, the development of new leader–member relationships, and the (indirect) deliverance of sermons. Another study highlighted how Buddhist leaders in Singapore practice various forms of 'strategic arbitration' by using the internet to facilitate the co-creation of information and expertise, under conditions where laity cooperation is elicited by retaining discretionary power among the leadership to determine informational and interpersonal outcomes and refrain from destabilizing the organization (Cheong, Huang, & Poon, 2011). Since these studies provide limited insight into the constitutive role of ICTs, we investigated the following research questions:

RQ1:   How do leaders of a Chinese transnational spiritual organization appropriate digital and social media to participate in the autopoietic co-constitution of their organization?
RQ2:   How do mediated interactions between organizational leaders, members, and non-members contribute to this co-constitution?

Case study

To examine these questions, we analyzed how Tzu Chi leaders account for their appropriation of digital and social media and how the mediated interactions they initiate play into the organization's co-constitution. Because we were interested in understanding Tzu Chi's broader communication ecology, given the importance of embedding communicative practices within the context of everyday work life as well as the contemporary convergence culture where different media systems interact amidst fluid media flows and the multiplicitous phenomenon of publishing online across platforms (Jenkins, 2006), we collected both offline and online data.

Data collection and analysis

The research for this article was part of a four-year, multidisciplinary, naturalistic study (Lindlof & Taylor, 2002), funded by the Social Sciences and Humanities Council of Canada and the A. T. Steel faculty grant, Center for Asian Research, Arizona State University. This study investigates Buddhist organizing via multiple methods, including extensive archival and literature research, interviewing, participant and nonparticipant observation, and the systematic analysis of the Tzu Chi website and social media interactions. For this article, we triangulated interview and online data (Markham & Baym, 2009) because it allowed us to develop a rich set of complementary insights into Tzu Chi's transnational co-constitution.

To understand how Tzu Chi leaders appropriate digital and social media to participate in the co-constitution of their organization (RQ1), we analyzed in-depth face-to-face interviews with 12 directors or senior managers of various departments of the Da Ai Cultural and Humanitarian Centre ('Da Ai'), conducted in Taipei in 2011. Da Ai ('great love' in Mandarin) plays a pivotal role in enacting the organization's missions and constitutes its heart in terms of all things related to media (see O'Neill, 2010). The interviews were semi-structured, lasted on average 60 minutes, and asked people to reflect on their management practices in view of their media use, work motivations and the role of Master Cheng in their work. Most interviews were conducted in Mandarin by the second author who fully masters Mandarin and Taiwan's cultural practices – some interviews included a mix of Mandarin and English. All interviews were transcribed (totaling approximately 200 pages), where necessary translated into English, and then analyzed thematically (see Lindlof, 1995; Ryan & Bernhard, 2003; Van Manen, 1990).

The latter implied that we 'reflectively [analyzed] the structural or thematic aspects [of Tzu Chi leaders' accounts]' (Van Manen, 1990, p. 78), focusing on those aspects that showed how leaders made sense of the role of their media appropriation in the co-constitution of their organization. To accomplish this, we repeatedly read our transcripts (often while simultaneously listening to our audio recordings and checking our field notes). This repeated reading allowed us to identify recurring points of reference in the data, such as 'compelling incidents, sequences of action, repetitive acts, and other critical details that inform[ed our] understanding of the scene' (Lindlof, 1995, pp. 219–220) – Van Manen (1990) refers to these reference points as 'fasteners, foci, or threads around which the phenomenological description is facilitated' (p. 91). Looking at the regularity with which these foci resurfaced then enabled us to define two related themes or '[essential] structures of experience' (Van Manen, 1990, p. 79), capturing leaders' specific ways of accounting for the role of their media appropriation Tzu Chi's coproduction (see first part of next section). While keeping these main themes in mind, we subsequently reexamined our data to uncover and correct any inconsistencies or misinterpretations in our initial analysis.

To understand how mediated interactions contribute to Tzu Chi's co-constitution as an operationally closed system (RQ2), we analyzed (1) Tzu Chi's Chinese and English Facebook sites (http://www.facebook.com/TzuChi.org?v=wall and http://www.facebook.com/pages/Tzu-Chi-Foundation/114315968643044?v=wall] and the Da Ai Facebook [http://www.facebook.com/Da AiTV]) for the 2011 calendar year (the Chinese Facebook started in November 2010 and currently has 35,990 'likes' or Facebook 'fans'; the English Facebook started in February 2011 and has 3609 'likes', 1 January 2013). To gain additional insight into Tzu Chi's engagement with the contemporary convergence culture, we also examined Tzu Chi's video channels (http://www. livestream.com/Da Aitv, which links to Facebook and Twitter, and http://www.youtube.com/ user/TzuChiDa Aitv/feed); the Da Ai Radio site (http://radio.newDaAi.tv/aod/index_in.php); and Tzu Chi's two official apps (i.e. one allows users to consume a wide range of Chinese media content through live TV/radio, podcasts, and RSS, and the other allows users to download and read the *Tzu Chi Monthly*). On Facebook, we located 176 (101 Chinese and 75 English) posts. We compared popular posts (i.e. posts that received a more than average number of likes or comments (i.e. $\geq 44,108/101 = 437$ likes or $\geq 2556/101 = 25$ comments for the Chinese Facebook; $\geq 1156/75 = 15$ likes and $\geq 87/75 = 1$ comment on the English site) to determine different types of appropriation. This analysis involved a constant comparative method of individually reading the online data to categorize data in view of our second research question, returning to the data for reexamination and confirmation, and then discussing our interpretations to ensure convergence and consistency. These research team discussions enabled us to select representative excerpts to illustrate our insights (Lindlof & Taylor, 2002). As we will show in the second part of the next section, our analysis of Tzu Chi's communication ecology revealed the central role of multiple types of social media appropriation in the organization's transnational autopoietic co-constitution.

Tzu Chi's autopoietic co-constitution through mediated communication

Tzu Chi is a remarkably advanced organization that uses media to incarnate Master Cheng Yen's particular Buddhist philosophy around the world. According to her,

> media should only report what is true and moreover, guide the public in the right direction. What our society needs is peace and harmony. We should use the media to educate people and teach them the right values by reporting the positive, wholesome elements of society and humanity. I hope that the

media can be the means of reviving moral values and ethics, purifying people's hearts and minds, and cleansing the unwholesomeness in our society. (Tzu Chi Foundation, 2010b, para. 8)

As indicated, Da Ai plays a central role in enacting the Master's philosophy transnationally. According to Da Ai's director, '[Da Ai] is her eyes and ears to Tzu Chi in the world' (O'Neill, 2010, p. 60). Instead of focusing on gossip and sensationalistic entertainment, Da Ai employees and volunteers work to purify the minds of audiences through 'wholesome media' (see Tzu Chi Foundation, 2010b). Hence, older and newer media are appropriated to reinforce a unique linguistic domain with more or less coherent symbolic and material features that reflects Tzu Chi's (and the Master's) philosophy. By communicating with people who are (or are not) Tzu Chi members through these media, Tzu Chi leaders, employees, and volunteers thus perpetuate their organization's way of making sense of the world and assure the continuity of their linguistic domain vis-à-vis ongoing environmental perturbations, as we will show next.

The role of leaders' media appropriation in Tzu Chi's autopoietic co-constitution

Our analyses indicate that Tzu Chi leaders engage the convergence culture in such a way that they embody and extend Tzu Chi's spiritual philosophy. Particularly, (1) they perceive digital media as extending karmic affinities and view digital media programming as sacramental; and (2) because they work in Master Cheng Yen's name, they consider their media work to be the enactment of her vision.

First, one concept that resurfaced frequently in Tzu Chi leaders' accounts was 'karmic affinities' (*yinyuan* in Mandarin). *Yinyuan* generally implies the idea that we are 'bound' to each other through cause-and-effect relationships, both in this life and in previous or future ones. For this reason, our positive or negative emotions and actions are believed to come to fruition in the form of positive or negative circumstances for ourselves and others.

In several accounts, interviewees shared how they work to construct 'positive news' and maintain 'open, universal and free' media access to foster *yinyuan* across the globe. For instance, one Da Ai program manager explained why she quit her work at a commercial media outlet to join Tzu Chi's leadership. Since she understood karmic affiliations and its emphasis on the meritorious relationship between cause and effect, she saw her work as fulfilling Tzu Chi's worldwide missions and, thus, as avoiding reincarnation to inferior states in future lives:

> Listening to the Master, I began to comprehend the importance of discerning between good and evil. Therefore, I gradually realized that my news occupation does not benefit society and may even stir up social unrest ... I began to fear because you reap what you sow. There is a story about an author who descended through eighteen levels of hell because his writings inspired others to think and do bad things. Therefore, since retribution is so miraculous, I decided not to harm society by resigning from my corporate job.

As this account shows, this manager believes that her work at Tzu Chi is sacramental, an act of redemptive purification. She appropriates digital media to tell stories that provide moral examples and contribute to society in positive ways. More specifically, she views her media work as a manifestation of Tzu Chi's philosophy, which is not primarily driven by audience ratings. In turn, this account shows how this manager's digital programming to create content that alleviates global suffering and advances well-being plays into the advancement of Tzu Chi's operationally closed universe of meaning.

Similarly, Da Ai's media operations manager justified open access to Da Ai's satellite television programming and a change in their digital media content production by framing their media development strategy in terms of *yinyuan*:

> How do we efficiently reach audiences now and in the future? Its terrestrial satellite, websites, mobile devices, everything, to let more people watch and receive our signals. We use nine satellite transponders to communicate to the whole world. Only places like the North Pole, and the middle of Africa cannot receive the signal. We don't lock the signal ... So if you want, if you have the *yinyuan*, you can receive it ... The other is new media ... [They] can reach the [whole] world, so we need to attract more people to our site ... because Da Ai TV is all about video and audio, so now we put more videos online. You can easily touch your mobile device to access ... so we connect everything and integrate content. For our future, we need to think about this experience and restructure.

While this statement illustrates how the global telecommunications infrastructure is consistently adapted to incarnate Tzu Chi's philosophy, it also demonstrates how digital media appropriation feeds into the communication through which the organization is co-constituted transnationally as an identifiable linguistic (and material) domain. Hence, we see how this manager views the appropriation of media in terms of the *yinyuan* concept, so that this appropriation makes sense in the context of Tzu Chi's languaging and serves the operationally closed dynamics through which Tzu Chi is constituted as a collective, organizational self in relation to its larger environment.

Another example of this autopoietic co-constitution was provided by the director of Tzu Chi's internet radio department. At the time of our research, the organization was in the midst of organizing the theatrical adaptation of the 'Water Repentance' text to show how 'human beings have created negative karma as a result of their afflictions and inner impurities and urge all to sincerely reflect and repent' (Tzu Chi Foundation, 2011b, para. 1). Referring to this major event, the director stated:

> Everyone is pure and good-natured. We can collectively unite this goodness to welcome peace, good fortune, and a nice climate. All these relate to everyone but not many know about it. Therefore, we use the show to explain Master's views. There are many people doing repentance. At Tzu Chi, this means: present my own body to speak about truth. So we will try our best to find these stories, hire someone to record something, help him or her with the editing. Then during the daily radio show, everybody can hear different repentance stories.

Here, we see that this Tzu Chi leader accounts for the use of internet radio to convey her organization's (and Master Cheng Yen's) message, both in Taiwan and abroad. By recording people who 'let their bodies speak about the truth' of their own experiences and playing these recordings during her show, they come to speak on behalf of Tzu Chi and make its worldview present. Also in this case, then, a particular medium is adapted to incarnate Tzu Chi's philosophy: internet radio becomes a channel for encouraging people to reflect on their own lives. As the Master stated, 'Their example inspires us to realize that the Buddhist teachings are in fact very connected to our everyday sufferings and can transform our lives if we practice them. These stories are truly modern sutras [canonical Buddhist texts]' (Tzu Chi Foundation, 2011c). Thus, by telling their stories, which are then made public through the internet, people also help to lay down Tzu Chi's path in communicating, and by using Tzu Chi's languaging, they sustain its operationally closed linguistic domain.

Second, interviewees noted that they do not appropriate digital media based on a set recipe dictated by the Master, but by using her teachings and mantras as guiding organizing principles. Thus, they feel emancipated in their work and 'empowered' in their leadership because they intervene in critical and pressing matters. The media operations department manager illustrated this by stating:

> The most important in Da Ai TV is the philosophy ... to attain our goals to purify people's hearts for harmony [in] society ... If we want to purify people's hearts, it is most important to use media. If we talk one by one, this cannot happen. So we [refer to] the Sutra of Immeasurable Meanings ... the seed,

one seed becomes [many seeds] ... So, [working at] Da Ai TV, I don't feel there is any limitation. We just feel what we need to do, we do, and report to the Master because we know we are doing things for Da Ai to promote and embody the words of the Master.

The sutra of reference here postulates that '[e]veryone has the same sincere pure heart as the Buddha'. Its aim is to inspire 'people to vow to unlock their intelligence, to attain purity in the chaotic life and to bring benefits to all sentient beings'. In turn, it can enable people to use 'this immeasurable power, to unleash others' good conscience and altruistic selves' (Tzu Chi Foundation – Australia, 2007, para. 7). This manager refers to this scripture to explain how Da Ai's appropriation of media can be seen as the incarnation of Master Cheng's view of 'whole-some media', but we also see how his work activities and sensemaking contribute to sustaining Tzu Chi's operationally closed linguistic and material domain.

Thus, our analysis shows that leaders appropriate various media in such a way that they carry out the Master's Buddhist philosophy around the world. Yet by engaging digital media they also partake in constituting their organization in ways that adapt their operationally closed system to the changing global media landscape and ensure the continuation of their collective, organizational self.

The role of social media interactions in Tzu Chi's autopoietic co-constitution

Our analysis of social media interactions revealed three types of digital appropriation, each playing an important role in the organization's transnational co-constitution: (1) posting updates to inform and celebrate Tzu Chi's activities and accomplishments, (2) forwarding prayer requests to galvanize members toward communal interaction, and (3) presenting Master Cheng in social media.

First, Tzu Chi leaders employ Facebook to inform users (who may or may not be Tzu Chi members) about its activities and accomplishments. On average, the Chinese Facebook page is updated at least once a day, whereas the English page is updated on a monthly basis. Users typically react by praising the organization and/or the Master. The following interaction illustrates this dynamic:

Tzu Chi Foundation
On October 2, the Tzu Chi Foundation held a tea party to celebrate completion of the second phase of a new community it built in south Taiwan. They built it for those who lost their homes to Typhoon Morakot in August 2009. At the ceremony, 250 homes at the Shanlin Da Ai Community, in a suburb of Kaohsiung, were handed over to their new residents, taking the total of 1,002 homes. Construction of the new homes began on March 12 this year.

Tzu Chi Completes Second Phase of Community for Taiwan Typhoon Victims
[http://tw.Tzu Chi.org/en/index.php?option=com_content&view=article&id=874%3Atzu-chi-completes-second-phase-of-community-for-taiwan-typhoon-victims&catid=42%3Atyphoon-morakot&Itemid=160&lang=en]

Like · Comment · October 12 at 2:58am ·

[Person 1], [Person 2], [Person 3] and 21 others like this.
1 share
6 comments

[Commentator 1] Keep it up the good work!
October 12 at 3:09am · Like 2

[Commentator 2] God bless you all for all the kindness and help you had given to my country Phi-lippines....from the bottom of my heart Thanks alot...Salute you all REAL LIVING HEROES;)
October 12 at 3:19am · Like 1

[Commentator 3] A humbling example of what our true purpose in life is.
October 12 at 7:42am · Like 1

[Commentator 4] our sincere Respect n Admiration to Tzu Chi members/volunteers n the dynamic Team ! Thank You all.
October 12 at 10:21am · Like 1

[Commentator 5] Keep it Up Tzu Chi.
October 13 at 6:23am · Like

[Commentator 6] I was very delight to meet with Tzu Chi members in United States during my recent tour... I feel really wonderful their activities…Thank you all for all members and followers... We will continue do our best the world. I'm very honor to organize very special prayer for World Peace here in our Sera Monastery in South India. Keep it Up Tzu Chi.
October 15 at 9:46am · Like

Examining this interaction, we see that this post does more than simply provide information about Tzu Chi's activities. It presents an instance of self-referential or 'auto-communication' (Cheney & Christensen, 2001), which is a pivotal communicative practice for the organization's self-pro-duction. By informing Facebook users about Tzu Chi's accomplishments, members around the world who post these kinds of messages enable the organization to 'pat itself (and its members) on the back', so to speak, and, thereby, legitimizes the organization's *raison d'être*. In turn, a post like this appears to 'call out' to Facebook users (who may be members or not) because their 'likes' and comments suggest that they are motivated to participate in Tzu Chi's enactment. This interaction thus illustrates how Facebook enables the autopoiesis through which this spiritual organization is constituted by showing how Tzu Chi's adaptation of this medium fortifies existing members' organizational identification and draws non-members into its universe of meaning.

This kind of interaction can be observed regularly on Tzu Chi's Chinese and English Face-book sites, although users participate much more actively on the Chinese site (where the most popular posts receive more than 437 'likes' and 25 comments). Moreover, we can see that this kind of mediated communication may facilitate transnational spiritual humanitarian work as it allows readers to draw inspiration from the organization's work and feel impelled to act in the name of the organization (and the Master) and carry out its (and her) missions. For example, in response to a post on Tzu Chi's earthquake victim relief efforts, one user got inspired to support the organization and wrote on 17 March 2011: 'I was touched the way Tzu Chi Foun-dation respond to the sufferings of people in Japan. My heart is saddened to see a lot of people suffer from the disasters. I am going to start collecting relief supplies to be donated to your foundation and I want to be part of the Tzu Chi Foundation. Buddha bless you all!'

Second, social media are appropriated to forward prayers requests. In so doing, members are galvanized to engage in collective intercession and action. The next interaction on the Chinese Tzu Chi Foundation Facebook site provides a telling example of this, demonstrating how the social media network is reinterpreted to incarnate the organization's philosophy:

Tzu Chi Foundation
[Forward] Everyone please pray for the student [student's name]! [http://vmedia2.TzuChi.net/pray2/index.htm]

[Content] I am a recent graduate from Tzu Chi High School. On June 11, we held a solemn graduation ceremony in the Jing-Si Meditation Hall. However, the day after, our student, [student's name] (she is currently in her 6th year), had a terrible car accident on the road near the school due to inattentive driving. Right now, he is in a coma in the intensive care unit of the Tzu Chi General Hospital.

I think, to be able to meet each other on this human path, making a connection, must be due to very special karma. I always believe what Master says: the rise of karma is never extinguished.

I know the power of prayer is very great. And today what we can do is accompany him silently, but also pray for him. I believe positive praying will become the power for his recovery. I would like my Tzu Chi aunts and uncles to spread this news to everybody and have everyone pray for him together. We will also recite the Heart Sutra for him and, if you have the habit of reciting the Heart Sutra, please don't forget to include him in the dedication.

Like · Share · June 14 at 8:36pm ·
522 people like this.
229 comments

[Commentator 1] Amitofo... [a prayer to Buddha Amithaba, Tzu Chi's principal Buddha]
June 15 at 1:53am · Like

[Commentator 2] sincerely praying be well soon:)
June 15 at 2:01am · Like

[Commentator 3] sincerely praying, praying for regaining your health soon!
June 15 at 2:07am · Like

[Commentator 4] praying for the student [last name]!
June 15 at 2:07am · Like

[Commentator 5] add oil!! [Chinese expression: keep going, you can do it]
June 15 at 2:17am · Like

[Commentator 6] _/_ [symbol representing two hands held together in Buddhist prayer]
June 15 at 2:23am · Like

[Commentator 7] I believe you will be able to overcome the difficulty – add oil!
June 15 at 2:23am · Like

Here, the user comments show how mediated communication plays into the coproduction of Tzu Chi's linguistic domain, characterized by its own particular terms (*Amitofo*; *Namo guan shi yin pusha*), expressions (*gan'en*, 'giving thanks'), symbols (e.g. _/_ signifying 'hands clasped together praying piously'), sutras, and aphorisms – the organization has even developed its own sign language. Thus, this excerpt illustrates how Tzu Chi leaders use Facebook posts to shape the organization, yet also how comments by online interactants help to coproduce and sustain Tzu Chi as an autopoietic unity. Multiple linguistic elements help to make the organization present and contribute to the constitution of the symbolic and material membrane that distinguishes it from its environment. By posting this message, liking, and posting positive comments and prayers, people appear to believe that they can put the organization's Buddhist philosophy into action. Many comments are indicative of their belief that their small communicative acts can actually make a difference in relieving the suffering of the injured student. Indeed, it is not uncommon to see Facebook posts that solicit (or respond to) prayers and intercessions, particularly for peace in the world, and for those who are suffering in different parts of the world. As the above example shows, Facebook communication thus contributes to the transnational enactment of Tzu Chi's philosophy and the worldwide co-constitution of the organization as a higher-order autopoietic system.

What is also interesting – although not shown in the interaction above – is that commentators start interacting among themselves. For instance, one commentator regularly posted updates about the student's recovery. We observed the same kind of interaction on the Da Ai internet radio site. On 10 June 2011, a popular radio host posted a message about his recovery from an illness, followed by many prayers in the form of comments. In this case, Da Ai internet radio, which enables listeners to interact with hosts while their program is going on, was transformed into an online venue for the expression of joy and exchange of encouragements and prayers.

Third, in line with our analysis of Tzu Chi leaders' accounts, our analysis of social media interactions reveals that the organization appropriates its social media sites and online video channels to make Master Cheng Yen present in the lives of ordinary people and to allow them to have more or less 'personal' contact with her. Although the Master does not have a personal Facebook account, Tzu Chi leaders adapt the site to make her part of people's social network and communicate 'directly' with them. Facebook thus enables leaders to make her speak – and to speak on her behalf – *in her absence*. This is accomplished, for example, by posting what they call 'Master's Teachings' on the English site, such as 'Our mind is very powerful; with one thought, we conjure up many things. The Buddha describes the mind as a dexterous artist' (Tzu Chi Foundation Facebook post 27 July 2011). On the Chinese site, leaders post the Master's daily address to Tzu Chi volunteers. While the Master's words can simply be taken as inspirational quotes, they actually give many users the sense that the Master is speaking to them and guiding their lives. As one user commented, 'The more I know about Tzu Chi and Master's thoughts, the more I admire Master! Looking at myself, I feel ignorant, small, and selfish' (Tzu Chi Foundation Facebook comment, 11 October 2011). Moreover, these daily posts are often complemented by links to her complete teachings and video clips of her speeches on particular topics or by songs that transform her teachings into music and thus enable people to incorporate her words by singing along. All these examples show how Tzu Chi leaders adapt the contemporary convergence culture to presentify their founder and enact her authority. And by enabling those who frequent these sites to interact with her in this way, organizational members and non-members across the globe are given the opportunity to partake in coproducing Tzu Chi's operationally closed universe of meaning.

Discussion

In this article, we have investigated how leaders of a Chinese transnational spiritual organization appropriate digital media to participate in the autopoietic co-constitution of their nonprofit organization and how social media interactions between various actors contribute to this co-constitution. The results of our analyses have several important implications for research on the internet, transnationalism, and civic engagement in Chinese societies.

First, Luisi (2003) noted in his review of research on autopoiesis that as open systems, living organisms must operate within 'an interesting contradiction between the biological autonomy and at the same time the dependence on the external medium' (p. 54). As our analyses have indicated, this same principle applies to higher-order unities like spiritual organizations: '[T]he perturbations brought about by the environment are seen as changes selected and triggered by the inner [organizing processes of these organizations]' (p. 49), which are enacted though mediated communication. Thus, social media appropriation and mediated communication by organizational leaders, members, and online interactants play a *vital* – in the literal sense of the word – role in these organizations' ongoing adaptation and autonomy by enabling (and constraining) the reproduction of their social collectivities, grounded in particular spiritual philosophies. As we have shown, these organizations are co-constituted through self-referential ('auto-')communicative practices, such as informing internal and external audiences about the organization's accomplishments or making spiritual leaders' mantras present on an iterative basis. What is particularly interesting, in this regard, is how essential seemingly ordinary, even trivial practices like posting Facebook messages are for the enactment of these organizations; they 'scale up', one social media post at a time, to reproduce the unity of its more or less coherent linguistic and material domain. Therefore, this article demonstrates how useful it is to see transnational spiritual organizations like Tzu Chi as autopoietic systems with specific symbolic and material features that emerge within our current convergence culture and are made present (Cooren et al., 2008) through ongoing appropriations of digital media.

Correspondingly, Castells (2009) has argued that contemporary communication networks are dialectically composed in that social actors program their goals and operating procedures while their structure evolves in a more or less flexible, fluid manner. Communicative power is thus expressed through local, national, and transnational socio-spatial networks that reproduce power relationships through a variety of social practices and organizational forms. The autopoietic co-constitution processes we have examined by studying the case of Tzu Chi are fueled by interactions between different actors, many of whom hail from Taiwan, but also other parts of the world. They show the subtle, complex exercise of power, predicated on communicative actions to build a consensual universe of meaning. Hence, Tzu Chi may be seen as an impressive organizational 'machine' with clear material artifacts, such as a sophisticated telecommunications infrastructure, hospitals, recycling stations, etc. in Taiwan and beyond. Our analyses illustrate, however, that 'the' organization only exists at the grace of ongoing and mediated interactions between leaders, members, and non-members, which make the social system present as an identifiable unity on a global stage. Tzu Chi is therefore not an abstract, objective entity, but a 'virtual self', a social collectivity that acts as a coherent whole, yet lacks a central agent (see Varela, 1999). In turn, we see that the notion of 'organizational membership' becomes increasingly vague, as diasporic and even non-members are called out to participate in this coproduction, which blurs the boundaries between the organization's internal and external stakeholders. ICTs play a significant role in this presentification, but their role is not causally determined. Rather, ongoing mediated communicative acts coproduce the transnational logics that manifest Tzu Chi's spiritual philosophy of universal love, and the success of the organization's global aspirations and operations depends on their constitutive force.

According to O'Neill (2010), since Tzu Chi's 'mediatization' puts Master Cheng Yen in the spotlight, it may seem like the organization's constitution depends on one central agent. However, the Master persistently denies that she constitutes Tzu Chi *by herself* and asserts that employees and volunteers should be credited for the organization's transnational co-constitution. Rather than appropriating media to create a cult of the personality, then, organizational leaders and members appropriate media 'to spread the message of Tzu Chi, especially overseas' and see 'the focus on Cheng Yen [as] a means to achieve this ... not an end' (O'Neill, 2010, p. 56).

These insights are important because they expand the catalogue of economic and relational behaviors commonly attributed to overseas Chinese by highlighting the divergent transnational engagements of Chinese actors in civic collaborations and spiritual humanitarian work to build global civil societies. According to Chan (2008), transnational networked organizations are often ideated as 'embodiments and carriers of global civil society, yet these assessments remain incomplete due to a lack of empirical research on their internal dynamics' (p. 232). In view of this observation, the rich case we have analyzed shows how digital media afford transnational practices and illuminates the role of a Chinese spiritual nonprofit organization in engendering social change for the betterment of people across the world.

Second, understanding the constitutive properties of ICTs is heuristically innovative, as digital media are popularly celebrated for their subversive potential to destabilize institutions and enervate authority. Our study demonstrates that spiritual networked organizations can provide the vision and resources to engender collaborative action and social change. As we have shown, investigating how mediated autopoietic processes enable spiritual philosophies to be incarnated in the form of transnational spiritual organizations illustrates how these kinds of organizations are brought and kept 'alive' through posting social media messages, online interactions, etc. – among other forms of communication. While social media certainly allow for contestation and debate, we observed comparatively few critical or contentious comments within the discursive domain of Tzu Chi's social media (in 2011, approximately 32% of the comments on the Chinese Facebook could be deemed as critical and within this subset, many were phrased as questions; 1% of the comments on the English Facebook were critical) – interestingly, Hutchings (2011) observed a similar operational closure in a Christian organization where the pastor's authority is reinforced by exhortative chatroom discourse. For example, on 2 July 2011, someone responded to a Tzu Chi Facebook post about karmic affinities by writing: 'not to be a fly in the ointment but I think these things – karmic affinities – probably have scientific explanations. If we want Buddha's healing message to reach the suffering in the world we need to abandon superstitious beliefs, such as karmic affinities.' There were no follow-up posts that critiqued the sender or this viewpoint, although we did observe posts that expressed how proud individuals felt to be a Tzu Chi member or volunteer. Moreover, on 27 September 2011, slightly critical comments were posted in response to Tzu Chi's disaster relief in North Korea. Of 25 comments, two expressed the view that Tzu Chi should not be working in North Korea, but most interactants supported the humanitarian efforts by expressing gratitude in the form of writing *gan'en* (giving thanks) multiple times. Interestingly, one post pointed out that Tzu Chi's 'universal love' principle should not preclude geographic areas and cultural groups, and attempted to 'correct' the prior dissenting posts' misperceptions by posting a rhetorical question about Tzu Chi's vision, thus reinforcing the coherence of its linguistic domain.

There are several plausible reasons for this focus on discursively maintaining harmony. One obvious reason is that Tzu Chi leaders and followers' desire for harmony and concatenate online-offline interactions reflects the Chinese culture of collectivism and conflict avoidance (see Leung, 1988). A more compelling reason, though, is that Master Cheng advises members not to become defensive or aggressive in view of critique, but to focus on creating understanding and expressing compassion. As she says, 'Only when we humble ourselves and respect others can our presence open other minds' (Tzu Chi Foundation – Philippines, 2011). Critical (or negative) comments on Facebook or other online forums are thus seen as opportunities for cultivating Tzu Chi's philosophy of mindfulness (see Brummans et al., 2013). However, the reason that corresponds most closely with our analyses is that Tzu Chi leaders and members are concerned about saving their organization's 'face' – and, accordingly, their own individual face. As we have shown, their mediated communicative activities concentrate on organizational *mianzi* (face-saving) by bolstering the reputation of their virtual collective self in a global environment from which it tries to distinguish itself, yet on which it also depends. Hence, our analyses indicate that Tzu Chi leaders and members are driven by their desire to present a coherent, positive collective self (see Goffman, 1959) by communicatively reinforcing the distinctness and uniqueness of their linguistic domain. For instance, the editor-in-chief of *Rhythms Monthly*, which is supported by Tzu Chi, told us that he hoped that Tzu Chi would become 'a future symbol of Taiwan', so that 'when [people] think of Tzu Chi, they think of Taiwan'. Furthermore, our field observations and interviews reveal how preoccupied 'Tzu Chi *ren*' (an often used Mandarin term, implying 'Tzu

Chi people') are with preserving their organization by creating an organizational history. For example, during our first visit to Tzu Chi in 2007, we observed how 'every event is recorded, particularly those events in which Master Cheng Yen participates' (Field notes, 15 July 2007). As one of the managers of Tzu Chi's public relations department explained, this is done 'for when Master Cheng Yen is no longer there'. In addition, the manager noted that Tzu Chi had recently been officially recognized as a 'new school in Buddhism', which was significant because it would allow people to see that Tzu Chi's humanistic Buddhism is, as he said, 'one of a kind'. Observations like these suggest that Tzu Chi leaders and members realize how essential it is to ensure the continuity of their organization in an environment with similar organizations, especially since they know that their leader and founder will pass on. Their archivization 'fever' (Derrida, 1995) originates, therefore, from their desire to preserve their organization's present and future existence within the ongoing processes of its erasure through their communicative practices.

Third, given that little research has looked at the role of digital technologies in the voluntary sector (Kenix, 2008), the autopoietic perspective we have developed and applied in this study presents an alternative lens for understanding the role of transnational Chinese nonprofit organizations in view of the technological affordances of emerging media. Our findings reveal that the autopoietic co-constitution of an organization goes beyond leaders' construction and framing of the internet as a suitable vehicle for the creation of sacred communal unity. Rather, leaders and members reinterpret and engage the convergence culture co-terminously. Hence, this study underlines the importance of examining how spiritual organizations' 'core beliefs and patterns' (Campbell, 2012) are incarnated *in* everyday mediated interactions that enable the co-constitution of these autopoietic social systems. Additionally, our research reveals how the Chinese spiritual principle of *yinyuan* facilitates the revitalized appropriation of digital and social media to sustain goodwill and retributive justice in this life and the next to secure merit for future generations.

In sum, the autopoietic processes we have analyzed illustrate the mediated coproduction through which a transnational spiritual organization emerges vis-à-vis a global convergence culture filled with social collectivities that are pursuing similar missions. They reveal the intricate interplay between mediated and organizational communication, thus providing valuable insights into the ways organizational autopoiesis works through everyday interactions. In turn, our work further underscores the importance of understanding the context of new media appropriation beyond the Web 2.0 hype and demonstrates what Horgan and Wellman (2012) propitiously name 'the immanent internet', embedded in concrete, quotidian, and socio-historical settings. In this context, the notion of transnational immanence emerges not merely as an ethereal paradox, but more significantly as a profound and hybridized online-offline phenomenon in our mediated epoch, worthy of continued systematic research.

Future studies should extend this exploratory research by investigating how members account for their digital appropriations in greater detail than space would permit here, as well as the different ways in which mediated autopoiesis expresses itself in different contexts, to yield even finer, more complex understandings. For instance, future studies may examine additional Tzu Chi Facebook sites, since beyond the two official sites analyzed in this article, Tzu Chi members worldwide have also started regional and/or local Facebook sites (e.g. Tzu Chi USA currently shows 945 likes and Tzu Chi UK 3153 likes). Moreover, at present, only a comparatively small number of Tzu Chi members actively use Facebook. Hence, analyzing other social media data will reveal their role in the organization's autopoietic co-constitution. Future scholarship could also focus on articulating the similarities and differences between transnational spiritual organizations and spiritual social movements that frame their collective identity through shared texts to mobilize potential adherents and activists. As Benford and Snow (2000) suggests, to rectify social conditions, social movements typically frame issues by pitting 'us' versus 'them', which resonates with the autopoietic perspective we have presented here. Correspondingly, it would be useful to examine how transnational spiritual organizations like Tzu Chi construct a 'repertoire of harmony' in contrast to a 'repertoire of contention' (i.e. a set of protest-related tools and actions that are available and developed within a particular time frame; see Tilly, 2003). Beyond this case, future research should also look at other transnational spiritual organizations that are adopting social media in their local and cross-border work, beyond those lodged in the Western hemisphere (see Tracey, 2012). Comparatively investigating the organizational incarnation of different spiritual philosophies is important, as it will help us understand more deeply how faith-based organizations lay down their paths in mediated communication.

Acknowledgements

Please direct all correspondences to Pauline.cheong@asu.edu. We are grateful for the support provided by the Social Sciences and Humanities Research Council of Canada, as well as the A.T. Steel Faculty grant award, Center for Asian Research, Arizona State University. We would like to acknowledge the kind participation of the research interviewees. In addition, we would like to thank James Taylor and Robert McPhee for helpful comments on an earlier draft which was presented at the 2012 meeting of the National Communication Association in Orlando, FL., as well as the editor and anonymous reviewers for their insightful recommendations on our paper.

References

Benford, R. D., & Snow, D. A. (2000). Framing processes and social movements: An overview and assessment. *Annual Review of Sociology, 26*, 611–639.

Brummans, B. H. J. M., Cooren, F., & Chaput, M. (2009). Discourse, communication, and organisational ontology. In F. Bargiela-Chiappini (Ed.), *The handbook of business discourse* (pp. 53–65). Edinburgh: Edinburgh University Press.

Brummans, B. H. J. M., Hwang, J. M., & Cheong, P. H. (2013). Mindful authoring through invocation: Leaders' constitution of a spiritual organization. *Management Communication Quarterly, 27*(3), 346–372.

Cadge, W., Levitt, P., & Smilde, D. (2011). De-centering and re-centering: Rethinking concepts and methods in the sociological study of religion. *Journal for the Scientific Study of Religion, 50*(3), 437–449.

Campbell, H. (2012). How religious communities negotiate new media religiously. In P. H. Cheong, P. Fischer-Nielsen, P. S. Gelfgren, & C. Ess. (Eds.), *Digital religion, social media and culture: Perspectives, practices, futures* (pp. 81–96). New York, NY: Peter Lang.

Castells, M. (2009). *Communication power*. New York, NY: Oxford University Press.

Chan, S. (2008). Cross-cultural civility in global civil society: Transnational cooperation in Chinese NGOs. *Global Networks, 8*, 232–252.

Chaput, M., Brummans, B. H. J. M., & Cooren, F. (2011). The role of organizational identification in the communicative constitution of an organization: A study of consubstantialization in a young political party. *Management Communication Quarterly, 25*(2), 252–282.

Chen, C. H. (2007). Building the pure land on earth: Ciji's media cultural discourse. *Journal of Media and Religion, 6*(3), 181–199.

Chen, W., & Wellman, B. (2009). Net and jet. *Information, Communication & Society*, *12*(4), 525–547.

Cheney, G., & Christensen, L. T. (2001). Organizational identity: Linkages between internal and external communication. In F. M. Jablin & L. L. Putnam (Eds.), *The new handbook of organizational communication: Advances in theory, research, and methods* (pp. 231–269). Thousand Oaks, CA: Sage.

Cheong, P. H., Huang, S. H., & Poon, J. P. H. (2011). Cultivating online and offline pathways to enlightenment: Religious authority in wired Buddhist organizations. *Information, Communication & Society*, *14*(8), 1160–1180.

Cheong, P. H., & Poon, J. P. H. (2009). Weaving webs of faith: Examining internet use and religious communication among Chinese Protestant transmigrants. *Journal of International and Intercultural Communication*, *2*(3), 189–207.

Cooren, F., Brummans, B. H. J. M., & Charrieras, D. (2008). The coproduction of organizational presence: A study of Médecins sans Frontières in action. *Human Relations*, *61*(10), 1339–1370.

Cooren, F., & Taylor, J. R. (1997). Organization as an effect of mediation: Redefining the link between organization and communication. *Communication Theory*, *7*(3), 219–260.

Derrida, J. (1995). *Archive fever: A Freudian impression* (E. Prenowitz, Trans.). Chicago, IL: The University of Chicago Press.

Eglash, R. (2004). Appropriating technology: An introduction. In R. Eglash, J. Croissant, G. Di Chiro, & R. Fouche (Eds.), *Appropriating technology: Vernacular science and social power* (p. vii–xxi). Minneapolis: University of Minnesota Press.

Goffman, E. (1959). *The presentation of self in everyday life*. Garden City, NY: Doubleday.

Ho, G. (2009). *Challenges: The life and teachings of venerable master Cheng Yen*. Vancouver: Douglas & McIntyre.

Horgan, B., & Wellman, B. (2012). The immanent internet redux. In P. H. Cheong, P. Fischer-Nielsen, P. S. Gelfgren, & C. Ess. (Eds.), *Digital religion, social media and culture: Perspectives, practices, futures* (pp. 43–62). New York, NY: Peter Lang.

Huang, C. J. (2009). *Charisma and compassion: Cheng Yen and the Buddhist Tzu Chi movement*. Cambridge, MA: Harvard University Press.

Hutchings, T. (2011). Contemporary religious community and the online church. *Information, Communication & Society*, *14*(8), 1118–1135.

Jenkins, J. (2006). *Convergence culture: Where old and new media collide*. New York, NY: New York University Press.

Kenix, L. J. (2008). Nonprofit organizations' perceptions and uses of the internet. *Television & New Media*, *9*(5), 407–428.

Khagram, S., & Levitt, P. (2008). Constructing transnational studies. In S. Khagram & P. Levitt (Eds.), *The transnational studies reader: Intersections and innovations* (pp. 1–22), New York, NY: Routledge.

Lee, J. (2009). Cultivating the self in cyberspace: The use of personal blogs among Buddhist priests. *Journal of Media and Religion*, *8*(2), 97–114.

Leung, K. (1988). Some determinants of conflict avoidance. *Journal of Cross-cultural Psychology*, *19*(1), 125–136.

Levitt, P. (2003). 'You know, Abraham was really the first immigrant': Religion and transnational migration. *International Migration Review*, *37*(3), 847–873.

Lewis, L. K., Hamel, S. A., & Richardson, B. K. (2001). Communicating change to nonprofit stakeholders: Models and predictors of implementers' approaches. *Management Communication Quarterly*, *15*(1), 5–41.

Liao, P. (2012). The mediating role of mediatized religious content: An example of Buddhist institutional use of prime-time dramas. *Australian Journal of Communication*, *39*(1), 37–52.

Lindlof, T. R. (1995). *Qualitative communication research*. Thousand Oaks, CA: Sage.

Lindlof, T. R., & Taylor, B. C. (2002). *Qualitative communication research methods*. Thousand Oaks, CA: Sage.

Luisi, P. L. (2003). Autopoiesis: A review and a reappraisal. *Naturwissenschaften*, *90*, 49–59.

Markham, A., & Baym, N. (2009). *Internet inquiry: Conversations about method*. London: Sage.

Maturana, H. R., & Varela, F. J. (1987). *The tree of knowledge: The biological roots of human understanding*. Boston, MA: Shambhala.

McPhee, R. D., & Iverson, J. (2009). Agents of constitution in communidad. In L. L. Putnam & A. M. Nicotera (Eds.), *Building theories of organization: The constitutive role of communication* (pp. 49–87). New York, NY: Routledge.

O'Neill, M. (2010). *Tzu Chi: Serving with compassion*. Singapore: John Wiley & Sons.

Ong, A., & Nonini, D. (Eds.). (1997). *Ungrounded empires: The cultural politics of modern Chinese transnationalism*. New York, NY: Routledge.

Ryan, G. W., & Bernhard, H. R. (2003). Techniques to identify themes. *Field Methods*, *15*(1), 85–109.

Stamatov, P. (2010). Activist religion, empire, and the emergence of modern long-distance advocacy networks. *American Sociological Review*, *75*(1), 607–628.

Taylor, J. R. (1995). Shifting from a heteronomous to an autonomous worldview of organizational communication: Communication theory on the cusp. *Communication Theory*, *5*(1), 1–35.

Taylor, J. R. (2001). The 'rational' organization reconsidered: An exploration of some of the organizational implications of self-organizing. *Communication Theory*, *11*(2), 137–177.

Tilly, C. (2003). *The politics of collective violence*. New York, NY: Cambridge University Press.

Tracey, P. (2012). Religion and organization: A critical review of current trends and future directions. *The Academy of Management Annals*, *6*(1), 87–134.

Turner, B. (2007). Religious authority and the new media. *Theory, Culture, Society*, *24*(2), 117–134.

Tzu Chi Foundation. (2010a). Introduction to Buddhist Tzu Chi Foundation. In *Introductory pamphlet to Tzu Chi*. Retrieved August 12, 2012, from http://www.scribd.com/doc/36043934/Introductory-pamphlet-to-Tzu-Chi

Tzu Chi Foundation. (2010b). *Wholesome media*. Retrieved January 8, 2012, from http://www.tw.TzuChi.org/en/index.php?option=com_content&view=article&id=485%3Awholesome-media&catid=80%3Amissionofculture&Itemid=180&lang=en

Tzu Chi Foundation. (2011a). Tzu Chi *missions*. Retrieved January 8, 2012, from http://tw.TzuChi.org/en/index.php?option=com_content&view=article&id=293%3Atzu-chi-missions&catid=58%3Atzuchi&Item id=283&lang=en

Tzu Chi Foundation. (2011b). *Synopsis of the sutra adaptation of the water repentance text*. Retrieved January 8, 2012, from http://www.tw.TzuChi.org/en/index.php?option=com_content&view=article&id=866&Itemid=328&lang=en

Tzu Chi Foundation. (2011c). *A modern sutra: Real-life stories of repentance*. Retrieved January 8, 2012, from http://www.tw.TzuChi.org/en/index.php?option=com_content&view=articlc&id=853%3Aa-modern-sutra-real-life-stories-of-repentance&catid=112%3Aseries-on-repentance&Itemid=322&lang=en

Tzu Chi Foundation – Australia. (2007). *Tzu Chi dharma teachings (sutra of immeasurable meanings)*. Retrieved January 8, 2012, from http://www.TzuChi.org.au/en/index.php?option=com_content&view=article&id=309%3Atzu-chi-dharma-teachings-sutra-of-immeasurable-meanings&catid=101%3Aphilosphy&Itemid=265&lang=en

Tzu Chi Foundation – Philippines. (2011). *Master Cheng Yen answer commonly-asked questions about Tzu Chi*. Retrieved August 12, 2012, from http://www.TzuChizam.org/Tzu Chi/about-tzu-chi/faq.html

Van Manen, M. (1990). *Researching lived experience: Human science for an action sensitive pedagogy*. London: The Althouse Press.

Varela, F. (1987). Laying down a path in walking. In W. I. Thompson (Ed.), *GAIA, a way of knowing: Political implications of the new biology* (pp. 48–64). Hudson, NY: Lindistarne Press.

Varela, F. J. (1999). *Ethical know-how: Action, wisdom, and cognition*. Stanford, CA: Stanford University Press.

Varela, F. J., Thompson, E., & Rosch, E. (1991). *The embodied mind: Cognitive science and human experience*. Boston, MA: MIT Press.

Online political participation, civic talk, and media multiplexity: how Taiwanese citizens express political opinions on the Web

Yuli Patrick Hsieh[a] and Meng-Hao Li[b]

[a]Media, Technology, and Society (MTS) Doctoral Program, Northwestern University; [b]Department of Public Administration, University of Illinois at Chicago

This study seeks to assess the implications of the social use of information and communication technologies (ICTs) for online political participation. Past research investigating the link between ICTs and political participation has emphasized the informational use of ICTs, overlooking their communication-enabling potentials for facilitating political talk in interpersonal spaces and subsequently, political participation in public domains. To understand further how ICTs as a means of communication may relate to political participation, we use data from the 2008 Taiwan Social Change Survey ($N = 1076$) to examine the relationship between the Internet and online political participation by looking at online media use for social interaction and engagement in civic talk online. Our findings suggest that interpersonal factors such as online civic talk and media multiplexity are positively associated with online political participation. Individuals who discuss politics with their friends via the Internet and those who use more types of online media for social interaction are more likely to contact legislators and elected officials directly via the Web and articulate their political thoughts in online public spaces such as forums, blogs, and websites of news media. We further offer an assessment of the findings' implications for political participation, political communication, and digital inequality.

Introduction

Civic and political engagement has been the focus of scholarly debates on the democratic potential of the Internet and other digital technologies, as engagement is foundational to the functioning of a democracy. Empirical evidence from past research in this area has indicated that Internet use may facilitate and even promote civic and political participation, finding that easy access to political information online may be able to modestly enhance political participation in the Web era (e.g. Bimber, 2001). However, the literature seems to consider primarily the informational function of the information and communication technologies (ICTs) as the mechanism connecting ICT use and civic and political participation, overlooking the potentials of the Internet and other digital technologies as a means for political communication. Consequently, the mechanism by which ICTs afford political communication within citizens' social networks and then enable civic and political engagement is still underdeveloped (Hampton, 2011; Valenzuela, Kim, & Gil de Zúñiga, 2011).

To understand how the Web's communicative functions may facilitate online political participation, this study examines the relationship between multiple media use for communication (i.e. media multiplexity) and engagement in informal discussion of public affairs (i.e. civic talk) in the online contexts. We use data from the 2008 Taiwan Social Change Survey (TSCS) to examine how Taiwanese Web users ($N = 1076$) engage in political participation online. Our findings suggest that interpersonal factors such as online civic talk and media multiplexity are positively associated with online political participation. Specifically, individuals who discuss politics with their friends via the Internet and those who use more types of online media for communicating with their personal networks tend to directly contact and express their political opinions to legislators and elected officials online. Additionally, political news enthusiasts and those who have high political efficacy are more likely to express their political opinions in online public spaces such as forums and blogs. We further offer an assessment of what these findings in Taiwan suggest about how instrumental, psychological, and interpersonal perspectives may explain online political participation.

How ICTs afford political participation

As one of the important foundations of healthy and functioning democratic societies, political participation can be defined broadly as both psychological engagement and behavioral involvement of civic and public affairs with a clear expectation of influencing government actions (Verba, Schlozman, & Brady, 1995). While Verba and his colleagues primarily look at the level of citizens' psychological engagement in politics: political interest, political efficacy, political knowledge and partisanship, other studies in this domain measure political participation by examining political behaviors: voting, attending civic events, contacting officials, volunteering or working in campaigns and donating money to political figures (Bimber, 2003; Boulianne, 2009; Brady, Verba, & Schlozman, 1995; Gil de Zúñiga, Veenstra, Vraga, & Shah, 2010; Mossberger, Tolbert, & McNeal, 2008; Xenos & Moy, 2007). The main advantage of these measures is that these political behaviors can be observed in public settings and even from public records (e.g. voting and tax-exempted donation). The past literature shows that the factors differentiating political participants from non-participants involve individuals' demographic characteristics and socioeconomic status, psychological engagement, and other tangible resources such as time and money (e.g. Brady et al., 1995; Verba et al., 1995). In this study, we consider online political participation to be the aforementioned political behaviors engaging in public domains on the Internet. As elaborated later in detail, focusing on online political participation allows us to explore further the extent to which factors like the communicative functions of ICTs may relate to political behaviors in online contexts.

ICTs as information sources for political information

Studies investigating the link between ICT use and political participation originate arguably from the traditional media effects research (e.g. Gerbner, Gross, Morgan, & Signorielli, 1982; Uslaner, 1998). Initially, scholarship theorizing the relationship between Internet use and political participation mainly considered the Internet as a source of political information similar to news media, suggesting that the easy access to political information is the key to enhancing political participation. The instrumental approach asserts that citizens who perceive low search costs of online political information are more likely to be politically informed and thus to participate in political affairs (Bimber, 2003; Tolbert & McNeal, 2003). At the same time, higher psychological engagement in politics may also motivate users to search for and retrieve information online for civic and political affairs (Bimber, 2001, 2003; O'Neill, 2010; Xenos & Moy, 2007). For example, by examining the data from the 2000 American National Election Studies (ANES), Bimber (2003) reported that citizens who have higher political efficacy and have used the Internet for political information were more likely to vote. Similarly, in their analysis of the subsequent 2004 ANES data, Xenos and Moy (2007) found that citizens accessing political information online were more likely to engage in political activities such as volunteering in campaigns and donating to certain candidates, and that such a positive tendency seemed to be stronger for those with higher political interests. Other work also found that political and informational Web use were positively related to civic and political participation, while recreational Web use seemed to be negatively related to civic and political activities (Kenski & Stroud, 2006; Shah, Cho, Eveland, & Kwak, 2005; Wang, 2007).

While a large body of research has examined rigorously how traditional socioeconomic status, psychological traits regarding politics, and instrumental Web use condition civic and political participation, only a few recent studies have empirically examined why interpersonal communication and social networks matter to political participation in the information age (Hampton, 2011; Klofstad, 2011). This line of work (e.g. Bimber, 2001) concentrates on ICTs' capabilities of information retrieval, seemingly paying less attention to the interactivity of digital technologies that may facilitate citizens' communication with their peers as well as their communication with public officials and political figures.

ICTs as communication media for political discussion

Beyond citizens' socioeconomic status and psychological characteristics, political scientists have already recognized that people are often reluctant to become involved in political activities (Eliasoph, 1998; Verba et al., 1995, p. 269). While often, citizens may not participate in political activities spontaneously in the public domain, past research also discovered that citizens may be influenced and motivated by their peers to do so (Huckfeldt & Sprague, 1991). Additionally, citizens may still engage in politics even though they do not necessarily express their political stance in public. For example, citizens may discuss politics with their friends in private settings although they do not participate in the campaign of their favorite candidate. Research in this area consistently shows that citizens' social networks serve an important role for their political information and opinion exchange, and subsequently, have positive implications for their political participation (Gil de Zúñiga, & Valenzuela, 2011; Huckfeldt & Sprague, 1987; Ikeda & Boase, 2011; Lake & Huckfeldt, 1998; Lazarsfeld, Berelson, & Gaudet, 1968; McLeod et al., 1999; Mutz, 2002; Rojas, Shah, & Friedland, 2011; Scheufele, Hardy, Brossard, Waismel-Manor, & Nisbet, 2006).

However, having personal networks with diverse information or opinions only presents the *potential* for information exchange or deliberation. A diverse interpersonal environment in and of itself is a necessary but insufficient condition for civic or political talk. Furthermore, political discussion may often be a by-product of conversations about other matters in daily routines (Klofstad, McClurg, & Rolfe, 2009). Citizens will not use such opportunities to be politically informed until they talk about public affairs with their peers. Therefore, Klofstad (2011) contends that civic talk – informal political discussion with peers in one's personal networks – is a distinctive type of political behaviors in the private sphere that may encourage citizens' political participation in the public sphere such as voting or contacting officials. In line with Klofstad's (2011) findings, a few other studies have also pointed out that individuals practicing civic talk were more likely to engage in civic and political activities (Best & Krueger, 2006; Nisbet & Scheufele, 2004; Shah, et al., 2005).

In addition, political participation varies in form between online and offline contexts (Di Gennaro & Dutton, 2006; Valenzuela et al., 2011). The Web's varying affordances, such as inter-activity, replicability, and portability, enable citizens to participate in political behaviors in different ways. For example, citizens are able to access candidates' websites anytime to view the multimedia content of their campaigns. They can contact elected officials and politicians directly via various Web services. More importantly, people can comment on political news directly on the websites of news media. They can debate about current political events or rant anonymously on discussion boards and web forums. Citizens can also share their opinions along with the URLs of the news articles with their personal networks via email, instant messaging, and popular social media.

Some recent work specifically examines the link between online communication and online political participation, finding that individuals interacting with online communities and participating in political discussion online were more likely to engage in civic and political activities (Gil de Zúñiga et al., 2010; Kobayashi, Ikeda, & Miyata, 2006; Shah et al., 2005; Valenzuela et al., 2011). Neverthe-less, citizens may require a certain degree of ICT usage proficiency to maneuver online contexts and to use ICT swiftly for communication before they seek to engage in civic talk and other types of political behaviors online (Di Gennaro & Dutton, 2006). As a result, it is unclear that whether the positive association between civic talk and political participation will persist in the current digital environment where ICTs and social media become increasingly pervasive in everyday life. Hence, we derive the following hypothesis regarding civic talk and political participation online:

H1: Practicing online civic talk is positively associated with online political participation, while con-trolling for other demographic and psychological antecedents.

Media multiplexity: how citizens use ICTs for communication and engagement

Although past research has started to recognize that online communication may have positive implications for civic and political participation, how and to what extent ICTs can be used for citizens' political discussion with their personal networks are under-theorized. In this section, we turn to the literature of Internet studies and communication research to further understand ICTs' role in political discussion. The implications of the Internet and other ICTs for social inter-action and social capital have been debated for years since the early days of the Web's mass diffu-sion, contrasting positive and negative outcomes related to digital technologies (e.g. see Haythornthwaite & Rice, 2006; Shklovski, Kiesler, & Kraut, 2006 for a review of this literature).

On the negative side of the debate is the capital-depletion perspective. Scholars have argued that use of new ICTs will undermine the way citizens communicate with others and disrupt individuals' social engagement with their interpersonal networks and society at large (Kraut et al., 1998; Nie, Hillygus, & Erbring, 2002; Putnam, 2001), given the zero-sum time allocation between media use and other social activities (e.g. Robinson, Barth, & Kohut, 1997). Conversely, the literature seems to offer more empirical support to the positive and capital-enhancing implications of ICTs (Bargh & McKenna, 2004; Boulianne, 2009). A considerable body of research has found evidence suggesting that using ICTs may increase civic participation (Katz & Rice, 2002; Kavanaugh, Carroll, Rosson, Zin, & Reese, 2005) as well as bonding and bridging social capital (Ellison, Stein-field, & Lampe, 2007, 2011; Norris, 2004). More importantly, social interaction in digital environ-ments tends to intensify existing social relationships and involvement in public affairs (Hampton, 2011; Hampton, Sessions, & Her, 2011; Hampton & Wellman, 2003; Stern & Adams, 2010).

Additionally, some recent work theorizes further the mechanisms connecting ICT with social interaction and public affairs (Wellman et al., 2003). Accounting for varying affordances associ-ated with different communication media, the 'media multiplexity' perspective (Boase, Horrigan, Wellman, & Rainie, 2006; Haythornthwaite, 2005) argues that individuals use various media interchangeably to maintain their social relationships as they see fit in different situations.

Findings from this line of work indicated that people were likely to use more types of media to keep in touch with those with whom they shared stronger ties in various social contexts (Boase, 2008; Haythornthwaite, 2005; Ledbetter, 2008, 2009). Hogan (2008) found from his urban Canadian participants that individuals were likely to be in touch with the most socially accessible contacts rather than those with whom they have the strongest ties while using multiple ICTs for networking with contacts of their social circles.

A growing body of work has discovered similar results regarding using multiple communication methods for maintaining social relationships and participating in civic activities (e.g. van Cleemput, 2010; Kim, Kim, Park, & Rice, 2007; Mesch, 2009; Shah et al., 2005; Stern & Adams, 2010), indicating that the ways users employ ICTs and the choices to use a certain medium rather another are the function of the features of technologies, the purposes of interaction (e.g. discussion topics), and the social contexts (e.g. the relational closeness between contacts, social roles, locality, etc.) of a particular interaction. Therefore, using multiple ICTs (i.e. practicing media multiplexity) allows citizens to access their social capital residing in their personal networks and to participate in public affairs under various circumstances.

Taken together, the media multiplexity perspective underscores the potential benefits of ICT use for connecting with their interpersonal environment and the general public sphere, given that various offline and online media afford individuals a forum for their social and civic activities under different situations and needs. Consequently, using multiple media allows citizens to tap into different opportunities for social interaction and civic participation associated with different media and diverse personal networks. In the context of the current study, using many different types of online media suggests that such individuals are more proficient in utilizing the various benefits of the Web: these citizens are more likely to express their opinions publicly as well as to communicate with others in their personal networks about public and civic affairs via online services. Hence we propose the following hypothesis:

H2: Using multiple online media for social interaction will be positively associated with online political participation, while controlling for other demographic and psychological antecedents.

Data and method

Research context

Since the 1990s, Taiwan has undergone massive political reform, and its political system has transformed from a 40-year and single-party monopoly to a multi-party representative democracy. In 1996, Taiwan conducted the first direct presidential election with a 76% voter turnout. The successful democratization continues to inspire Taiwanese citizens' political participation. The voter turnout of the following presidential elections remained approximately 80% (Central Election Commission Taiwan, 2012). Taiwan has also undergone two administration transitions between the China Nationalist Party (i.e. Kuomingtang) and Democratic Progressive Party since both major parties have won the past presidential elections in the past two decades.

In addition to the encouraging environment for political participation, the Internet adoption rate in Taiwan is the fourth highest in Asia. Data from the past TSCSs indicate that Internet users in Taiwan have increased gradually from 31.0% in 1998 to 54.3% in 2008. It is worth noting that Taiwan has a unique participatory culture regarding the use of Bulletin Board System (BBS), similar to the use of Usenet or Web forums in other Western countries. However, while many text-based online communication services (such as Usenet) have become obsolete and lost their users to social media and other Web 2.0 sites in other countries, text-based bulletin boards remain popular online destinations in Taiwan. To date, the most prevalent BBS (i.e. telnet://ptt.cc) attracts heavy Internet traffic and is ranked constantly as one of the top 50 websites in Taiwan.[1] At the same time, while the blogosphere has become another important public sphere for information and commentaries of current events and politics in some countries (e.g. Adamic & Glance, 2005; Hargittai, Gallo, & Kane, 2008), ptt.cc remains one of the most popular online venues where users tend to discuss political and social issues vehemently. Users sometimes use this non-profit BBS as the platform for citizen journalism, where they may disseminate information about ongoing public affairs to attract public attention or to organize civic and political activities. Consequently, news media cover public opinion on this popular BBS on a regular basis, frequently reading the comments of netizens on television.

Given the political progress, the high Internet penetration, and the prevalent practices of online public discourse, we consider the social context of Taiwan particularly appropriate for studying the implications of the Web for political participation in a non-Western democracy. More importantly, the unique participatory culture in Taiwan can help researchers investigate whether different types of Web use may have different effects on political participation online, which in turn allows researchers to unpack further the positive relationship between general Internet use and political participation in Taiwan (Wang, 2007).

Data source and descriptive statistics

To examine the aforementioned hypotheses, we conduct a secondary analysis on data from the Mass Communication Module (MCM) of the 2008 TSCS,[2] the largest nationwide social survey series in Taiwan. To account for the geographic hierarchy and urbanization status, a three-stage[3] stratified probability proportionate to the size sampling procedure was used to obtain a nationally representative sample of adults living in households in Taiwan. The face-to-face interviews were conducted between July and August 2008 by the Academia Sinica Taiwan. The response rate for the MCM in the 2008 survey was 43.0%, consisting of a research sample of 1980 adult respondents. The entire sample was 50.7% male and 49.3% female, with a mean age of 46.20 (SD = 17.32, range = 19–93). Almost two-thirds (62.9%) of the sample were either married or living with a partner. The average education level of the respondents was 11.2 years (SD = 4.6) and their average monthly personal income was 28,323 NTD (SD = 33,665). Approximately half of the participants (47.8%) lived in the main urban areas. Slightly more than half (54.3%) of them reported using the Internet in the past year.

Questions about Internet use and online behaviors such as news consumption and political participation online were one of the core components of the MCM. However, such questions were administered only to Internet users during the interview. As a result, the final sample for our study comprises 1076 Taiwanese Web users. Not surprisingly, compared with the general population in Taiwan, this Web-user sub-sample biases toward urbanites and those with higher socioeconomic status: Web users had an average of 14.2 years of education, and a mean monthly personal income of 36,000 NTD (SD = 36,901), and more than half (54.3%) of this group lived in the main urban areas. Given that our goal is to analyze users' online behaviors and the subsequent implications for their political participation online, we consider this national sample of Internet users suitable for our study.

Measurement construction and description

Online political participation

The 2008 TSCS included a set of questions regarding online political participation and online civic talk, which instructed respondents to recall their political behaviors by social contexts. First, we use three four-point scale (i.e. never, seldom, sometimes or often) questions to measure two types of citizens' online activities: articulating political opinions directly to the government (one item) or indirectly to the general public (two items combined). Given that only less than 5% of the participants were moderately engaged (i.e. reported sometimes or often) across all three questions, we construct two binary variables to indicate whether respondents had engaged in the following political activities online. The first variable measures whether respondents express political opinions directly to elected officials, legislators, or political figures via the Internet (11.2%). The second variable denotes whether respondents express political opinions in either one of the following online public spaces: (1) BBS, Web forums, blogs, or (2) websites of news media[4] (24.7%). Leaving opinions on the publicly accessible 'comment' section on web pages of news coverage is a clear example of this political practice. These binary variables of online political participation comprise the outcome variables of this study.

Online civic talk

Following the definition put forth by Klofstad (2011), we define online civic talk as informal discussions of politics within the private sphere (e.g. social ties in one's personal networks) that occur in online domains. Respondents were asked in another four-point scale question to report the extent to which they had 'discussed political issues with friends via the Internet'. Similarly to the treatment of the online political participation variables, we construct a binary variable denoting whether respondents had engaged in online civic talk (34.5%).

Online media multiplexity

Based on the media multiplexity perspective (Boase, 2008; Haythornthwaite, 2005), we define online media multiplexity as the number of online media people use to communicate with their personal networks. Given that 98.2% of the survey participants reported using telephone to contact their personal networks while the 2008 TSCS did not differentiate the usage of landline and mobile phone in the question, we focus mainly on Web-based media in the current study and do not include the invariant telephone usage in the variable. To measure online media multiplexity, we first transform the responses to six four-point scale questions of online media use into six binary measures to identify whether participants use the following online domains for social interaction: (1) chat with someone on BBS, post a message or response to a post on the board (31.4%), (2) visit chat rooms or websites that provide services for making friends (22.6%), (3) use email (85.6%), (4) use instant messaging services (64.6%), (5) use Internet phone like Skype (36.3%), and (6) browse or use blogs (69.1%). Then we construct the online media multiplexity index by summing the responses to these six binary indicators. Consequently, this measure (range = 0–6) provides a robust description of participants' online media usage patterns. Worthy of note is that this measure denotes the technological context of communication practices: the extent to which respondents engaged in technology-mediated communication regardless of the nature of interaction. On average, Taiwanese Web users employed three different online media to interact with others (mean = 3.1, SD = 1.8), while only a small proportion of these users either did not use any online media (8.6%) or used all six (8.4%) for social interaction.

Background characteristics

To test both hypotheses in our study appropriately, we need to take into account a number of factors that may affect the level of political participation, and more importantly, the associations between civic talk, media multiplexity, and political participation in online contexts. Demographic and socioeconomic characteristics such gender, age, education, income, and marital status have all been implicated as factors conditioning citizens' level of civic or political participation (e.g. Brady et al., 1995; Burns, Schlozman, & Verba, 2001). We use two binary variables classifying respondents' gender and marital status, where 1 denotes female and being married or living with a partner accordingly, and 0 indicates otherwise. We also control for respondents' age, years of education, and monthly personal income[5] in the analysis.

Psychological and behavioral antecedents of political participation

In addition, we include a series of psychological and behavioral antecedents of political participation as control variables in the analysis. Specifically, we use political efficacy, political trust, political knowledge, and political news consumption to account for the association between people's psychological engagement in politics and their political participation (Finkel, 1985; Levi & Stoker, 2000; Verba et al., 1995). To measure political efficacy, we construct an index variable by averaging the responses to four five-point scale (i.e. from 1 = strongly disagree to 5 = strongly agree) questions of participants' beliefs about their own competence to understand and to participate in politics and the responsiveness of governmental authorities (mean = 3.1, SD = 0.6, Cronbach's α = .51). Similarly, we construct a political trust index by averaging the responses to four five-point scale questions of participants' beliefs about whether or not the government is functioning in accord with citizens' expectations (mean = 2.6, SD = 0.8, Cronbach's α = .85). To measure political knowledge, we look at participants' responses to four factual questions about political affairs at the time, such as the tenure of presidency, countries with official diplomatic relationship with Taiwan, the president of China, and the executive chief of Hong Kong; we then create a political knowledge measure by calculating the number of correct answers provided from respondents, where 0 indicates little political knowledge, and 4 suggests a great understanding of the current politics in Taiwan (mean = 2.1 SD = 1.0).

To account for the instrumental effect of ICTs on political participation (Bimber, 2001; Jennings & Zeitner, 2003; Kenski & Stroud, 2006), we first include political news consumption as a proxy measure observing respondents' overall political information search activities. We construct an index measure by summing the responses to three four-point scale questions that inquire respondents' frequency of accessing political news via newspapers, television, and the Internet (range = 0–9, mean = 3.4, SD = 2.3, Cronbach's α = .68). Worthy of note is that looking at the overall political news consumption across media (i.e. counting both common mass media and the Web) is appropriate for our analysis since it does not bias the results further toward the heavy users in our Web user sample.

Furthermore, we employ two Internet experience variables – the hours spent online weekly as well as the familiarity of the Internet – as proxy measures capturing respondents' Internet usage intensity and their reliance on the Web. Time spent online weekly is derived from answers to two questions asking about hours spent online on an average day and days used the Internet in a typical week in the past year. This measure ranges from .017 (about 7 minutes a week) to 105 hours and is logged in the analyses because of the idea that there are diminishing returns of potential benefits to additional time as the time spent online increases (Hargittai, 2010; Hargittai & Hsieh, 2010).

Internet familiarity is constructed by averaging the answers to nine five-point scale questions of respondents' familiarity about different aspects of the Web (mean = 3.6, SD = 0.6). Respondents were asked to what extent they agree with the following: (1) the Internet can broaden their horizon, (2) using the Internet makes them feel happy, (3) if possible, I will go online every day, (4) I can freely express my opinions since I do not have to use my real name going online, (5) since I cannot see people in person online, I can chat more freely and without pressure, (6) using the Internet can strengthen my interpersonal relationships, (7) I can make more friends online, (8) by going online, my friends and I have more contact with each other, and (9) Internet makes it easier to communicate with people around the world. We consider these two variables as appropriate proxy measures for the instrumental effect of the Web, given the idea that respondents may go online more frequently and have more positive attitudes toward the Internet if they obtain more benefits from the low search cost and easy access to information while they are online.

Given the limitation posted by the original questions in the questionnaire, the respondents might not be able to indicate their engagement in different types of online political activities separately, as suggested in theory. The Pearson's correlations documented in Table 1 suggest that the two online political participation variables exhibit weak or moderate relationship with the key political traits and Internet experiences variables. However, the correlations between online civic talk, online media multiplexity, and expressing political opinions in online public spaces could suggest a problem with multicollinearity. We further conduct the variance inflation factor (VIF) tests to detect the potential multicollinearity among the aforementioned explanatory variables included in our models. The results suggest that the VIF factors of all our variables are smaller than 2^6, suggesting that our models do not suffer from the multicollinearity problem.

Analysis procedure

Given the binary form of our outcome variables, we conduct a series of logistic regressions to investigate the relationship between online civic talk, online media multiplexity, and online political participation while controlling for a set of socioeconomic, psychological and behavioral variables. The first set of models (Model 1–4 in Table 2) examines whether the aforementioned factors relate to contacting political figures online directly, while holding other antecedents constant. The second set (Model 5–8 in Table 3) looks at whether these factors also relate to expressing political opinions in online public spaces. In both tables, we begin by presenting the baseline models including only the control variables (Models 1 and 5), followed by the inclusion of online civic talk (Models 2 and 6), online media multiplexity (Models 3 and 7), and the interaction between these two variables of interest (Models 4 and 8).

In order to demonstrate the directionality of the relationships between our variables, we present the unstandardized coefficients and the standard errors in our tables. However, to better interpret the magnitude of the relationship between these variables, we describe the relationship using odds ratios in our discussion.

Findings

What explains online political participation

We observe similar patterns regarding the relationship between online civic talk, online media multiplexity, and both measures of online political participation. The first model in Table 2 indicates that, males, those who were younger and better educated, accessed more political news, and those who had a more positive attitude toward the Web were more likely to do so than their counterparts. As hypothesized, Model 2 suggests a positive relationship between online civic talk and contacting political figures directly, while only gender and political news consumption continue to exhibit a statistically significant association with this online political activity. Holding all other variables constant at their means, the corresponding odds ratio is 42.0 (exp. 3.738) in Model 2, suggesting that respondents who had discussed politics with their friends online were about 42 times more likely to contact political figures such as elected officials or legislators directly via online channels than those who had not done so.

Model 3 indicates that, as hypothesized, online media multiplexity is positively related to contacting politicians directly while controlling for other factors. Comparing to the respondents

Table 1. Correlation between respondents' political traits and online experiences.

	Political knowledge	Political efficacy	Political trust	Political news consumption	Internet attitude	Online civic talk	Online media multiplexity	Contacting political figures directly
Political knowledge	–							
Political efficacy	.113 (.000)	–						
Political trust	.008 (.772)	.485 (.000)	–					
Political news consumption	.447 (.000)	.177 (.000)	.066 (.003)	–				
Internet attitude	−.052 (.085)	.140 (.000)	.053 (.081)	.124 (.000)	–			
Online civic talk	.055 (.071)	.110 (.000)	.013 (.677)	.310 (.000)	.320 (.000)	–		
Online media multiplexity	−.009 (.764)	.036 (.239)	−.029 (.350)	.148 (.000)	.439 (.000)	.443 (.000)	–	
Contacting political figures directly	.068 (.026)	.065 (.033)	−.028 (.364)	.200 (.000)	.136 (.000)	.398 (.000)	.253 (.000)	–
Expressing political opinions in online public spaces	.066 (.031)	.130 (.000)	.015 (.635)	.270 (.000)	.260 (.000)	.625 (.000)	.398 (.000)	.643 (.000)

Note: *p*-Values are presented in parentheses.

Table 2.   Logistic regressions on contacting political figures directly.

	Contacting political figures directly			
	Model 1 Coefficient (SE)	Model 2 Coefficient (SE)	Model 3 Coefficient (SE)	Model 4 Coefficient (SE)
Female (female = 1)	−.575** (.219)	−.548* (.236)	−.552* (.240)	−.552* (.240)
Age	−.031* (.014)	−.004 (.016)	.006 (.017)	.007 (.017)
Years of education	.117** (.053)	.024 (.058)	.001 (.060)	.002 (.060)
Married/cohabitation	.402 (.295)	.489 (.315)	.603 (.326)	.591 (.326)
Personal income (logged)	−.022 (.015)	−.025 (.016)	−.027 (.017)	−.027 (.017)
Political efficacy	.368 (.201)	.254 (.219)	.212 (.220)	.214 (.220)
Political trust	−.256 (.149)	−.251 (.166)	−.254 (.169)	−.257 (.169)
Political knowledge	.058 (.135)	.065 (.148)	.059 (.151)	.058 (.151)
Political news consumption	.259*** (.052)	.123* (.057)	.110 (.059)	.110 (.059)
Hours online per week (logged)	.030 (.074)	−.093 (.079)	−.119 (.082)	−.125 (.083)
Internet attitude	.617** (.218)	.041 (.252)	−.170 (.263)	−.169 (.263)
Online civic talk with friends		3.738*** (.435)	3.449*** (.436)	4.018*** (.983)
Online media multiplexity			.357*** (.097)	.500* (.234)
Online civic talk × Online media multiplexity				−.166 (.247)
Constant	−6.703*** (1.245)	−5.437*** (1.404)	−5.598*** (1.437)	−6.074*** (1.627)
N	1060	1060	1060	1060
McFadden's R^2	.119	.315	.334	.335
Deviance	648.682	504.426	490.094	489.638
LR test	87.601	231.857	246.189	246.645
AIC	672.683	530.427	518.094	519.639
BIC	732.275	594.985	587.618	594.129

*$p < 0.05$.
**$p < 0.01$.
***$p < 0.001$.

who used three (mean = 3.1) types of online media to communicate with their social ties, the odds of directly contacting political figures via the Internet were as almost twice as large (197%) for those using five (one stand deviation above average, 4.84) different online media for interaction. Based on the non-significant interaction term, Model 4 shows that the association between online civic talk and contacting political figures directly is not moderated by online media multiplexity.

Similarly, Model 5 in Table 3 shows that, respondents who were younger, had higher education as well as political efficacy, accessed more political news, and had a more positive attitude toward the Web were more likely to express political opinions in online public spaces than their counterparts. Also as hypothesized, Model 6 indicates that respondents who had discussed politics with their friends via online channels were 24.7 times more likely than their counterparts to articulate their thoughts about politics on forums, blogs, websites of news media, or other similar online destinations.

Model 7 indicates that, compared with respondents who used three types of online media, the odds of expressing political opinions publicly online were also as almost twice as large (187%) for

Table 3.   Logistic regressions on expressing political opinions in online public spaces.

	Expressing political opinions in online public spaces							
	Model 5 coefficient (SE)		Model 6 coefficient (SE)		Model 7 coefficient (SE)		Model 8 coefficient (SE)	
Female (female = 1)	−.170	(.162)	−.061	(.193)	−.058	(.197)	−.058	(.197)
Age	−.022*	(.011)	.008	(.013)	.021	(.014)	.022	(.014)
Years of education	.126**	(.040)	.035	(.048)	.007	(.049)	.008	(.049)
Married/cohabitation	−.351	(.221)	−.435	(.262)	−.328	(.268)	−.332	(.268)
Personal income (logged)	−.009	(.012)	−.011	(.014)	−.014	(.015)	−.014	(.015)
Political efficacy	.494**	(.154)	.429*	(.182)	.416*	(.186)	.416*	(.186)
Political trust	−.208	(.115)	−.223	(.138)	−.223	(.139)	−.224	(.139)
Political knowledge	.071	(.102)	.100	(.122)	.093	(.126)	.093	(.126)
Political news consumption	.267***	(.040)	.141**	(.048)	.128**	(.049)	.128**	(.049)
Hours online per week (logged)	.072	(.055)	−.024	(.063)	−.074	(.067)	−.077	(.068)
Internet attitude	.852***	(.170)	.384	(.207)	.194	(.214)	.195	(.214)
Online civic talk with friends			3.208***	(.232)	3.004***	(.234)	3.151***	(.581)
Online media multiplexity					.380***	(.080)	.405***	(.122)
Online civic talk × online media multiplexity							−.040	(.144)
Constant	−7.549***	(.969)	−6.293***	(1.159)	−6.695***	(1.184)	−6.789***	(1.235)
N	1060		1060		1060		1060	
McFadden's R^2	.167		.393		.413		.413	
Deviance	989.484		720.958		697.282		697.206	
LR test	198.251		466.779		490.454		490.531	
AIC	1013.485		746.957		725.282		727.205	
BIC	1073.077		811.515		794.806		801.696	

*$p < 0.05$.
**$p < 0.01$.
***$p < 0.001$.

those using five different media to contact their social ties online. Only political efficacy and political news consumption continue to be positively associated with expressing political opinions online once we include online civic talk and online media multiplexity in Models 6 and 7. Lastly, Model 8 also suggests that the association between online civic talk and expressing political opinions publicly is not moderated by online media multiplexity.

Based on the similar results regarding both contacting political figures directly and expressing political opinions in online public spaces, we find that online civic talk and online media multiplexity are consistently and positively related to online political participation, either privately or publicly. Therefore, both H1 and H2 are supported by our analyses. More importantly, the positive relationship of online civic talk with these online political activities seems to remain at a similarly high level when we include online media multiplexity in the analyses. This suggests that, in addition to the variances explained by online civic talk, online media multiplexity is indeed able to explain further the differences in propensity toward online political participation.

Another interesting finding is that, when explaining whether citizens may engage in online political activities, demographic backgrounds, psychological traits, and Internet experience

Table 4.   Predicted probabilities of online political participation by online civic talk.

	Contacting political figures directly		Expressing political opinions in online public spaces	
	Model 2	Model 3	Model 6	Model 7
Diff. in online civic talk[a]				
Have not discussed politics with social ties via the Web	.009	.009	.049	.049
Have discussed politics with social ties via the Web	.275	.227	.561	.512
Diff. in online media multiplexity[a]				
Using 2 online media for social interaction	–	.020	–	.088
Using 3 online media for social interaction	–	.029	–	.123
Using 4 online media for social interaction	–	.041	–	.170
Using 5 online media for social interaction	–	.057	–	.231

[a]Holding all other variables at their mean when generating the predicted probabilities.

may not be as important as online civic talk and online media multiplexity. For example, education and Internet familiarity only exhibit a relationship with both online political activities in the baseline models (Models 1 and 5). Although our findings are consistent with the literature demonstrating the gender difference in direct political participation (Verba et al., 1995), showing that females were consistently less likely than males to directly contact political figures via the Web in all four models, we do not find gender difference regarding expressing political thoughts publicly online. Similarly, only one of the three psychological antecedents and the level of political news consumption exhibit a relationship with the odds of articulating political thoughts in online public spheres. The result is consistent with previous work indicating that politically efficacious Taiwanese citizens were more likely to be politically involved (Chen & Lo, 2006).

The large coefficients of online civic talk and online media multiplexity may be due to the overall political disengagement of some respondents, resulting in a low propensity to practice any political activities. The predicted probabilities presented in Table 4 illustrate such a tendency. Looking at the results generated from Models 2 and 6 in the top panel of Table 4, for those who had never engaged in civic talk online, their predicted probability of contacting political figures online directly is less than 1% and their predicted probability of expressing political opinion in online public spaces is only about 5%.

In sharp contrast, if respondents had discussed politics with their social ties online, there is about a 28% chance that they would contact political figures directly via the Internet, and the predicted probability of expressing political opinions publicly in online destinations is also fairly high (56%).[7] When controlling further for online media multiplexity, the predicted probabilities generated from Models 3 and 7 resemble the similarly large discrepancy between the people who had engaged in online civic talk and those had not done so.

The bottom panel of Table 4 presents the discrete change in the predicted probability in relation to the types of online media used for communication. While such changes in the predicted probabilities are less pronounced than the differences induced by online civic talk, using more online media for social interaction increases the odds of online political participation noticeably.

Importance of social factors in conditioning online political participation

The results presented in the previous section indicate that Taiwanese citizens engaging in online civic talk with their friends and those using multiple online media for social interaction are more likely to participate in online political activities, either directly or indirectly. The findings further provide four revealing insights into the link between ICT and political participation in the digitalized civic life in Taiwan. Our first contribution is to extend the understanding of the implications of political discussion for other politically expressive activities, as we confirm the positive link in online contexts using a nationally representative sample of Taiwan. We find that articulating political opinions online is not a political behavior reserved for politically enthusiastic bloggers (Gil de Zúñiga et al., 2010). Taiwanese citizens who use multiple online media regularly for social interaction are also likely to engage in these politically expressive activities via the Web. Note that although we did not have any variable specifically measuring the participatory online culture in Taiwan, the use of BBS was captured in the measure of online media multiplexity and in one of the online political activities. Therefore, our findings were able to represent the general ICT usage pattern of interests sufficiently.

Second, and perhaps most importantly, we find that ICTs as a means of communication play a prominent role in facilitating Web users' online political participation, given the strong and positive association of online media multiplexity and online civic talk with both direct and indirect online expressive participation. Our analyses also indicate that the novel effect of instrumental Web use appears to be wearing off (Xenos & Moy, 2007), given that there is no statistically significant relationship between the Internet experience variables and online political participation. This means that the media or technologies per se may not necessarily relate to citizens' political engagement. The specific ways in which citizens use online media can have crucial implications for their participation in public affairs (e.g. Shah *et al.*, 2005). In other words, using different online media (such as BBSs versus social network sites) does not necessarily differentiate the patterns of Taiwanese citizens' political participation since they may visit these online venues for only entertainment purposes. However, if Taiwanese citizens use multiple ICTs to communicate with their friends, then they are more likely to engage in expressive political activities online than their counterparts.

Third, our findings about online political participation in Taiwan also support the claims by Di Gennaro and Dutton (2006) regarding the factors explaining the difference in online political participation in the UK. The significance of online media multiplexity suggests that Taiwanese citizens can extend the political communication in their private spheres to general public spheres by using available communication tools, which marks a potential path to directly or indirectly influence policy processes. We also suspect that the extent of online media multiplexity appears to be a good indicator of new communication or civic skills allowing citizens to engage in politics in digital domains.

The perspective of civic skills (Verba et al., 1995) implies two underlying issues for digital divide research and e-government studies. We discover that once citizens adopted ICTs in their daily routines, the traditional fault lines such as socioeconomic status and Internet experience may not necessarily be able to differentiate politically involved, from politically disengaged, persons in online contexts. Consistent with the work highlighting the digital inequality in ICT use (Hargittai, 2008), our findings indicate that Taiwanese citizens who use more ICTs for social interaction in private domains are more likely to contact political figures via online channels and voice their political opinions in public spheres, suggesting that online media multiplexity – the usage intensity of online media for social interaction – is related to the democratic potentials of ICTs. Similarly, as citizens start to rely on digital technologies for social interaction as well as civic and political participation, governments, officials, and other political figures should not merely equate e-government initiatives with information dissemination or service digitalization (Li & Feeney, 2012). They should also consider utilizing the interactivity of ICTs to solicit and encourage citizens' participation in public affairs.

Conclusions and limitations of current study

Our study seeks to assess the implications of ICTs as a means of communication for online political participation. While we present some robust evidence showing how ICTs facilitate new types of expressive political participation in online contexts, much empirical work remains to be done to address the nuances and limitations in detail. There are inherent constraints of the TSCS data, which limit the interpretation of the findings. First, the cross-sectional nature of the 2008 TSCS data prevents us from investigating the causality between ICT use and political participation. In other words, we cannot determine whether the relationship suggests that political enthusiasts were likely to use ICTs more intensively, or that heavy Web users were likely to encounter more opportunities to express their opinions or participate in political activities.

Second, given that the 2008 TSCS mainly focused on media use and online behaviors, we do not have any traditional measures of respondents' civic and political behaviors, such as membership in voluntary organizations or participation in campaigns; nor do we have information regarding respondents' personal networks. Given that the original questionnaire primarily asked respondents to report the overall estimates of online political activities and ICT usage, we could only construct proxy measures capturing the general patterns of online civic talk and online media multiplexity. Without a more refined observation with the necessary details about these behaviors, we are not able to account for these important variables and further examine the interaction effects among these constructs noted by some recent studies (Gil de Zúñiga & Valenzuela, 2011; Kim, Hsu, & Gil de Zúñiga, 2013; Rojas, et al., 2011; Tian, 2011). We are also not able to explore the implications of social Web use for political participation in both online and offline contexts. Another limitation of our study is that we could only include Internet users in our models and we acknowledge that the selection bias may be unavoidable. We cannot explore whether there is a difference in general political participation between Internet users and non-users, nor can we examine whether online public spheres may have become the main venues for users to engage in public affairs. Future work in this area should seek to collect detailed information regarding citizens' experience with ICTs and their civic and political engagement in various domains to investigate further the link between ICT use and political participation.

Despite its limitations, our study's unique approach allows us to make distinct contributions to the literature. Our study produces robust findings consistent with prior research in Western societies regarding how ICTs facilitate online political participation. More importantly, our findings suggest that communication affordances of ICTs may have notable implications for political communication and participation in online contexts. However, the extent to which citizens can benefit from the democratic potentials may depend largely on their ability to employ and utilize ICTs for social interaction under different situations and needs (Hsieh, 2012). Future work in this area is also encouraged to explore the inequality implications of online political activities.

Notes

1. Internet traffic ranking is based on statistics from Alexa (http://www.alexa.com/siteinfo/ptt.cc). The ranking may be fluctuating given that Alexa updates their tracking statistics daily.
2. The survey questionnaire was designed by the Institute of Sociology at Academia Sinica Taiwan.
3. In the first stage, cities and counties were randomly selected based on a seven-tier stratum classifying their traits of geography and urbanization. In the second stage, a random sample of townships from selected cities and counties was drawn. In the third stage, a random sample of individual household addresses was drawn from the household registration records of selected townships.
4. For example, emailing letters to editors or commenting news articles on the news media website.
5. We apply logarithmic transformation to the monthly personal income to adjust its distribution to normality.

6. The general rule of thumb is that, a VIF factor larger than 10 indicates a multicollinearity problem. A low threshold (VIF = 5) is often used for a more robust detection (O'brien, 2007).
7. Given the low predicted probabilities for those who did not discuss politics with social ties online (online civic talk = 0), the discrete change (from 0 to 1 in online civic talk) in predicted probability for both outcome variables of online political activities does not correspond closely to the constant factor change in probability. For more details, please see Long (1997).

References

Adamic, L. A., & Glance, N. (2005). *The political blogosphere and the 2004 U.S. election: Divided they blog*. Paper presented at the Proceedings of the 3rd international workshop on Link discovery, Chicago, IL.

Bargh, J. A., & McKenna, K. Y. A. (2004). The internet and social life. *Annual Review of Psychology, 55*(1), 573–590. doi: 10.1146/annurev.psych.55.090902.141922

Best, S. J., & Krueger, B. S. (2006). Online interactions and social capital: Distinguishing between new and existing ties. *Social Science Computer Review, 24*(4), 395–410. doi: 10.1177/0894439306286855

Bimber, B. A. (2001). Information and political engagement in America: The search for effects of information technology at the individual level. *Political Research Quarterly, 54*(1), 53–67. doi: 10.1177/106591290105400103

Bimber, B. A. (2003). *Information and American democracy: Technology in the evolution of politcial power*. New York, NY: Cambridge University Press.

Boase, J. (2008). Personal networks and the personal comunication system: Using multiple media to connect. *Information, Communication & Society, 11*(4), 490–508. doi: 10.1080/13691180801999001

Boase, J., Horrigan, J., Wellman, B., & Rainie, L. (2006). *The strength of internet ties*. Washington, DC: Pew Internet and American Life Project.

Boulianne, S. (2009). Does internet use affect engagement? A meta-Analysis of research. *Political Communication, 26*(2), 193–211. doi: 10.1080/10584600902854363

Brady, H. E., Verba, S., & Schlozman, K. L. (1995). Beyond SES: A resource model of political participation. *The American Political Science Review, 89*(2), 271–294.

Burns, N., Schlozman, K. L., & Verba, S. (2001). *The private roots of public action: Gender, equality, and political participation*. Cambridge, MA: Harvard University Press.

Central Election Commission Taiwan. (2012). Database of presidential elections. available from central election commission database of elections Retrieved January 25, 2013, from central election commission Taiwan. Retrieved from http://db.cec.gov.tw/

Chen, Y.-N. K., & Lo, V.-H. (2006). Media use and political capital. *Mass Communication Research (Xinwenxue Yanjiu in Chinese), 88*, 83–134.

van Cleemput, K. (2010). 'I'll see you on IM, text, or call you': A social network approach of adolescents' use of communication media. *Bulletin of Science, Technology & Society, 30*(2), 75–85. doi: 10.1177/0270467610363143

Di Gennaro, C., & Dutton, W. (2006). The internet and the public: Online and offline oolitical participation in the United Kingdom. *Parliamentary Affairs, 59*(2), 299–313. doi: 10.1093/pa/gsl004

Eliasoph, N. (1998). *Avoiding politics: How Americans produce apathy in everyday life*. Cambridge: New York, NY: Cambridge University Press.

Ellison, N. B., Steinfield, C., & Lampe, C. (2007). The benefits of facebook 'Friends': Social capital and college students' use of online social network sites. *Journal of Computer-Mediated Communication*, *12*(4), 1143–1168. doi: 10.1111/j.1083–6101.2007.00367.x

Ellison, N. B., Steinfield, C., & Lampe, C. (2011). Connection strategies: Social capital implications of Facebook-enabled communication practices. *New Media & Society*, *13*(6), 873–892. doi: 10.1177/1461444810385389

Finkel, S. E. (1985). Reciprocal effects of participation and political efficacy: A panel analysis. *American Journal of Political Science*, *29*(4), 891–913.

Gerbner, G., Gross, L., Morgan, M., & Signorielli, N. (1982). Charting the mainstream: Television's contributions to political orientations. *Journal of Communication*, *32*(2), 100–127. doi: 10.1111/j.1460–2466.1982.tb00500.x

Gil de Zúñiga, H., & Valenzuela, S. (2011). The mediating path to a stronger citizenship: Online and offline networks, weak ties, and civic engagement. *Communication Research*, *38*(3), 397–421. doi: 10.1177/0093650210384984

Gil de Zúñiga, H., Veenstra, A., Vraga, E., & Shah, D. (2010). Digital democracy: Reimagining pathways to political participation. *Journal of Information Technology & Politics*, *7*(1), 36–51. doi: 10.1080/19331680903316742

Hampton, K. N. (2011). Comparing bonding and bridging ties for democratic engagement – everyday use of communication technologies within social networks for civic and civil behaviors. *Information, Communication & Society*, *14*(4), 510–528. doi: 10.1080/1369118x.2011.562219

Hampton, K. N., Sessions, L. F., & Her, E. J. (2011). Core networks, social isolation, and new media: Internet and mobile phone use, network size, and diversity. *Information, Communication and Society*, *14*(1), 130–155. doi: 10.1080/1369118x.2010.513417

Hampton, K. N., & Wellman, B. (2003). Neighboring in netville: How the internet supports community and social capital in a wired suburb. *City and Community*, *2*(4), 277–311.

Hargittai, E. (2008). The digital reproduction of inequality. In D. B. Grusky, M. C. Ku, & S. Szelényi (Eds.), *Social stratification: Class, race, and gender in sociological perspective* (pp. 936–944). Boulder, CO: Westview Press.

Hargittai, E. (2010). Digital na(t)ives? Variation in internet skills and uses among members of the 'Net Generation'. *Sociological Inquiry*, *80*(1), 92–113.

Hargittai, E., Gallo, J., & Kane, M. (2008). Cross-ideological discussions among conservative and liberal bloggers. *Public Choice*, *134*(1), 67–86.

Hargittai, E., & Hsieh, Y. P. (2010). Predictors and consequences of differentiated practices on social network sites. *Information, Communication and Society*, *13*(4), 515–536. doi: 10.1080/13691181003639866

Haythornthwaite, C. (2005). Social networks and Internet connectivity effects. *Information, Communication & Society*, *8*(2), 125–147.

Haythornthwaite, C., & Rice, R. E. (2006). Perspectives on Internet Use: Access, Involvement and Interaction. In L. A. Lievrouw & S. Livingstone (Eds.), *The handbook of new media: Social shaping and social consequences of ICTs* (Updated Student ed., pp. 92–113). Thousand Oaks, CA: Sage.

Hogan, B. (2008). *Networking in everyday life* (Doctoral dissertation), University of Toronto, Toronto. Retrieved from http://individual.utoronto.ca/berniehogan/Hogan_NIEL_10–29–2008_FINAL.pdf

Hsieh, Y. P. (2012). Online social networking skills: The social affordances approach to digital inequality. *First Monday*, *17*(4). Retrieved from http://firstmonday.org/ojs/index.php/fm/article/view/3893/3192

Huckfeldt, R., & Sprague, J. (1987). Networks in context: The social flow of political information. *The American Political Science Review*, *81*(4), 1197–1216.

Huckfeldt, R., & Sprague, J. (1991). Discussant effects on vote choice: Intimacy, structure, and interdependence. *The Journal of Politics*, *53*(1), 122–158.

Ikeda, K. I., & Boase, J. (2011). Multiple discussion networks and their consequence for political participation. *Communication Research*, *38*(5), 660–683. doi: 10.1177/0093650210395063

Jennings, M. K., & Zeitner, V. (2003). Internet use and civic engagement: A longitudinal analysis. *The Public Opinion Quarterly*, *67*(3), 311–334.

Katz, J. E., & Rice, R. E. (2002). Syntopia: Access, civic involvement and social interaction on the internet. In B. Wellman & C. Haythornthwaite (Eds.), *The internet in everyday life* (pp. 114–138). Oxford: Blackwell.

Kavanaugh, A., Carroll, J. M., Rosson, M. B., Zin, T. T., & Reese, D. D. (2005). Community networks: Where offline communities meet online. *Journal of Computer-Mediated Communication*, *10*(4), 0–0. doi:10.1111/j.1083–6101.2005.tb00266.x

Kenski, K., & Stroud, N. J. (2006). Connections between internet use and political efficacy, knowledge, and participation. *Journal of broadcasting & electronic media*, *50*(2), 173–192. doi: 10.1207/s15506878jobem5002_1

Kim, H., Kim, G. J., Park, H. W., & Rice, R. E. (2007). Configurations of relationships in different media: FtF, email, instant messenger, mobile phone, and SMS. *Journal of Computer-Mediated Communication*, *12*(4), 1183–1207.

Kim, Y., Hsu, S.-H., Gil de Zúñiga, H. (2013). Influence of social media use on discussion network heterogeneity and civic engagement: The moderating role of personality traits. *Journal of Communication*, *63*, 498–516. doi: 10.1111/jcom.12034

Klofstad, C. A. (2011). *Civic talk: Peers, politics, and the future of democracy*. Philadelphia, PA: Temple University Press.

Klofstad, C. A., McClurg, S. D., & Rolfe, M. (2009). Measurement of political discussion networks: A comparison of two 'Name Generator' procedures. *Public Opinion Quarterly*, *73*(3), 462–483. doi: 10.1093/poq/nfp032

Kobayashi, T., Ikeda, K. I., & Miyata, K. (2006). Social capital online: Collective use of the internet and reciprocity as lubricants of democracy. *Information, Communication & Society*, *9*(5), 582–611.

Kraut, R., Patterson, M., Lundmark, V., Kiesler, S., Tridas, M., & Scherlis, W. (1998). Internet paradox: A social technology that reduces social involvement and psychological well-being?. *American Psychologist*, *53*(9), 1017–1031.

Lake, R. L. D., & Huckfeldt, R. (1998). Social capital, social networks, and political participation. *Political Psychology*, *19*(3), 567–584. doi: 10.1111/0162–895x.00118

Lazarsfeld, P. F., Berelson, B., & Gaudet, H. (1968). *The people's choice: How the voter makes up his mind in a presidential campaign*. New York, NY: Columbia University Press.

Ledbetter, A. M. (2008). Media use and relational closeness in long-term friendships: Interpreting patterns of multimodality. *New Media & Society*, *10*(4), 547–564. doi: 10.1177/1461444808091224

Ledbetter, A. M. (2009). Patterns of media use and multiplexity: Associations with sex, geographic distance and friendship interdependence. *New Media & Society*, *11*(7), 1187–1208. doi: 10.1177/1461444809342057

Levi, M., & Stoker, L. (2000). Political trust and trustworthiness. *Annual Review of Political Science*, *3*(1), 475–507. doi:10.1146/annurev.polisci.3.1.475

Li, M.-H., & Feeney, M. K. (2012). Adoption of electronic technologies in local U.S. governments: Distinguishing between E-Services and communication technologies. *The American Review of Public Administration*. doi: 10.1177/0275074012460910

Long, J. S. (1997). *Regression models for categorical and limited dependent variables*. Thousand Oaks, CA: Sage.

McLeod, J. M., Scheufele, D. A., Moy, P., Horowitz, E. M., Holbert, R. L., Zhang, W., ... Zubric, J. (1999). Understanding deliberation: The effects of discussion networks on participation in a public forum. *Communication Research*, *26*(6), 743–774. doi: 10.1177/009365099026006005

Mesch, G. S. (2009). Social context and communication channels choice among adolescents. *Computers in Human Behavior*, *25*(1), 244–251.

Mossberger, K., Tolbert, C. J., & McNeal, R. S. (2008). *Digital citizenship: The Internet, society, and participation*. Cambridge, MA: MIT Press.

Mutz, D. C. (2002). Cross-cutting social networks: Testing democratic theory in practice. *American Political Science Review*, *96*(01), 111–126. doi: 10.1017/S0003055402004264

Nie, N., Hillygus, S., & Erbring, L. (2002). Internet use, interpersonal relations and sociability: A time diary study. In B. Wellman & C. Haythornthwaite (Eds.), *The internet in everyday life* (pp. 244–262). Oxford: Blackwell.

Nisbet, M. C., & Scheufele, D. A. (2004). Political talks as a catalyst for online citizenship. *Journalism & Mass Communication Quarterly*, *81*(4), 877–896.

Norris, P. (2004). The bridging and bonding role of online communities. In P. N. Howard & S. G. Jones (Eds.), *Society online: The interaction in context* (pp. 31–42). Thousand Oaks, CA: Sage.

O'brien, R. (2007). A caution regarding rules of thumb for variance inflation factors. *Quality & Quantity*, *41* (5), 673–690. doi: 10.1007/s11135–006–9018–6

O'Neill, B. (2010). The media's role in shaping canadian civic and political engagement. *Policy and Society*, *29*(1), 37–51. doi: 10.1016/j.polsoc.2009.11.004

Putnam, R. D. (2001). *Bowling alone: The collapse and revival of American community*. New York, NY: Simon and Schuster.

Robinson, J. P., Barth, K., & Kohut, A. (1997). Social impact research: Personal computers, mass media, and use of time. *Social Science Computer Review*, *15*(1), 65–82.

Rojas, H., Shah, D. V., & Friedland, L. A. (2011). A communicative approach to social capital. *Journal of Communication, 61*(4), 689–712. doi: 10.1111/j.1460–2466.2011.01571.x

Scheufele, D. A., Hardy, B. W., Brossard, D., Waismel-Manor, I. S., & Nisbet, E. (2006). Democracy based on difference: Examining the links between structural heterogeneity, heterogeneity of discussion networks, and democratic citizenship. *Journal of Communication, 56*(4), 728–753. doi: 10.1111/j.1460–2466.2006.00317.x

Shah, D. V., Cho, J., Eveland, W. P. J. R., & Kwak, N. (2005). Information and expression in a digital age: Modeling internet effects on civic participation. *Communication Research, 32*(5), 531–565. doi: 10.1177/0093650205279209

Shklovski, I., Kiesler, S., & Kraut, R. E. (2006). The internet and social interaction: A meta-Analysis and critique of studies, 1995–2003. In R. E. Kraut, M. Brynin, & S. Kiesler (Eds.), *Computers, phones, and the internet: Domesticating information technology* (pp. 251–264). Oxford: Oxford University Press.

Stern, M. J., & Adams, A. E. (2010). Do rural residents really use the internet to build social capital? An empirical investigation. *American Behavioral Scientist, 53*(9), 1389–1422. doi: 10.1177/0002764210361692

Tian, Y. (2011). Communication behaviors as mediators: Examining links between political orientation, political communication, and political participation. *Communication Quarterly, 59*(3), 380–394. doi: 10.1080/01463373.2011.583503

Tolbert, C. J., & McNeal, R. S. (2003). Unraveling the effects of the internet on political participation? *Political Research Quarterly, 56*(2), 175–185.

Uslaner, E. M. (1998). Social capital, television, and the 'mean world': Trust, optimism, and civic participation. *Political Psychology, 19*(3), 441–467. doi: 10.1111/0162–895x.00113

Valenzuela, S., Kim, Y., & Gil de Zúñiga, H. (2012). Social networks that matter: Exploring the role of political discussion for online political participation. *International Journal of Public Opinion Research, 24*(2), 163–184. doi: 10.1093/ijpor/edr037

Verba, S., Schlozman, K. L., & Brady, H. E. (1995). *Voice and equality: Civic voluntarism in American politics.* Cambridge, MA: Harvard University Press.

Wang, S.-I. (2007). Political use of the internet, political attitudes and political participation. [Article]. *Asian Journal of Communication, 17*(4), 381–395. doi: 10.1080/01292980701636993

Wellman, B., Quan-Haase, A., Boase, J., Chen, W.-H., Hampton, K., Díaz, I., & Miyata, K. (2003). The social affordances of the internet for networked individualism. *Journal of Computer-Mediated Communication, 8*(3). doi: 10.1111/j.1083-6101.2003.tb00216.x

Xenos, M., & Moy, P. (2007). Direct and differential effects of the internet on political and civic engagement. *Journal of Communication, 57*(4), 704–718. doi: 10.1111/j.1460-2466.2007.00364.x

Derailed emotions: The transformation of claims and targets during the Wenzhou online incident

Maria Bondes and Günter Schucher

GIGA German Institute of Global and Area Studies, Institute of Asian Studies

Social media have both enabled and reinforced a shift towards the personalization of politics and collective action that is also occurring in China. In addition to street actions, the country is seeing a continuously growing number of so-called online mass incidents. While they have been attracting growing scholarly attention, most analyses have been based on anecdotal evidence and have treated netizens as a uniform group without evaluating the event's internal discursive dynamics. In order to assess such micro-blogging incidents' actual potential for political change, we investigate the case of the largest 'online mass incident' in China since the advent of Chinese micro-blogging services in 2009, prompted by the crash of two high-speed trains near the city of Wenzhou in July 2011. Drawing on the systematic content analysis of more than 4600 micro-blog posts published in the aftermath of the accident, we analyse the events' discursive dynamics, focusing on the composition, transformation, and radicalization of claims and targets. Our analysis demonstrates that the level of radicalism of the Wenzhou online mass incident is rather moderate and that no radicalization took place before the debate levelled down. While the incident significantly enhanced the tendency in Chinese online activism towards the broadening of the critical debate on national affairs, expectations about a democratizing impact of online debates might be premature.

Introduction

The Copenhagen protests on climate change, the Occupy movement, the 'indignados' in Spain, and not the least, the uprisings in the Arab region have demonstrated new forms of social struggle. In particular, social media have both enabled and reinforced a shift towards the personalization of politics and collective action that have been termed as 'connective action' (Bennett & Segerberg, 2012), 'digitally networked action' (Bennett & Segerberg, 2011), 'e-movements' (Earl & Kimport, 2011), a 'logic of aggregation' (Juris, 2012), or 'cloud protesting' (Milan, 2011). These new forms of social activism are built around loosely connected networked individuals, based on the individual expression of emotions and personalized interpretations of the world, and centre on issues of social justice. They are often short-lived, attract large numbers of partici-pants, and fade away rapidly.

These shifts have also occurred in China, the country with the most Internet users worldwide and the most refined system of Internet control and manipulation (Franzosi, 2008; Krippendorff, 1989), where a rapid diffusion of social media is met with 'forced' individualization (Hansen & Svarverud, 2010; Yan, 2010) and growing social discontent (Göbel & Ong, 2012). In addition to street actions, the country is seeing a continuously growing number of so-called online mass incidents – online debates that evolve around issues of social justice, corruption, and other problems associated with China's rapid economic development (Neuendorf, 2002; Tong & Lei, 2013; Yang, 2009). Other than digitally enabled 'connective action' in democratic countries, however, the majority of Chinese 'online mass incidents' develop entirely without the orchestration or engagement of any organization.

In a restrictive political setting like China, where organizations disconnected from the Communist Party have limited scope for action and where collective action is strictly controlled and channelled by an anxious party-state, the potential of social media, and particularly micro-blogs, to enable large-scale online events have electrified many observers (Herold & Marolt, 2011; Yang, 2009; Zheng, 2008; Zhou, 2009). Social media have been said to push the boundaries of public engagement in the vein of a 'liberation technology' (Diamond & Plattner, 2012). However, it is precisely this lack of organizational instances, which would mobilize discontents, channel personalized expressions, generate a focused agenda or orchestrate sustainable action, that has prompted less optimistic scholars to criticize such online events as mere cacophony and a short-lived venting of emotions in a fragmented online sphere that do not generate 'real offline events' (Farrell, 2012; Gladwell, 2010; Leibold, 2012).

While Chinese 'online mass incidents' and their potential to promote political change in China have been attracting growing scholarly attention, most analyses have been based on anecdotal evidence or online surveys and self-selection-biased snowball sampling. They have focused on the events' overarching characteristics regarding participants, causes, issues (Jiang, forthcoming, 2013; Yang, 2009), their relation with media, public, and political discourses (Hassid, 2012; Tong & Lei, 2013), or the mechanisms of state intervention via Internet control and censorship (Berg, 2001; King, Pan, & Roberts, 2013; Lombard, Snyder-Duch, & Bracken, 2004).

First and foremost, all these studies treat the participating netizens as a uniform group. Little attention has been paid to the events' internal discursive composition and development, although the participants' sentiments and opinions are the key factors in promoting the evolution of Internet events (Tan, Li, & Mao, 2012). To assess the political change potential of 'online mass incidents' in China, it is less important how many netizens participate. The most radical development happens when despite the absence of organizational entities participation in the debate leads individual netizens to the perception that the government is no longer answerable to its critics (Craig, 1980). Thus, systematic content analyses of single events are needed to shed light on the actual level of radicalism of the claims and targets produced in such unorchestrated online incidents and to disclose whether claims and targets change during the course of events. Answering these questions not only furthers our understanding of 'online mass incidents' and their potential for social mobilization in China, it contributes to the overall debate on the prospects for political change in China.

We investigate these questions by looking at the case of the largest 'online mass incident' in China since the advent of Chinese micro-blogging services in 2009, the massive online debate that was prompted by the crash of two high-speed trains near the city of Wenzhou in July 2011. Due to its unprecedented scale and set in the wake of the Arab Spring, the incident encouraged many observers to eagerly draw parallels with the so-called Twitter revolutions (Chin, 2011; Yi, 2011). Drawing on the content analysis of more than 4600 micro-blog posts, we evaluate the event's level of radicalism and its discursive dynamics, focusing on the composition, transformation, and radicalization of claims and targets.

In the following section, we will locate Chinese 'online mass incidents' in the broader context of digitally enabled action and discuss the core characteristics and limitations of the new forms of personalized connective action. We will then explain the emergence, transformation, and radicalization of claims and targets as the analytical framework for our analysis, before turning to the case of the Wenzhou incident. We will briefly outline the background and trajectory of the Wenzhou incident in the fourth section and introduce our data and methods thereafter. In the sixth and seventh sections we will present and discuss our findings. We conclude with a reflection on the political implications of 'online mass incidents' in authoritarian China.

Social media, personalized connective action, and 'online mass incidents'

In the last few decades, theorists and researchers have traced the rise of the networked individual in modern society (Castells, 1996; Giddens, 1994; Krippendorff, 2011). Social media and personalized communication technologies have both empowered and reinforced the personalization of politics and collective action (Bennett, 2012; Bennett & Segerberg, 2011). The global justice movements of the late 1990s and 2000s, empowered by new Web applications, marked a first shift towards networked and decentralized collective action based on informal groups, horizontal leadership, and decentralized networks with multiple and flexible identities that easily connected across national boundaries (Clark & Themudo, 2006; Della Porta & Mosca, 2005). The new technologies increased the speed and scope of mobilization and the dissemination of information and protest (Ayres, 1999; Bimber, Flanagin, & Stohl, 2005), eased linkages and collaborations among social movements and organizations (van de Donk, Loader, Nixon, & Rucht, 2004; Langman, 2005), and promoted meso-mobilization and the effective coordination of short-term commitments and small-scale acts of support (Garrett, 2006). While increasing the number and variety of actors and targets (Earl & Schussman, 2003), this networked form of collective action was still tied to more or less formal groups and collectives (Milan, 2011).

Social media have since contributed to a further individualization and personalization of collective action. Particularly, micro-blogs enable viral information flows based on the cascading of real-time and user-generated information through personal networks (Kaplan & Haenlein, 2011). These empower the rapid aggregation of large crowds of loosely connected individuals that can nonetheless share a strong sense of connectedness, co-presence, and a powerful feeling of solidarity (Juris, 2012). In what Milan (2011) calls 'cloud protesting', each individual can tailor his or her participation and contribute to the broad narrative and identity of the 'cloud'. Identities, resources, and narratives are individually negotiated and mediated by the social media platforms that take over the role of organizational instances. While the overall issues tackled may still resemble those of conventional forms of collective action, these new forms of 'connective action' (Bennett & Segerberg, 2012) centre on the large-scale expression of personal hopes, lifestyles and grievances, and 'personal action frames' or memes that invite personalized interpretations of a multitude of issues and are aim at a variety of targets.

Such personalized connective action has severe limitations, however. The most crucial impediment relates to sustainability. Social media and particularly micro-blogs are far less facilitative of lasting organizational networks and sustainable collective action than prior networking tools (Juris, 2012). The large crowds of individuals aggregated through the viral flows of social media disaggregate just as rapidly unless complemented with alternative tactics, strategies, and means of networking. Another major challenge concerns the issue of claims and goals. The aggregation of personalized expressions renders the emergence of concise demands and unified contentious claims highly unlikely. Various authors have thus suggested that the political impact of connective action enabled by social media that does not generate a more sustainable movement might be limited to shifts in public and political discourse (Bennett, 2012; Juris, 2012). Moreover, such connective action is highly dependent on the spaces and organizational function provided by social media platforms, making it vulnerable to Internet control and censorship.

Chinese 'online mass incidents' – 'public events where large numbers of netizens participate in often *unorganized, autonomous* online efforts to express their sentiments and opinion, address collective needs, or influence public opinion and policy' (Jiang, forthcoming, 2013) – reflect similar logics. Particularly since the advent and rapid spread of Chinese micro-blogging services (*weibo*) in 2009,[1] these incidents have seen a rapid growth both in terms of frequency and numbers of participants. The largest 'online mass incident' in 2011, the Wenzhou incident under investigation, had at least 10 million participants (Zhu, Shan, & Hu, 2012). Reflecting the broader development of personalized politics, such online events tend to be concerned with issues of social justice and the direction in which society is headed (Jiang, forthcoming, 2013; Lee, 2012; Yang, 2009).

Despite the multi-layered censorship of China's Internet that is particularly directed at curtailing collective action (King et al., 2013), the cost of participating in such personalized connective action can be regarded as almost negligible for the majority of netizens when compared to the cost of traditional collective action. The rapid aggregation of participants is facilitated by the exceptionally high percentage of Chinese Internet users employing mobile communication devices – 420 million out of a total of 564 million total Internet users and more than 65% of Weibo users (CNNIC, 2013) – and by the specifics of Chinese micro-blogging services. Sina Weibo's commenting function, the direct inclusion of pictures and videos in posts – not possible on Twitter – and the richer content that can be transmitted in the Chinese language within the prescribed maximum of 140 characters enable much more structured and centralized discussions when compared to the rather chaotic and multidimensional conversation structures on Twitter (Sam, 2010).

However, the limitations of this form of digitally enabled action also apply to China. Unless the online events are either appropriated by pre-established groups and actors such as China's rights defence (*weiquan*) movement (Hung, 2010; Teng, 2012), social organizations, activists and dissidents (Sima, 2011; Sullivan & Xie, 2009; Yang, 2008, 2009) or emerging opinion leaders (Tong & Lei, 2013), or unless they are directed at specific problems that might trigger offline actions such as in the case of recent (so-called 'NIMBY') environmental protests, they disaggregate as rapidly as they aggregated. While the cost of participating in online events might be low, the cost of complementing digitally networked action with alternative (offline) tactics, strategies, and forms of organization has not experienced a significant decline. Moreover, highly dependent on the spaces and organizational function provided by social media platforms, such online events have been vulnerable to official censorship and intervention. In recent years, China has thus seen a long line of massive but fragmented and short-lived online debates about a multitude of issues that have flared up ever more frequently without generating a sustainable social movement.

While the events have been credited with contributing to public agenda setting and impacting political and public discourse by pushing the boundaries of the discursive permissible and constituting spaces for public deliberation (Esarey & Qiang, 2008; Jiang, forthcoming, 2013; Lee, 2012; Neuendorf, 2002; Wang & Hong, 2010), critics have decried them as cacophony and a mere venting of steam in a fragmented online sphere (Hassid, 2012; Leibold, 2012). The absence of organizational instances and unified contentious claims, however, does not preclude that expressions of anger and individual thoughts transform into the attribution of blame or even one step further into mobilization efforts and calls for action – processes rendered vital in social movement theory.

Consequently, our questions are: Who or what are these claims targeted at? and: Do claims transform and radicalize? To answer these questions, we have to disassemble 'online activism' and analyse the online events' internal discourse development. But first we need criteria to measure different levels of radicalism.

The radicalization of claims and targets

The ubiquitous use of the terms radical and radicalization in protest literature suggests a consensus about there meaning that does not exist since the terms are used in different contexts. But in any case radicalization refers to patterns of both attitudes and behaviour, both in democracies and authoritarian regimes. In research on political violence, 'the term radicalization emerged to stress the interactive (social movements/state) and processual (gradual escalation) dynamics in the formation of violent, often clandestine groups' (Porta & LaFree, 2012). In social movement literature, radicalization is the development of extreme ideology and/or the adoption of violent forms of contention (McAdam, Tarrow, & Tilly, 2001). It is understood as an escalation process leading to the articulation of increasingly 'radical' aims and objectives and the use of violent means and strategies – often in interaction between those radicalized and their targets (Alimi, Bosi, & Demetriou, 2012; Larziellière, 2012; Moskalenko & McCauley, 2009).

Drawing on Tarrow's (2011) competition model of claim 'radicalization', Mueller (1999) explains 'radicalization' in the Leninist regime of the German Democratic Republic in 1989 as a shift in both the types of claims and targets. Motivated by a 'logic of grievances', claims shifted from the reactive defence of traditional rights to proactive demands for new rights; primarily material claims for changes in regime policies transformed into claims for the access to decision-making and later into open opposition to the regime (Mueller, 1999; Tarrow, 2011). While the most radical form of claims in China would be regime challenging and their manifestation the transformation from authoritarian rule, claim radicalization also happens on lower levels of contention.

In practice, it is not possible to distinguish claim radicalization and the shift of targets. However, in our analysis we treat them separately. For each of these processes, we define a three-step ladder. Explaining the emergence and transformation of disputes, Felstiner, Abel, and Sarat (1980/1981) have argued that in a first transformation called 'naming', 'an unperceived injurious experience […] must be transformed into a perceived injurious experience'. Research on 'mass incidents' in China has demonstrated that anger-venting has become a common form of protest (Yu, 2009). Participants in anger-venting activities do not display clear interest demands and direct their frustration at authorities or those who assumedly inflicted harm. We thus call the first category of claims 'anger' – expressions of anger and frustration without clear demands or interests. A second step, which Felstiner et al. (1980/1981) term 'blaming', occurs 'when a person attributes an injury to the fault of another individual or social entity'. Several studies have certified that the attribution of blame plays an important role in collective action (Commercio, 2009; Javeline, 2003). We include the *inquiry* for the cause or the responsible agent of a problem in our second claim category and call it 'causality and blame'. The third transformation occurs when someone knowing about the problem and its cause takes action and/or tries to mobilize others. We call this third category 'mobilization'.

With regard to targets, anger such as the complaints described by Felstiner et al. (1980/1981) is often not directed at any individual or a social entity in particular. We therefore call the first step of our ladder of targets 'none'. Attribution of blame, however, demands the identification of a culprit. Here, narrowly attributed blame 'is a more powerful motivator than diffuse blame' (Javeline, 2003). In authoritarian regimes, there is a qualitative difference between blame attributed to, or discontent directed at, specific officials or targets and those directed at the political system or regime as such. Easton's seminal distinction between specific and diffuse system support can be understood as a continuum rather than as a dichotomous typology, going from the approval of incumbent office-holders, confidence in regime institutions, positive evaluation of regime performance, and approval of the regime's core values to lasting bonds with the nation-state, exemplified by feelings of patriotism and national pride. According to this conceptualization, people can approve some institutions while rejecting others (Easton, 1975; Norris, 2011). As the flipside of the coin, specific discontent with certain officials or even institutions does not necessarily create generalized discontent weakening the support of the nation-state. Following Norris, we differentiate between claims targeted at specific institutions – in our case the Ministry of Railways (MOR) or its representatives – and the extension of criticism to other ministries, the central government and its representatives, or the party-state in general. We call the first category 'specific' and the latter 'systemic' – although we are aware that extending criticism beyond the MOR does not necessarily mean challenging the system of governance, i.e. the political regime.

We thus have a two-dimensional chart that reflects the radicalization of claims on the one axis and the radicalization of targets on the other (see Figure 1). The targets are plotted on the horizontal axis from 'none' to 'specific' to 'system', while the vertical axis reflects the radicalization of claims from 'anger' to 'causality/blame' to 'mobilization'. Rectilinear radicalization would lead from non-specified anger to mobilization against the system of governance.

Radicalization in authoritarian regimes is not necessarily rectilinear, the more so as it develops in interaction with repression. Due to the limited spaces for and available forms of opposition, criticism in China is often framed in legitimate terms and targeted at specific culprits to avoid the attention of the regime itself (O'Brien, 2008; O'Brien & Li, 2006).

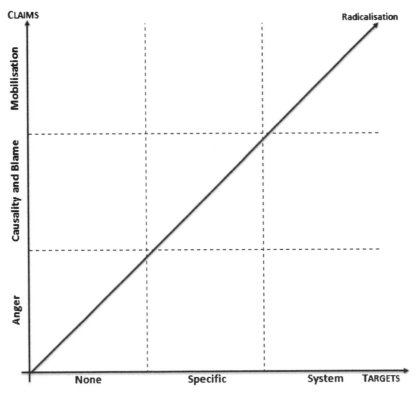

Figure 1. The radicalization of claims and targets.
Source: Authors' own illustration.

The Wenzhou online incident

On 23 July 2011, the crash between two high-speed trains triggered the largest 'online mass incident' since the advent of micro-blogging in China. Around 8:30 pm, high-speed train D3115 travelling along China's eastern coast from the city of Hangzhou to Fuzhou came to a halt over a viaduct near the city of Wenzhou. Shortly thereafter, high-speed train D301, also travelling to Fuzhou from Beijing, crashed into its rear end. Four train cars fell off the viaduct, killing 39 and injuring around 200 passengers. Minutes later, a message posted on Sina Weibo calling for help started to draw a lot of attention. After 10 hours, the message had been reposted more than 100,000 times and received more than 18,000 comments. The number of posts related to the Wenzhou train crash exploded on Chinese social media almost immediately after the accident. Within less than an hour, staff at Sina Weibo had set up a page devoted to the train crash that served as a major platform for the online debate. In the following week, there were 10 million messages, including reposts, related to the accident on Sina Weibo and a total of 26 million posts across Chinese micro-blogging platforms (Johnson, 2012; Osnos, 2012; Wines & LaFraniere, 2011; Xinhua, 2011).

While the scale of the online debate was unprecedented, it can be understood as the culmination of a long line of public doubts and anger about China's massive high-speed railway (HSR) programme. Initially designed as a practical solution to the long-standing problems of China's railway system, the Chinese Communist Party (CCP) soon elevated the enormous programme, designed and implemented by the MOR, to a symbol of national pride, an embodiment of the 'Chinese dream' and 'a miracle on earth created by the Chinese people' (Century Weekly, 2011) in an attempt to boost its legitimacy. All high-speed trains were named 'Harmony' (*hexie*), in reference to General Secretary Hu Jintao's ideological core concept of a 'Harmonious Socialist Society'. The Beijing–Shanghai line, which went into service only weeks before the train crash on 1 July 2011, just in time for the CCP's 90th anniversary, was promoted as an embodiment of Hu's second ideological core concept, his 'Outlook on a Scientific Development'.

From its early stages, however, the project's image was severely shaken by a high-level corruption scandal that had led to the dismissal of former minister of railways, Liu Zhijun, in February 2011, by massive safety concerns, and a series of technical failures that preceded the Wenzhou train crash. The MOR had rushed ahead with the implementation of the project, which was criticized as 'excessive' by a research team of the Chinese Academy of Sciences and compared to the 'Great Leap Forward' during the Mao era (Yue, 2011). Criticism mounted that overly rapid construction and the lack of independent quality controls had led to severe safety oversights. After the opening of the Beijing–Shanghai track, daily malfunctions and delays irritated passengers (Bandurski, 2011). In the weeks leading up to the Wenzhou accident, public anger boiled over on Chinese micro-blogs. The unprecedented scale of posts and the number of participants during the Wenzhou incident have to be seen in light of these prior developments.

The turbulent unfolding of events in the aftermath of the crash was characterized by interactions between the authorities, the netizens, and the media. The major events during the incident, which were widely debated on Sina Weibo, were: (1) the burial of a wrecked carriage at the site of the accident on the early morning of 24 July; (2) the rescue of a toddler from the wreckage on the same day, hours after the official rescue efforts had been concluded; (3) a late evening press conference on the same day given by MOR spokesman Wang Yongping; (4) the unearthing of the buried car on 25 July, which was attributed to online public opinion in state media; (5) Prime Minister Wen Jiabao's visit to the site on 28 July and his press conference, at which he announced that railway safety was a top priority; and (6) the publishing of a critical editorial written by the CCP's flagship newspaper, the *People's Daily*, which called on China to say no to a 'blood-smeared

GDP' (*daixue de GDP*) on the same day (Custer, 2011; Wines & LaFraniere, 2011; Xinhua, 2011).

The train crash remained a central issue on Sina Weibo until 2 August, when topics related to the accident, which had occupied the top three of Sina Weibo's hottest topics list for 10 straight days, were suddenly toppled by other trends (Li, 2011; RedTech Advisors, 2011), suggesting official intervention. While fierce censorship efforts were also directed at traditional state media who reported exceptionally critically about the accident – particularly via a media directive issued by the Central Propaganda Department on 29 July that was termed a 'media blackout' by the *New York Times* (LaFraniere, 2011) – the online debate could unfold relatively unimpeded by official intervention during the first 10 days after the accident. The term 'Wenzhou' and other central keywords were at no point in time censored on Sina Weibo.

Similar to the development of prior Chinese 'online mass incidents' and other instances of digitally enabled connective action, the number of participants had already started to level down before the official intervention on 2 August, however. Micro-blog users were never remobilized on a considerable scale at a later time, not even by a deadly subway crash in Shanghai on 27 September that was traced back to a failure of the same safety system used on the Wenzhou trains. Even the release of the official investigation report on the Wenzhou accident on 28 December 2011 – which found 54 officials as well as the design of the local control centre and on-board components responsible for the accident – did not prompt a significant increase in related posts.

Data and methods

To investigate the internal discourse on the events, we analysed micro-blog posts published on Sina Weibo in the aftermath of the accident. Although the online debate ignited by the train crash was not restricted to Sina Weibo (Zhu et al., 2012), we concentrated on the platform as it is the leading micro-blogging service in China (RedTech Advisors, 2011). Most scholars studying online debates rely on non-probability sampling like online surveys and snowball sampling or just anecdotally select single prominent posts, methods that are affected by self-selection and non-representative sampling (Dumitrica, 2011). In contrast to these rather impressionistic approaches, we combined a stratified random sample provided by WeiboScope and a systematic sample based on interval sampling to create an appropriate body of data for the systematic and quantitative analysis of the posts' special characteristics (Franzosi, 2008; Neuendorf, 2002).

Social media research is still faced with severe methodological difficulties particularly with regard to the samples' representativeness in light of the vast amounts of posts inhibiting social media spaces. This is particularly the case for Chinese social media research, where most auspicious tools applied in Internet research are thus far of limited use for reasons of both language and technology. While inferences drawn from content analyses of micro-blogging posts are thus arguably limited in scope, systematic random sampling allows some valuable insights despite its limitations. Undeniably, better analytical tools are needed for Chinese social media research. We understand our approach as a contribution in this direction.

In a first step, we relied on data provided by the WeiboScope Search archive, a project established by the Journalism and Media Studies Centre at the University of Hong Kong. The project uses the information retrieval software Lucene as an indexer to conduct full-text searches on Sina Weibo, indexing every four hours and storing all linked information in a standard database.[2] Unless censored within the time period before the initial indexing (at a maximum of four hours), our sample thus contains all the posts made, regardless of whether they were deleted after initial indexing.[3]

WeiboScope's subsample, and thus also our coded sample, consists of users with more than 1000 followers, which is a rather low threshold for the Chinese micro-blogging community, but excludes all first-time users. Since three quarters of Chinese micro-bloggers have less than 20 followers or inactive accounts and particularly incidents like the Wenzhou crash draw many 'light users', the subsample does not reflect the complete picture of the micro-blogging universe (Fu & Chau, 2013). Nevertheless, the selection is appropriate since we asked about radicalization, which was expected to be more distinct with active users.

The WeiboScope archive features a search engine that allows keyword searches. Since the Wenzhou incident did not produce any central hashtags, we chose the Chinese term for 'high-speed train' (*gaotie*) as our keyword since it showed the best returns in terms of numbers and relevancy. We conducted a search request for each day for the first month after the train collision, starting from 23 July, and stored all posts in an internal database in chronological order. The downloaded posts totalled 70,255. Starting almost immediately after the train crash on the evening of 23 July, the number of posts in our sample displays a sharp increase, peaking on 24 July at 11,183 posts. From 25 July onwards, posts start to decline and level off at about 1000 posts per day after 2 August, reflecting the overall development of the Wenzhou incident (see Figure 2). Due to the large amount of data and the fact that the number of posts declined rapidly after 29 July, we restricted our coding to the first nine days after the accident (23–31 July).

To capture variation in time in order to be able to investigate the incident's diachronic development, we then selected a systematic random sample based on interval sampling and coded the first 20 posts after each half-hour according to their publication date (i.e. the first 20 posts posted after 11:00, after 11:30, after 12:00, etc.), amounting to a total of 4635 posts. Due to downloading problems with the search engine, our data contain some gaps in terms of the timeline.

In a first round of binary coding we then excluded all posts that were not related to the Wenzhou incident, thus restricting the sample to 4001 relevant posts or approximately 85% of the total number of posts. Coding was not confined to the posts' original text, but also included re-tweets and attached pictures – but no comments.

For this definitive sample, content coding was conducted by focusing on participants' claims and targets. After preliminary coder training and informal assessment of agreement, all posts

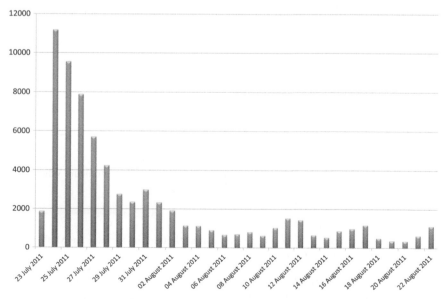

Figure 2. Number of posts on WeiboScope containing Gaotie, 23 July–22 August 2011.
Source: WeiboScope, authors' own calculations.

related to the Wenzhou incident were coded by two native Chinese coders, proficient in the language as well as the subtext of Chinese micro-blog posts. We tested inter-coder agreement in a pilot test of 60 posts before we started coding of the full set. Since we opted for different sets of units for both coders with an overlap of over 10%, we assessed agreement for the overlapping units during coding using per cent agreement – although disputed – and calculated the number of agreed codings to the full sample by hand (Krippendorff, 2011; Lombard et al., 2004). Coding resulted in different rates of agreement for rather manifest (participants and targets) and rather latent categories (claims) (Berg, 2001). Nevertheless, we reached an average accuracy of over 80% which is considered acceptable (Neuendorf, 2002). Recoding of inconsistent codes by the authors raised accuracy further.

The various tests of agreement helped us to refine our coding instructions, adjust and reduce the codes and improve the coding scheme. While our initial round of coding included various categories of claimants such as social organizations, media representatives, officials, or members of the Fifty Cent Party, most claimants were coded as simple netizens since the other categories were extremely hard to detect. We thus altogether dropped the claimant category for our analysis due to its limited explanatory power. Nonetheless, claimant coding displayed one relevant result, i.e. that in fact no social organizations or comparable organizational instances were engaged in the online event. Not a single post was found written by a conventional social organization. Moreover, we could not detect any 'opinion leaders' (Tong & Lei, 2013), defined by us as netizens with an amount of postings above average.

As to claims and targets, our initial categories exceeded those used for our analysis with regard to the radicalization of claims and targets. Claim categories also included the mere statement of 'information', amounting to 13.7% of all posts. Targets included 'media' institutions. For the evaluation of the debate's radicalization in this article, all related posts were re-coded by the authors according to the three categories developed for claims and targets, respectively, based on our analytical framework (cp. coding scheme given in Table 1). Previously separated target codes for government institutions and their representatives were merged. Examples of each category are given in the results section.

In addition to the coding just described, the central issues and topics discussed in the posts were determined during two iterations of open coding by the authors and the two coders and the resulting coding scheme was then used for definitive content coding and analysed in another article (Schucher & Bondes, forthcoming, 2014). The results of this issue coding serve

Table 1. Coding scheme.

Code	Description
Claim	
Anger	Expressions of anger, sorrow, grief, disbelief, or doubts
Causality/ blame	Attributions of causality or blame: what is the cause of the problem? Who is responsible for the problem? Who should solve the problem?
Mobilization	Mobilization, calls for action
Target	
None	No explicit target
Specific	Claims directed at a specific government institution, in our case the MOR and/or its representatives (name or position)
System	Claims extended to more than one institution at the national level of party or government and/or its representatives (name or position), as well as national policies and responsibilities such as GDP growth or China's development path

Source: Authors' own compilation.

as background information for the present analysis and to give a better impression of the discussion during the incident.

Results

In the following sections we will first outline the overall discursive composition of the online event with regard to the three analytical categories of claims and targets, respectively, to display the general level of radicalism across all days under investigation and determine the level of it from the claims and targets raised during the incident. To give a better impression of the discussion, we display examples for each category. Percentage figures given here refer to the total number of posts in order not to distort the general view. We will then turn to the debate's internal dynamics and the question of a dynamic radicalization throughout the incident, following our 'ladder of radicalization', in order to assess the incident's potential for political change within the given Chinese setting.

Claims

With regard to claims, not surprisingly the majority of posts are expressions of anger at the lowest level of radicalization. At an average of 49.8% across all days between 23 July and 31 July, this category makes up almost half of the posts. The venting of anger ranges from moderate statements of frustration or grief to expressive outbursts of anger such as by user @Erdongqiang: '//@Beijingbingren: Son-of-a-bitch of stupid Xinhuanet, listen well: HSR is not for the state's benefit, it's for the entire people's benefit! If the entire people's benefit got damaged, the entire people have the right to investigate!' (24 July, 18:02).[4]

Central objects of anger are safety issues, corruption, the opaque handling of the crash and rescue measures, as well as the official boasting about the trains' superiority. Criticizing a lack of safety concerns, user @Lisakong-Konglisha for instance posted: '#Wenzhou train tailgated# Don't run too fast – since your soul cannot keep pace – trains, HSR and aeroplanes are not reliable – the world is very chaotic, very dangerous – (we) have no sense of security!! […]' (24 July, 23:31). Denouncing the official opacity in handling the case and related rescue efforts, user @QuanqiuJingdianFengyunBang complained:

> HSR-rail crash in Germany, made public! Transparent! Rescue work continued for 3 days! Using 2800 people! […] China's HSR, 5 hours after the end of rescue efforts they found a small girl was still alive! … this crime is a shame for China! Prompting the whole world to laugh! (28 July, 13:00)

Posts by no means halt at the mere expression of anger, however. Almost a quarter of the posts or 22.3%, asked for reasons and responsibilities and attributed causality and blame, such as user @Bianzixinxin: 'Concrete responsibility? //@tuqianmei: Was HSR approved by the director of the Shanghai Railway Bureau hastily loaded with people?' (24 July, 17:21). Sometimes they are clearly addressed to those assumedly responsible:

> [Questions to the Premier] 1. What is the nature of the crash? 2. How many people died? […] 4. Was evidence hastily destroyed? 5. Why were rescue efforts stopped after 72 hours? […] 7. Why were the media anxiously instructed to hide the facts? 9. How was the safety of HSR and trains evaluated? 10. Will the State Council ask about the responsibility? (@Hanzhiguo, 28 July, 12:00)

Looking for culprits, netizens blamed managers of railway bureaus, the MOR, Premier Wen and state institutions, as well as the government in general: '//@maqiji: If the HSR has no problems, then the political power and the government have problems' (@Shushengyiqi, 24 July, 18:32).

While only a few made the step towards mobilization – a total of 6.4% of all coded posts – the online incident produced three calls for, protest actions. The first was a public vote for the resignation of the Railway Minister Cheng Guangzu and the HSR Chief Engineer He Huawu. The second was a consumer boycott of the HSR, calling to avoid the trains in the future and to return tickets already bought. The latter posts were often accompanied by pictures of heaps of 'returned' HSR tickets. Both mobilizations, calls for participation in the public vote and the HSR ticket boycott, started on 24 July but never caught real momentum. On 28 July, another call for a boycott, which became one of the dominant issues in our sample on 31 July, took off. Micro-bloggers called for the collective return of mineral water produced by the Tibetan company Xizang 5100 Glacier Mineral Water, which had been distributed free of charge on the high-speed trains. Ecological concerns turned into large-scale indignation when netizens realized that the wife of the dismissed minister of railways, Liu Zhijun, had been a member of the company's executive board.

Targets

While only 9.6% of posts had no explicit target, the great majority of 86% were targeted at the MOR and/or its representatives, which is not surprising in the case of a train crash. However, 11.8% of posts moved beyond the MOR to the 'systemic' level, targeting also other ministries, the government, national leaders (mostly Premier Wen), or even addressed the political system. Those posts often linked the train crash to broader societal issues such as the chain of safety scandals, nationwide corruption, or even China's development path, such as the following two posts:

> From food safety to all kinds of hardware equipment, elevator and HSR, all of the repeated accidents prove that excessively fast development results in not reaching the desired speed. […] It's time now for slowing down the pace, take your time, life is precious! (@XingyueyueYaonuliaqianxing, 24 July, 10:00)
>
> //@Xuxiaonian: Crash in the rear of the 'Great Leap Forward'. […] //@Daibangyinfei: Corruption stops at nothing and is unbridled. […] (@Shishiluantan, 24 July, 22:59)

Many of these posts pleaded to slow down the 'Chinese speed' (@Sunxiaoninzaieryue, 24 July, 10:01). Appeals to slow down GDP growth particularly gained in number after the publication of a critical editorial by the CCP's flagship newspaper, the *People's Daily*, which called on China to say no to a 'blood-smeared GDP' (*daixue de GDP*) on 28 July. While these appeals can be considered to be compliant with the aims of the "twelfth five-year plan"?, some posts called for political reforms like that of user @Liusong – Jiaguwen: '//@Gator: The reform of our system is actually too slow. That is the reason why the HSR is too fast. As long as the system does not change, everything that should be slow is not able to slow down' (29 July, 19:12).

Radicalism and radicalization during the course of the incident

When taking a closer look at the level of radicalism displayed during the online debate, anger is the dominant expression among the claims. Taking only those posts relevant to our three-step ladder of claim radicalization, posts coded as 'anger' make up 63.4%, those coded as 'causality and blame' account for 28.4%, and the 'mobilizing' posts amount to 8.2%. As for the three-step ladder of target radicalization, the posts without any target make up only 9%, whereas those aimed at the 'specific' target MOR account for 80%. Those blaming the 'system' make up a significant share of 11%. That means that neither claims nor targets reveal a very high level of radicalism. However, compared to 28 million posts over the course of the debate, 8% of posts calling for action and 11% extending their criticism beyond the MOR and attributing blame to the government or even the political system are still a vast number. Nevertheless, the debate is far from being a political debate about the faults of the system.

This becomes much clearer when we link claims to targets. The huge majority of all claims in our three-step scheme are directed at the MOR: when we look at the three categories individually, those posts expressing anger at the MOR make up 82.1%, those attributing causality and blame to the MOR amount to 74.8%, and 100% of mobilization efforts are targeted at the MOR since mobilization was limited to consumer boycotts and did not turn into further political action. When moving to the systemic level, the share of posts targeting the system is somewhat higher for 'causality and blame' than for anger (19.4% compared to 11.5%). This means that netizens who considered the question of responsibility were more likely to link the problems to the systemic level.

To analyse the radicalization of claims and targets across time, we looked at the development and shifts in the three categories, respectively, over the observed time span from 23 July to 31 July; results are presented in Figures 3–5. Figure 3 shows the development of claims with regard to the three categories of claim radicalization throughout the incident. Figure 4 presents the development of targets. And Figure 5 displays the development of those shares of posts in all categories of claims that target the 'systemic' level.

Both claims and targets display some variation between the days, but none of them experience any noticeable or continuous shift towards radicalization. The only exception is the last day, 31 July, when appeals to return the mineral water bottles distributed on the HSR took off. We do not take this as an evidence of radicalization, however, but only as a short-term surge. This reading is supported by Figure 5, which reveals that the share of claims targeted at the 'system' declines after 26 July.

To sum up, our analysis demonstrates that the level of radicalism of the Wenzhou online mass incident is rather moderate and that no radicalization in claims or targets took place during the first nine days before the debate levelled down. This is illustrated by Figure 6, in which we located the

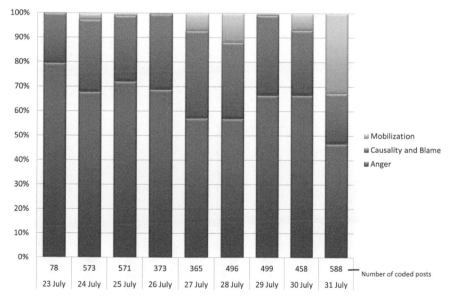

Figure 3. Development of claims (in per cent).
Source: Authors' own calculations.

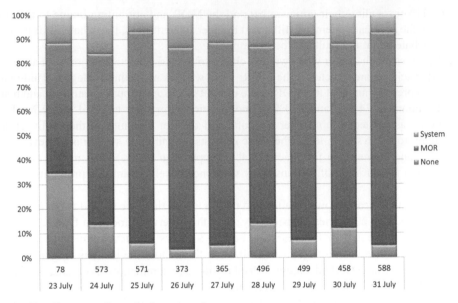

Figure 4. Development of targets (in per cent).
Source: Authors' own calculations.

posts published on the first full day (24 July) of events, towards the middle of the incident (27 July) and on the last day of coding (31 July) in our 'radicalization scheme'. All three ellipses display almost the same position. The share of posts targeted at the system is larger on 24 July, reflecting that 'systemic criticism' even diminished throughout the incident across all categories of claims. On 31 July, a larger share of posts is aimed at mobilization, which remains targeted at the specific target MOR, however.

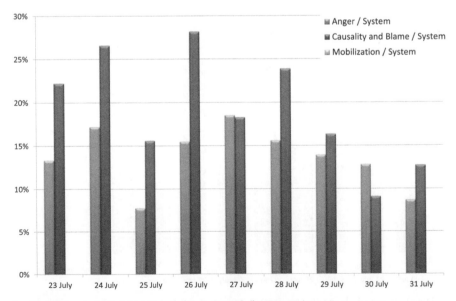

Figure 5. Development of claims targeted to 'system' (in per cent).
Source: Authors' own calculations.

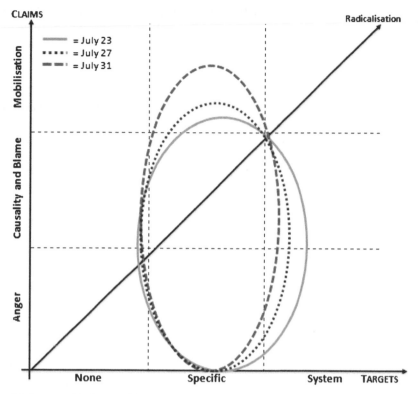

Figure 6.   Moderate radicalism and lacking radicalization of the Wenzhou online Debate. Source: Authors' own illustration.

Discussion

Most studies on 'online mass incidents' in China and particularly those on micro-blogging campaigns have focused on the Internet's power to promote digital political participation, expand the public sphere into online space, express online public opinion, challenge offline agendas, and put pressure on governments to change policy. These features have been confirmed by the Wenzhou incident. Moreover, our analysis revealed a comparatively large share of proactive claims that are rated as evidence of radicalization in social movement theory. A similar development has only recently been described for offline protests, particularly those of the urban middle class (Cai, 2010; Johnson, 2010) and of workers (Elfstrom & Kuruvilla, 2012). But the proactive attitude of the Wenzhou bloggers was not systematically linked with more radical targets. Nor did it transform into mobilizing; the consumer boycotts – which have been a rather defensive part of China's repertoire of contention for a long time – remained reactive.

Radicalization, however, is not limited to a shift from rather reactive defence to proactive demands. It also involves a shift of targets that might finally transform grievances into regime-challenging claims. During this process the level of political discontent rises and the participation in or approval of unconventional behaviour increases. Disagreement translates into the erosion of diffuse support (Craig, 1980).

While the large majority of studies on online activism treat netizens as a uniform group, we were able – based on our unique sample – to analyse not only the overall level of radicalism during the Wenzhou incident, but also a possible transformation of claims and targets. If radicalization was to happen, this would support arguments that online activism gives new impetus to political participation in China and is a force of political change under conditions of lacking organizational opposition to the ruling Communist Party. We did, however, only detect a moderate level of radicalism and almost no radicalization, which implies that expectations about the democratizing impact of online activism might be premature. We assume this result to have four main reasons.

First, online activism is not fundamentally different from offline activism. The Wenzhou online incident exhibits features that are common for offline contention in China. On the one hand, a large group of people expresses emotions like anger, frustration, sorrow or doubt without having any clear interest demands, characterized as social anger-venting by the Chinese scholar Yu Jianrong (Yu, 2009); on the other hand, people raise clear interest demands aimed at fixing specific problems. While they are increasingly aware of rules and rights, their claims are more reactive than proactive, targeted against specific public authorities that are assumed to have inflicted harm. Incidents are isolated and crowds dissolve when the problems seem to be fixed. This kind of fragmented contention, stimulated by concrete and predominantly material interests and directed at specific targets, has been depicted by many scholars (Cai, 2010; Chen, 2012; O'Brien, 2008). Online contention seems not to make any difference (Herold & Marolt, 2011; Yang, 2009). Our study, however, shows that the quantitative relationship between these two groups has been inverted. While in offline contention rights defending activities account for up to four-fifths of mass incidents (Yu, 2009), the Wenzhou online debate was dominated by anger-venting netizens. One reason might be that the crash itself did not provoke any particular material interest, another one is that the low costs of participation in online contention attract larger crowds of discontented people.

Second, even though online contention comes at very low costs compared to offline actions, there remains a constant threat of repression, although we could not detect any clear signs of censorship until 2 August. The media directives issued by the Central Propaganda Department circulated on Sina Weibo, however, as well as orders by the Wenzhou Judicial Bureau and the Wenzhou Lawyers Association to lawyers not to take on cases involving victims' families. The Damocles sword of repression hanging over the netizens likely led the participants of the debate to act like their fellow countrymen in other incidents and stick to rather concrete claims and specific targets (Li, 2013).

Third, like other online incidents this debate, though large, was also too episodic to enable radicalization and rather followed the 'logic of aggregation' (Earl & Kimport, 2011; Juris, 2012; Zhou, 2009). The sharp increase in participation and its rapid decline resembles flash activism or 'smart mobs' (Lee, 2012; Rheingold, 2004), where a user's self-understanding as an 'activist' or the construction of a united 'we' is no longer necessary and where action is primarily based on personalized action. While the overall issues tackled still resemble those of conventional forms of collective action, digitally networked contention tends to be based more on the large-scale expression of personal feelings and individualized concerns regarding common issues. Participants are co-present and connected, but they are rarely interacting.

Fourth, it is true that with sharply reduced costs for participating in popular contention and with participants not having to be simultaneously present in time and space, traditional organizations are no longer required to start and coordinate contention. While we could not find any organization intervening in the debate, communication on *weibo* itself was the central organizing principle. The netizen community did not decide on coherent hashtags, but the staff of Sina Weibo set up a page devoted to the train crash shortly after the accident. But like physical space in the recent occupy movements, online space is a rather fragile form of 'organization'. Aggregation in vulnerable social media spaces is not enough to generate sustainable action. Etling, Faris, and Palfrey (2010) conclude that the upturn in bottom-up spontaneous protests focusing on specific high-profile issues, local events, and visible abuses of power – a trend we can clearly discern in China – is the logical consequence of the lack of organizations in closed regimes combined with decentralized digital reporting. In a similar vein, Yang (2009) observed that the more outrageous incidents are, the more spontaneous the protests.

Conclusion

The Wenzhou incident impressively demonstrated that the networked forms of contention enabled by micro-blogs have become a new and formidable element of Chinese popular contention. Without any engagement by conventional organizations or the construction of a collective identity, action evolved through the aggregation of millions of participants via micro-blogs. Like other online actions, this self-organized form of networked action exploded within hours and faded away equally quickly after a few days. During the incident, the micro-blogging platforms took over the role of organizing agents, magnifying the voices of individual bloggers.

Though unprecedented in its scale, the Wenzhou incident also sustained common features in Chinese popular contention. Refraining from direct criticism of the central government, the netizens mainly targeted the MOR and tackled issues that drew on broader debates in society and official discourse about safety, corruption, or lacking transparency. Thus, the Wenzhou incident significantly enhanced the tendency in Chinese online activism towards the broadening of the critical debate on national affairs. Unlike the local or material claims that primarily drive offline protests, criticism was not constrained to the accident itself but also questioned the political and economic logic behind the tragedy. Many netizens critically commented on social ills and core national policies and raised proactive demands to slow down the push for growth.

Micro-blogging during the Wenzhou incident did not radicalize to produce collective claims or stipulate offline action, which means that the potential of online activism to instigate political change has to be re-evaluated, however. Although in large numbers, participants still mainly express their individual emotions and personalized interpretations. Taking the 'crash course on public opinion' (GlobalTimes, 2011) seriously, China's leadership has decided to take a two-pronged approach by improving the 'guidance' of public opinion, while also raising the bar for the outright posting of individual opinions through the introduction of stricter regulations for micro-blogging such as a real-name registration system.

This less optimistic conclusion of the political change potential of micro-blogging activism in China has its limitations, however, and cannot be generalized without further case studies. We only analysed a single event, albeit the largest one so far, and sampled posts from Sina Weibo only. Moreover, by relying on WeiboScope we restricted the analysis to the most active users. Therefore, it would be necessary to analyse radicalization of other online incidents and investigate in longitudinal studies whether there is radicalization over time and/or whether memory traces and action repertoires are left that can be remobilized later on.

Notes

1. Western social media applications such as Facebook, Twitter, and Youtube have been blocked in China since 2009. Chinese Internet corporations such as Sina and Tencent were quick to come up with their own products, however. China now has a multifaceted social media landscape with a multitude of micro-blogging services, social networks, and other applications.
2. WeiboScope search can be found at http://research.jmsc.hku.hk/social/search.py/sinaweibo/. Information on building and deploying the system is given on Cedric Sam's blog 'The Rice Cooker' at http://jmsc.hku.hk/blogs/ricecooker/ and JMSC's page on the content-sharing platform GitHub at https://github.com/JMSCHKU/Social.
3. There is no suitable way of including posts that were generally blocked from publishing, e.g. via keyword-based censorship, however.

4. The double slash // indicates a repost. Other than on Twitter, Sina Weibo users can comment on posts with all their comments displayed underneath the original post, thereby facilitating conversation. Each post contains information about the number of reposts and comments. All of the English quotes of micro-blog posts mentioned in this paper are the authors' own translations.

References

Alimi, E. Y., Bosi, L., & Demetriou, C. (2012). Relational dynamics and processes of radicalization: A comparative framework. *Mobilization: An International Journal, 17*(1), 7–26.

Ayres, J. M. (1999). From the streets to the internet: The cyber-diffusion of contention. *The Annals of the American Academy of Political and Social Science, 566*(1), 132–143.

Bandurski, D. (2011, July 21). *Inside the murky plans of 'Great Leap Liu'*. Retrieved 18 March 2012, from http://cmp.hku.hk/2011/07/21/13951/

Bennett, W. L. (2012). The personalization of politics: Political identity, social media, and changing patterns of participation. *The Annals of the American Academy of Political and Social Science, 644*, 20–39.

Bennett, W. L., & Segerberg, A. (2011). Digital media and the personalization of collective action. Social technology and the organization of protests against the global economic crisis. *Information, Communication & Society, 14*(6), 770–799.

Bennett, W. L., & Segerberg, A. (2012). The logic of connective action. Digital media and the personalization of contentious politics. *Information, Communication & Society, 15*(5), 739–768.

Berg, B. L. (2001). *Qualitative research methods for the social sciences*. Boston, MA: Allyn and Bacon.

Bimber, B., Flanagin, A. J., & Stohl, C. (2005). Reconceptualizing collective action in the contemporary media environment. *Communication Theory, 15*(4), 365–388.

Cai, Y. (2010). *Collective resistance in China: Why popular protests succeed or fail*. Redwood City, CA: Stanford University Press.

Castells, M. (1996). *The rise of the network society. The information age: Economy, society and culture*. Malden, MA: Blackwell.

Century Weekly, E. (2011, August 26). Our bullet train lesson: Look before leaping. *A Century Weekly*. Retrieved from http://english.caixin.com/2011-08-26/100295367_all.html

Chen, X. (2012). *Social protest and contentious authoritarianism in China*. Cambridge: Cambridge University Press.

Chin, J. (2011, July 26). Weibo watershed? Train collision anger explodes online. China real time report. *The Wall Street Journal*. Retrieved from http://blogs.wsj.com/chinarealtime/2011/07/26/weibo-watershed-train-collision-anger-explodes-online/

Clark, J. D., & Themudo, N. S. (2006). Linking the web and the street: Internet-based dotcauses' and the anti-globalization' movement. *World Development, 34*(1), 50–74.

CNNIC. (2013). *CNNIC released the 31st statistical report on Internet development*. Retrieved 24 January 2013, from http://www1.cnnic.cn/AU/MediaC/rdxw/2012nrd/201301/t20130116_38529.htm

Commercio, M. E. (2009). Emotion and blame in collective action: Russian voice in Kyrgyzstan and Latvia. *Political Science Quarterly, 124*(3), 489–512.

Craig, S. C. (1980). The mobilization of political discontent. *Political Behavior, 2*(2), 189–209.

Custer, C. (2011). Death on the high speed rail, Day 2. *China Geeks*. Retrieved from http://chinageeks.org/2011/07/death-on-the-high-speed-rail-day-2/

Della Porta, D., & Mosca, L. (2005). Global-net for global movements? A network of networks for a movement of movements. *Journal of Public Policy, 25*(1), 165–190.

Diamond, L., & Plattner, M. F. (Eds.). (2012). *Liberation technology: Social media and the struggle for democracy*. Baltimore, MD: Johns Hopkins University Press.

van de Donk, W., Loader, B. D., Nixon, P. G., & Rucht, D. (2004). Introduction: Social movements and ICTs. In W. van de Donk, B. D. Loader, P. G. Nixon, & D. Rucht (Eds.), *Cyberprotest: New media, citizens and social movements* (pp. 1–25). London: Routledge.

Dumitrica, D. (2011). Editorial: Special issue: Methodological approaches to the study of virtual environments and online social networks. *Graduate Journal of Social Science, 8*(3), 9–13.

Earl, J., & Kimport, K. (2011). *Digitally enabled social change. Activism in the internet age*. Boston: The MIT Press.

Earl, J., & Schussman, A. (2003). The new site of activism: On-line organizations, movement entrepreneurs, and the changing location of social movement decision making. In P. Coy (Ed.), *Consensus Decision Making, Northern Ireland and Indigenous Movements (Research in social movements, conflicts and change)* (Vol. 24, pp. 155–187). Bingley: Emerald Group Publishing Limited. Retrieved from http://www.emeraldinsight.com/books.htm?chapterid=1783714&show=pdf

Easton, D. (1975). A re-assessment of the concept of political support. *British Journal of Political Science, 5*(4), 435–457.

Elfstrom, M., & Kuruvilla, S. (2012, July). *The changing nature of labor unrest in China*. Paper presented at the International Labor and Employment Relations conference, Philadelphia. http://ilera2012.wharton.upenn.edu/NonRefereedPapers/Kuruvilla,%20Sarosh%20and%20Elfstrom,%20Manfred.pdf

Esarey, A., & Qiang, X. (2008). Political expression in the Chinese blogosphere: Below the radar. *Asian Survey, 48*(5), 752–772.

Etling, B., Faris, R., & Palfrey, J. (2010). Political change in the digital age: The fragility and promise of online organizing. *SAIS Review, 30*(2), 37–49.

Farrell, H. (2012). The consequences of the internet for politics. *Annual Review of Political Science, 15*, 35–52.

Felstiner, W. L. F., Abel, R. L., & Sarat, A. (1980/1981). The emergence and transformation of disputes: Naming, blaming, claiming. *Law and Society Review, 15*(3/4), 631–654.

Franzosi, R. (2008). Content analysis: Objective, systematic, and quantitative description of content. In R. Franzosi (Ed.), *Content analysis* (Vol. 1, pp. XXI–XLX). Thousand Oaks, CA: Sage.

Fu, K.-w., & Chau, M. (2013). Reality check for the Chinese microblog space: A random sampling approach. *PLOS ONE, 8*(3), e58356. doi: 10.1371/journal.pone.0058356

Garrett, R. K. (2006). Protest in an information society: A review of literature on social movements and new ICTs. *Information, Communication & Society, 9*(2), 202–224.

Giddens, A. (1994). *Modernity and self-identity*. Cambridge: Polity Press.

Gladwell, M. (2010, October 4). Small change. Why the revolution will not be tweeted. *The New Yorker*. Retrieved from http://www.newyorker.com/reporting/2010/10/04/101004fa_fact_gladwell?currentPage=all

GlobalTimes. (2011, December 29). Govt gets crash course on public opinion, *Global Times*. Retrieved from www.globaltimes.cn

Göbel, C., & Ong, L. H. (2012). *Social unrest in China* (65 pp.). London: ECRAN.

Hansen, M. H., & Svarverud, R. (Eds.). (2010). *iChina: The rise of the individual in modern Chinese society*. Copenhagen: NIAS.

Hassid, J. (2012, August/September). *The politics of China's emerging micro-blogs: Something new or more of the same?* Paper presented at the APSA 2012 annual meeting, New Orleans. http://ssrn.com/abstract=2106459

Herold, D. K., & Marolt, P. (Eds.). (2011). *Online society in China. Creating, celebrating, and instrumentalising the online carnival*. London: Routledge.

Hung, C.-f. (2010). The politics of China's Wei-Quan movement in the internet age. *International Journal of China Studies, 1*(2), 331–349.

Javeline, D. (2003). The role of blame in collective action: Evidence from Russia. *American Political Science Review, 97*(1), 107–121.

Jiang, M. (forthcoming, 2013). Chinese internet events. Wang luo shi jian. In A. Esarey & R. Kluver (Eds.), *Internet in China: Online business, information, distribution, and social connectivity*. New York, NY: Berkshire.

Johnson, I. (2012, October 5). China advances high-speed rail amid safety, corruption concerns. *National Geographic Daily News*. Retrieved from http://news.nationalgeographic.com/news/2012/10/121005-china-high-speed-rail-trains-transportation-world/

Johnson, T. (2010). Environmentalism and NIMBYism in China: Promoting a rules-based approach to public participation. *Environmental Politics, 19*(3), 430–448.

Juris, J. S. (2012). Reflections on #Occupy everywhere: Social media, public space, and emerging logics of aggregation. *American Ethnologist, 39*(2), 259–279.

Kaplan, A. M., & Haenlein, M. (2011). The early bird catches the news: Nine things you should know about micro-blogging. *Business Horizon, 54*(2), 105–113.

King, G., Pan, J., & Roberts, M. E. (2013). How censorship in China allows government criticism but silences collective expression. *American Political Science Review, 107*(2), 326–343. doi:10.1017/S0003055413000014

Krippendorff, K. (1989). Content analysis. In E. Barnouw, G. Gerbner, W. Schramm, T. L. Worth, & L. Gross (Eds.), *International encyclopedia of communications* (pp. 403–407). New York, NY: Oxford University Press.

Krippendorff, K. (2011). *Agreement and information in the reliability of coding* (16 pp.). Annenberg School of Communication, University of Pennsylvania.

LaFraniere, S. (2011, July 31). Media blackout in China after wreck. *New York Times*. Retrieved from http://www.nytimes.com/2011/08/01/world/asia/01crackdown.html

Langman, L. (2005). From virtual public spheres to global justice. A critical theory of internetworked social movements. *Sociological Theory, 23*(1), 42–74.

Larzielličre, P. (2012). Political commitment under an authoritarian regime: Professional associations and the Islamist movement as alternative arenas in Jordan. *International Journal of Conflict and Violence, 6*(1), 11–25.

Lee, M. (2012). Online activism by smart mobs and political change in southern China. *Issues and Studies, 48*(4), 1–35.

Leibold, J. (2012). Blogging alone: China, the internet, and the democratic illusion? *The Journal of Asian Studies, 70*(4), 1023–1041.

Li, L. (2013). The magnitude and resilience of trust in the center: Evidence from interviews with petitioners in Beijing and a local survey in rural China. *Modern China, 39*(1), 3–36.

Li, M. (2011). Rising voice. *China Daily*, published in *Washington Post* online, August 30. Retrieved from http://chinawatch.washingtonpost.com/2011/08/rising-voice.php

Lombard, M., Snyder-Duch, J., & Bracken, C. C. (2004). *Practical resources for assessing and reporting intercoder reliability in content analysis research projects*. Retrieved February 12, 2013, from http://www.temple.edu/sct/mmc/reliability/

McAdam, D., Tarrow, S., & Tilly, C. (2001). *Dynamics of contention*. Cambridge: Cambridge University Press.

Milan, S. (2011). *Cloud protesting: Dissent in times of social media*. Retrieved December 28, 2012, from https://citizenlab.org/2011/10/cloud-protesting-dissent-in-times-of-social-media/

Moskalenko, S., & McCauley, C. (2009). Measuring political mobilization: The distinction between activism and radicalism. *Terrorism and Political Violence, 21*(2), 239–260.

Mueller, C. (1999). Claim 'radicalization?' The 1989 protest cycle in the GDR. *Social Problems, 46*(4), 528–547.

Neuendorf, K. A. (2002). *The content analysis guidebook*. Thousand Oaks, CA: Sage.

Norris, P. (2011). *Democractic deficit: Critical citizens revisited*. Cambridge: Cambridge University Press.

O'Brien, K. J. (Ed.). (2008). *Popular protest in China*. Cambridge, MA: Harvard University Press.

O'Brien, K. J., & Li, L. (2006). *Rightful resistance in rural China*. Cambridge: Cambridge University Press.

Osnos, E. (2012, October 22). Boss rail. The disaster that exposed the underside of the boom. *The New Yorker*. Retrieved from http://www.newyorker.com/reporting/2012/10/22/121022fa_fact_osnos

Porta, D. D., & LaFree, G. (2012). Guest editorial: Processes of radicalization and de-radicalization. *International Journal of Conflict and Violence, 6*(1), 4–10.

RedTech Advisors. (2011). *Risky business: Sina Weibo intensifies censorship of tragic train crash*. Research note. Retrieved from http://www.slideshare.net/sinocismblog/redtech-advisors-on-sina-weibo-regulatory-risk-and-censorship

Rheingold, H. (2004). Smart mobs. The power of the mobile many. In H. McCarthy, P. Miller, & P. Skidmore (Eds.), *Network logic. Who governs in an interconnected world?* (pp. 191–202). London: Demos.

Sam, C. (2010). Sina Weibo and Twitter: Comparing data and conversation structures. *The Rice Cooker*. Retrieved from http://jmsc.hku.hk/blogs/ricecooker/2010/12/02/sina-weibo-and-twitter-comparing-data-and-conversation-structures/

Schucher, G., & Bondes, M. (forthcoming, 2014). China's dream of high-speed growth gets rear-ended: The 'Wenzhou 723' microblogging incident and the erosion of public confidence. In P. Marolt & D. Herold (Eds.), *Online China: Locating society in online spaces*. London: Routledge.

Sima, Y. (2011). Grassroots environmental activism and the internet: Constructing a green public sphere in China. *Asian Studies Review, 35*(4), 477–497.

Sullivan, J., & Xie, L. (2009). Environmental activism, social networks and the internet. *The China Quarterly, 198*, 422–432. doi:10.1017/S0305741009000381.

Tan, Z., Li, X., & Mao, W. (2012). Agent-based modeling of netizen groups in Chinese internet events. *SCS M&S Magazine*, 39–46.

Tarrow, S. (2011). *Power in movement: Social movements and contentious politics*. Cambridge: Cambridge University Press.

Teng, B. (2012). Rights defence (weiquan), microblogs (weibo), and the surrounding gaze (weiguan). The rights defence movement online and offline. *China Perspectives, 2012/3*, 29–41.

Tong, Y., & Lei, S. (2013). War of position and microblogging in China. *Journal of Contemporary China, 32*(80), 292–311.

Wang, S. S., & Hong, J. (2010). Discourse behind the forbidden realm: Internet surveillance and its implications on China's blogosphere. *Telematics and Informatics, 27*(1), 67–78.

Wines, M., & LaFraniere, S. (2011, July 28). In baring facts of train crash, blogs Erode China censorship. *The New York Times*. Retrieved from http://www.nytimes.com/2011/07/29/world/asia/29china.html

Xinhua. (2011, July 24). Xinhua insight: Microblogs reveal the healing power of 'We-Media' in wake of deadly high-speed train crash in East China, *Xinhua*. Retrieved from http://news.xinhuanet.com/english2010/indepth/2011-07/24/c_131006431.htm

Yan, Y. (2010). The Chinese path to individualization. *The British Journal of Sociology, 61*(3), 489–512.

Yang, G. (2009). *The power of the internet in China. Citizen activism online*. New York, NY: Columbia University Press.

Yi, Y. (2011, August 12). China's micro-blog revolution. *The Diplomat*. Retrieved from http://the-diplomat.com

Yang, G. (2008). *The rise of internet activists in China*. East Asian Institute, National University of Singapore.

Yu, J. (2009). Maintaining a baseline of social stability (speech before the Beijing Lawyers Association, translated by CDT). *Dongnan xinwen wang* [Tr. in *China Digital Times*]. Retrieved March 14, 2010, from http://chinadigitaltimes.net/2010/03/yu-jianrong-maintaining-a-baseline-of-social-stability-part-i/

Yue, Z. (2011). Expressways of excess. *Caixin Online*. Retrieved from http://english.caixin.cn/2011-10-31/100319471.html

Zheng, Y. (2008). *Technological empowerment. The internet, state, and society in China*. Redwood City, CA: Stanford University Press.

Zhou, X. (2009). The political blogosphere in China: A content analysis of the blogs regarding the dismissal of Shanghai leader Chen Liangyu. *New Media & Society, 11*(6), 1003–1022.

Zhu, H., Shan, X., & Hu, J. (2012). 2011 nian Zhongguo hulianwang yuqing fenxi baogao [Analysis on Internet-based public opinion in China, 2011). In R. Xin, L. Xueyi, & L. Peilin (Eds.), *2012 nian Zhongguo shehui xingshi fenxi yu yuce* [Society of China. Analysis and forecast [2012]) (pp. 194–214). Beijing: Shehui kexue wenxian chubanshe.

Weibo communication and government legitimacy in China:
a computer-assisted analysis of Weibo messages on two 'mass incidents'[†]

Jingrong Tong[a] and Landong Zuo[b]

[a]Media and Communication, University of Leicester; [b]IT Consultant and Data Scientist

This article, based on a computer-assisted analysis of Weibo communications about two recent 'mass incidents' in China, offers a model for understanding online communication's influence on government legitimacy. This study explores the discourse of Weibo discussions on social protests and what impacts this discourse may have on the legitimacy of Chinese government in the digital environment. The Weibo discourses on the two mass incidents suggest two modes of online communication: one-way communication, where local residents have taken the initiative and two-way communication, initiated by both local residents and national elites. Different themes the discourses have touched suggest different types and levels of impacts Weibo discussions have on government legitimacy. More precisely, the discourse in which there is a critique of the current national political system in China is more challenging to government legitimacy than the one in which there are only demands for local changes. The online discourse about the Haimen incident on Weibo even can be seen as reinforcing government legitimacy. Therefore, the impact of online communication on government legitimacy is relative and depends on specific cases. To understand the power of online communication requires us to analyse the nature of online discourses about specific cases and then examine them within external social and political contexts and by comparing them with one another. Contextual dynamics such as social problems and tensions can function as an indicator for understanding the type and level of impact of online communication on government legitimacy.

With the proliferation of online communication, there has been an intensive research interest in examining its impact on the legitimacy of government. Nevertheless, researches of this kind often involve analysis of large-scale and transient online data, which requires interdisciplinary knowledge and expertises. Therefore, relatively little research has been undertaken to assess this impact due to the lacking of effective methodologies, quantitative data analysis tools and frameworks.

[†]Weibo is a Chinese microblogging social media site where users disseminate and read short messages (up to 140 Chinese words) to/from the public or among a particular circle of contacts. Sina's Weibo was the first Weibo, appearing in 2009, and was immediately embraced by Chinese people. It had 195 million users by mid-2011. Various Internet portals now have their own Weibo websites, among which Sina's and Tencent's Weibo are the most influential. These explain why we selected Sina's Weibo in the present study.

This paper offers a model for understanding online communication's influence on government legitimacy, drawing from a computer-assisted analysis of data collected from Sina's Weibo about the 2011 Wukan and Haimen mass incidents[1] in China. We regard such impact as being relative, dynamic and depending on specific cases, rather than suggesting an objective measuring of the precise impact of online communication. We compare these two independent social events and seek to understand what kind of impact each case has and which case may have stronger impact on government legitimacy than the other one.

In this study, the data collected real time by using computational methods are unique and irre-plicable. The computer-assisted analysis of the 278,980 tweets outlines the key themes of online discourses emerging in Weibo communication about the incidents. Online communication is more critical when it addresses national fundamental socio-political problems (beyond local concerns) and attracts national attention in the Wukan incident than that in the Haimen incident, as the latter predominantly concerns local issues. To understand the power of online communication thus requires us to examine the nature of online discourses about specific cases within their social and political contexts and by comparing them with one another. Contextual dynamics such as social problems and tensions can act as an indicator for understanding the type and level of impact of online communication on government legitimacy.

Online communication, government legitimacy and social protests

Online communication may impact on government legitimacy in various manners and the level of its impacts is uncertain. The promise of free online communication consolidates government legitimacy in democratic societies for increasing transparency and democracy (Schesser, 2006; Trachtman, 1998), while failing to open online public spaces would lead to doubts on the legitimacy of governments (Schesser, 2006). Even authoritarian regimes, such as China and Saudi Arabia, promote e-government projects and allow a certain level of online participation in order to build legitimacy for their rule (Boas, 2006; Jiang, 2010; Lagerkvist, 2010). However, online communication on topics, such as corruption, may result in a crisis of government legitimacy in both democratic and non-democratic countries (Castells, 2009).

Government legitimacy is the capacity of a government to justify its rule and decisions, make them acceptable by its people and bring people together to be united (Gilley, 2005). Government legitimacy depends on 'the consent of the governed' (Rosenfeld, 2001, p. 1311), and thus would be impaired if the consent was broken down. Currently, societies where social tensions are aggravated to the level of open conflict have seen the outbreak of social protests. Social protests are open expressions of collective disagreement with governments that challenge a government's legitimacy (Mitsztal, 1985). From 'Occupy Wall Street' movements to Arab Spring uprisings, social protests have become a tough issue governments in both democratic and authoritarian societies are facing.

The use of the Internet may amplify the impact of social protests on government legitimacy. First, the Internet is regarded as offering enormous potential for organizing social protests and getting protest messages across the global public (Van de Donk, Loader, Nixon, & Rucht, 2004). Second, the Internet fosters public discussion about protests that may encourage the public to reflect on the status quo in society and even develop resonance with social protests. The public's sympathy for and support to protests may turn public opinion against governments involved (Arquilla & Ronfeldt, 2001).

However, it is unsure how and to what extent online communication about social protests would impact on government legitimacy. Conventional social protests are criticized as being frag-mented or even disorganized (Gerlach & Hine, 1970). This has not been corrected in cyberspace. Despite the connectivity of the Internet, it is unclear whether a stable and strong relationship can be established and effective social pressures can be conveyed through the use of the Internet to organize social protests and send message out (Garrett, 2006). The impact would be further limited by the quality of online communication. If the nature of online communication was like what is described as 'faceless one-dimensional stranger to stranger interaction' (Stoecker, 2000), its impact on government legitimacy would be limited.

China's government legitimacy in crisis

Though retaining 'political supremacy' in the economic reform process (Heberer & Schubert, 2006), the party leadership is unable to guarantee legitimacy for its rule in the new century. The dominant Communist ideology that the party is dependent on is dying in the face of economic reform and the dismantling of the old socialist system. Other ideologies, such as liberalism, are rising, which enable a critique of the regime's legitimacy (Gilley & Holbig, 2009; Guo, 2003; Holbig, 2006). Besides, the slim possibility of having political reforms puts governments' political legitimacy in danger (Schubert, 2008). Social problems, such as corruption, social inequality and injustice, and environmental problems, have further reduced the level of popular consent to the political legitimacy of the regime (Chen, Zhong, Hillard, & Scheb, 1997; He, 2000; Potter, 1994; Wong, 2004).

The central government increasingly relies on stirring popular emotion, through nationalism, for example, and on domestic economic achievements to regain and maintain its legitimacy (Downs & Saunders, 1998/1999; Shue, 2004). A unique 'political structural reform' has been launched as part of an attempt to secure more legitimacy, introducing an idea of 'socialist democracy with Chinese characteristics', though with the one-party leadership untouched (Dickson, 2004; Heberer & Schubert, 2006). Village elections, for example, are being promoted in rural China, helping to solve problems at local level and gaining new legitimacy for the party (Schubert, 2009; Xu, 1997).

The central–local government relationship, where powers are decentralized, is especially utilized for the sake of consolidating government legitimacy. The current political arrangement that separates the central government from local governments' activities keeps the central government from being blamed for repressing popular resistance (Cai, 2008). The multi-layered power structure of the government is thought of having saved the regime from collapse by leaving local governments to be held responsible for the failure in governance (Cai, 2008). 'Inner-party purity' is maintained through punishing local governments and officials for their wrongdoing (He, 2000).

However, the literature has also developed a critique of these efforts, hardly considering them as successful. These initiatives are thought to be limited by various national factors including 'the tensions between the central and local governments, institutional weaknesses, inconsistent policies, and the inability or unwillingness to undertake fundamental political reforms' (Lum, 2006, p. 8). Moreover, scholars (e.g. Dickson, 2004; Heberer & Schubert, 2006) argue that the lack of a dominant ideology, the absence of substantial political reforms leading to democracy, the persistence of social problems in reality, such as corruption and growing inequality and injustice, undermine the Chinese Communist Party's ability to retain its legitimacy, as these are the fundamental threats to it. This provides some implications for the present study: it would cast more doubts on government legitimacy if online discussions address issues concerning national socio-political problems rather than others.

Information and Communication Technologies, mass incidents and government legitimacy

The last few years have witnessed the proliferation of grassroots social protests generally, and mass incidents in particular, across China, as an expression of the public's demands that cannot be fulfilled in other ways (Gilboy & Read, 2008). Farmers, workers and home owners are among the most prominent protest groups. Contextual factors such as 'inequality and corruption', 'growing rights consciousness, organizational skill' and 'comparisons with other social movements' are responsible for growing mass incidents (Gilboy & Read, 2008; Lum, 2006).

The spread of information about mass incidents is facilitated by the fast growth of the Internet in China. The number of Internet users increased to 564 million by December 2012 and around 42% of the Chinese population is now connected to the Internet.[2] Compared with traditional media that are banned from reporting topics like mass incidents, the online medium enjoys relatively more autonomy. The Internet has been used to organize social protests, to disseminate information about protests and to interact with the press (Fewsmith, 2008). Recent cases, such as the Weng'an mass incident[3] in 2008, have drawn the Chinese leadership's attention to the online medium.

Nevertheless, the impact of online expressions about social protests on government legitimacy is precarious. First, online world is not completely free. Both the physical network and web content are under state control (Dong, 2012; Harwit & Clark, 2001). Internet censorship primarily aims to suppress social unrest and eliminate the possibility that online discussions will lead to collective action (Orcutt, 2012). Posts about collective action or social protest are among the top banned topics that are required to be removed from the Internet (Hunt, 2012).

Second, Chinese social protests are thought of as being short lived, curtailed by the repressive actions of local governments and by a weak connection between social unrest and organized political opposition, as well as being 'largely incoherent and disorganized' and 'fragmented' in themselves (Cai, 2008; Gilboy & Read, 2008). The Internet is even seen as reinforcing the existing social structure and conditions, as it does not directly encourage the kind of political activism that might bring democracy to China (MacKinnon, 2008).

Such impact becomes even more precarious when the social media age comes. Most recently, social media sites have been playing an increasingly important role in China's social and political life, through means such as eroding government censorship (Wines & LaFraniere, 2011), and providing a platform for Internet users to call into question government policies, decisions and actions (MacKinnon, 2012). Weibo, for example, has become an effective field for publicizing and discussing social events, such as protests (AFP, 2011). However, Weibo communication could be more fragmented and unsystematic than that on Internet forums due to its technical structure and 140 words limitation.

Despite its importance, the content on social media sites remains under-researched as a whole, let alone research specifically into posts about social protests. Few previous studies that have examined web content to understand the nature of online communication have mainly looked at blogs and forums (e.g. Hassid, 2012; MacKinnon, 2008; Wu, 2008; Yang, 2003; Zhou, 2009), leaving the content of social media sites a virgin area for research. This gap in the existing literature limits our ability to understand the nature of online communication and its challenge to government legitimacy. This study aims to fill the gap by analysing Sina's Weibo data about the Wukan and Haimen mass incidents.

Methodology

The two incidents were selected for our study because (1) both were mass incidents that were known by domestic and international worlds and (2) both took place in the Guangdong Province but had different patterns in their development, thus provided good examples for comparison.

The research was undertaken in a dynamic and agile style. We had little knowledge about what story the data set would tell us at the outset. The data exploration led us to develop the conceptual framework of the study. The whole process of carrying out the research was divided into small work tasks, which were executed iteratively until the conceptual framework clearly emerged. This was a reiterative process in which the researchers repeatedly conducted data mining, inductive logic and reasoning. The output or feedback of previous work tasks helped set tasks for next iterations. The researchers, who entered the field open-minded and unbiased regarding the impact of online communication, witnessed the full research walk-path and literally developed the research perception in the process.

This iterative process of data analysis allows us to define and refine the four open-ended research questions (enumerated below) that are initially predetermined based on the existing literature. Scholars (e.g. Davidov, Tsur, & Rappoport, 2010; Diakopoulos & Shamma, 2010; Go, Bhayani, & Huang, 2009; Hughes & Palen, 2009; Jansen, Zhang, Sobel, & Chowdury, 2009; Mendoza, Poblete, & Castillo, 2010; Pak & Paroubek, 2010) have studied the content on Twitter, such as patterns, sentiment and opinions, as well as the activities of Twitter users. Given the similar features of Twitter and Weibo, these previous researches provide a basis for this present study to develop its research design, with the aim of answering the following four research questions:

(1) What are the overall and overtime patterns of Weibo users' activities in tweeting the two incidents?
(2) What themes have emerged in the tweets about the two incidents? Are they fragmented? And how have these changed over time?
(3) Can the discourse about the two incidents be seen as bringing government legitimacy into question?
(4) Are there any differences between the two cases in terms of overall patterns, themes and development?

Guided by the insights gained from the data analysis and the literature, we regard how and to what extent online discussion of social protests can challenge government legitimacy lies in whether online discussion generates themes that threaten government legitimacy or not. Themes on national fundamental socio-political problems are thought of as more threatening government legitimacy than those on local issues.

Data collection and sampling

Sophisticated tools have been developed and utilized for data collection and sampling, data storing and querying, as well as data analysis and visualization. Sina's Weibo tweets on these two incidents were collected between December 2011 and June 2012, when the most dramatic and comparable trends were present in both incidents. The data collection was completed via Web request to the Weibo search Application Programming Interface (API). This routine task was executed on a daily basis throughout the collection period with relevant keywords (such as 'wukan'/'wk village'/'lufeng'/'china wukan'/'wukan event'; 'haimen'/'chaoshan haimen'/ 'HM town'/'guangdong haimen'/'haimen event'). The keyword list was first suggested by Weibo trends and then manually amended, working around the search censorship of Weibo APIs.[4] Pre-selection and filtering was applied to test the quality and reliability of data collection and prepare for the data set that will be used for further analysis. The data set was verified by extracting the most influential factors, such as popular trends, active persons and frequent word clusters. The outcome was semi-automatically audited and noise in terms of irrelevant topics and tweets was minimized. The final fully examined data set includes 278,980 tweets.

Data analysis and visualization

The data analysis comprises two parts. One examines the content of Weibo tweets and makes reference from the content to the context. This research method has been used in analysing a variety of media content including Internet, broadcasting and newspaper content (e.g. Hassid, 2012; Kiri-lenko & Stepchenkova, 2012; Popping, 2000; Tian & Stewart, 2005). Second is the analysis of tweets and of the activities of Weibo users, in the way that the studies on Twitter content cited above have done. Computer-assisted analysis was deployed in these studies because of its effi-ciency over manual coding and the higher reliability and functional flexibility of data processing.

The data storing and querying were driven by the analytical cases, that is, the key information demanded from the data collection. MySQL, a relational database system, was used to discover the tweet/user and tweet/retweet relationships, while Apache Solr[5] was used to perform the Natural Language Processing (NLP) of Chinese Language and data analysis, that is, facet numbers of terms across timeline or categories, and SPSS was employed for clustering analysis. The analysis and visualization tools used in the process enable the specific data insights over the data stored by illustrating the influential factors, for example, term frequency analysis and scheme clustering.

Given the scale of nearly 280 k Weibo posts, discourse analysis via manual coding is difficult to conduct. The clustering analysis in this research was based on collections of statistical models such as Term Frequency–Inverse Document Frequency and co-occurrence of most frequent and mean-ingful terms. The sophisticated NLP tools specialized for Chinese language was deployed in deter-mining the word tokenization and constructing the meaningful thesaurus lists separately for Haimen and Wukan. The statistics-based and NLP conformable method offers an easy and efficient way to access the contextual meaning of data. Besides, the research design in this practice intends to develop a common framework, in which data analysis can be generalized at certain level to inter-rogate data collections across different stories and conclude the analysis with comparable outcome.

There is a three-step operation in the data analysis. First, the quantitative data insight revealed the basic facts of Weibo activities, the top 100[6] most active users ranked by the amount of posts they made and grouped by profile types, the ratio of original tweets against retweets and the top 100 most popular retweets, in order to answer Q1. Second, the content analysis of Weibo tweets answered Q2 and Q3. The data query crossed all tweets to develop the frequency list of words. And then a group of words with the top 100 frequencies were statistically clustered by the co-occurrence possibilities within the same tweet. The approaches of hierarchical clustering analysis (creating dendrograms using Ward's method) were used. The clustering analysis, which has been used in previous studies (Balasubramanyan, Lin, & Cohen, 2010; Murphy, 2001; Tian & Stewart, 2005), offered an understanding of themes and semantic relations among these words. The event developments include several phrases. Clustering analysis for each phase was conducted to find more subtle themes emerging in different stages to identify the changes over time in the discourse on Weibo. Thirdly, research findings for the two incidents were compared, to measure the simi-larities and differences, in order to answer Q4.

Findings: two modes of Weibo communication

An overall image

Overall, communication on Weibo about the two incidents has been very active. During the sampling period, 159,902 Internet users have posted a total number of 278,980 tweets about the two incidents with a mean of 1.52 tweets per user. In addition, the number of retweets (186,545) was about twice the number of original tweets (92,435). The Wukan case (Wukan for short) saw much more active user participation than the Haimen case (Haimen for short), in respect both to the numbers of tweets and the numbers of participants; 136,907 users posted 243,309 tweets in Wukan, while 35,671 tweets were sent by 22,995 users in Haimen.

Four types[7] of Internet users – local residents or someone who has personal connections to the place, elites,[8] news organizations (both new media companies such as Sina and traditional media such as newspapers) and ordinary people whose identity cannot be identified – are found to be most active users (Figures 1 and 2). Notably most traditional news organizations participating are from the print media rather than television. Among the top 100 most active users, local residents and ordinary people were responsible for the majority of the posts: around 72% in Wukan and 81% in Haimen. They were more likely to retweet posts made by other users rather than tweet original posts made by themselves.

By contrast, elites and news organizations were more likely to send their original messages. In both cases, except for only 22 messages in Wukan, most tweets posted by news organizations were original. Elites behaved differently in the two cases. Elites tweeted and retweeted a nearly equal number of tweets in Wukan, but only posted the messages they themselves generated in Haimen. That is to say, more messages produced by other users were regarded as credible by elites and news organizations in Wukan than in Haimen.

The distribution of tweets in the two incidents displays similarities as well as differences in their trends, viewed on a daily basis (Figure 3). On the one hand, Weibo communication in both incidents reached a peak at 22 December 2011. This date was crucial, as it marked the final day of consecutive protests in Haimen and of confrontation between the villagers and the authorities in Wukan. On the other hand, the attention given to Haimen was rose sharply to a peak and then fell abruptly, dropping to trough within a short period of time, while the attention to Wukan lasted for a longer period of time, with ups and downs within the overall pattern. The longer the online attention lasted, the stronger the impact it potentially had on the real world.

Attention to both cases on Weibo showed variations in accordance with the development of actual events over the sampling time. The peaks more or less match the turning points of the events. As noted already, in Wukan the highest peak occurred on 22 December 2001, when the government came to negotiate with the villagers. Other peaks corresponded to the start of the December protest, the election of the village committee and the village elections (respectively, on 7 December 2011, 1 and 11 February, 3 and 4 March 2012). In Haimen, the highest peak matched the occurrence of the protests from 20 to 23 December 2011.

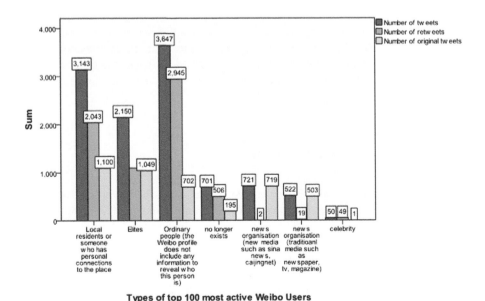

Figure 1. Sum number of tweets by top 100 most active Weibo users in the Wukan case.

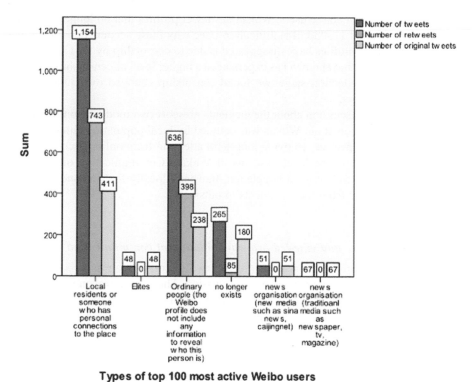

Figure 2.   Sum number of tweets by top 100 most active Weibo users in the Haimen case.

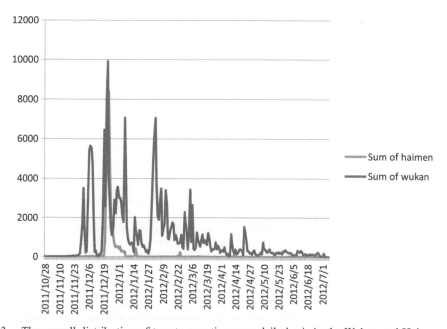

Figure 3.   The overall distribution of tweets over time on a daily basis in the Wukan and Haimen cases.

Among the top 100 most active users, Wukan has fewer profiles that no longer exist (around 6.4%) than Haimen (around 11.4%). It is difficult to trace why these accounts no longer exist. If the main reason why these profiles have disappeared is due to censorship by the Chinese government, then one could argue that Haimen has experienced a higher level of censorship than Wukan. But, indeed, in the data collection stage, we found censorship changed over time, sometimes lighter, but sometimes tighter.

In general, the Weibo discussion about the incidents presents two modes of online communication. Online communication about Wukan was both led by local population elites and featured themes with a national perspective, enjoying long-term attention from online users and two-way interaction between elites and the local residents of Wukan. Communication on Weibo about Haimen, however, was led by the local population, transient, locally focused and characterized by one-way communication from local residents to outsiders.

Wukan on Weibo: populace and elite-led two-way initiation of communication

Communication on Weibo in Wukan was elite led for two reasons. One reason is the active participation of elites and news organizations in the discussion. The second reason is the association of elite names with the themes of the discourse, which implies the role of elites in giving the Weibo discourse national meaning. The elite-led nature of the discussion suggests that the online communication was initiated by both local residents and those from outside.

Elites and news organizations both appeared to be active in the Wukan discussion. Nearly a third (31.3%) of the top 100 most active users and two out of the top 10 most active users (Table 1) were elites and news organizations. Despite the fact that ordinary people were most active type of users, elites were the category of users whose messages were most frequently retweeted by other users (Figure 4). Users preferred to retweet messages created by elites (accounting for 60%), followed by those by local residents (14%) and news organizations (13%). The more intensive attention from elites and news organizations in Wukan gives the incident a more national dimension.

Wukan has a discourse with focuses on keywords such as 'democracy', 'enlightenment', 'reform', 'rights', 'hope' and 'China'. Its seven clusters (Table 2) emphasize the aftermath

Table 1.   The top 10 most active Weibo users[a] in the Wukan case.

No.	Number of tweets	Types of Weibo users
1	1345	Local Wukan villager or someone who has personal connections to Wukan
2	525	Elites, including culture elites (such as journalists, university academics and writers) and economic elites (such as CEOs and other business people)
3	477	Ordinary people (the Weibo profile does not include any information to reveal who this person is)
4	368	Local Wukan villager or someone who has personal connections to Wukan
5	266	Ordinary people (the Weibo profile does not include any information to reveal who this person is)
6	258	Profile no longer exists
7	227	Local Wukan villager or someone who has personal connections to Wukan
8	197	News organization (new media such as Sina news, caijingnet)
9	186	Profile no longer exists
10	177	Ordinary people (the Weibo profile does not include any information to reveal who this person is)

[a]All the real names of profiles have been removed with a concern over possible ethics issues. Types of Weibo users were used instead.

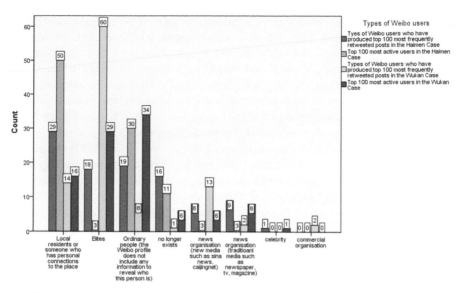

Figure 4.   The comparison of types of users between 'top 100 most active users' and 'users who have produced top 100 most frequently retweeted posts' in the Wukan and Haimen cases.

Table 2.   Wukan clusters.

Clusters	Cluster themes	Keywords
Cluster 1	Democracy and Weibo	Election, Xiong Wei, China, democracy, http, cn, Enlightenment, support, one, retweet
Cluster 2	Weibo and reform	Weibo, reform, attention, do not have, we, they, people (renmin), increasing pace, society, problem, solve, land, representatives, need, now, no, hope
Cluster 3	Elites	Xue Manzi, change, Xiaoshu, one time (yici), everybody (gewei)
Cluster 4	Meaning	Quality, young people, Xiaogang village, important, basic levels, start, peasants, Han Zhiguo
Cluster 5	Election	Village committee, vote, share, news, work, secretary, village, politics
Cluster 6	Justice	Interests (liyi), lawyers, Xue Jinbo, worth (zhide), today (jintian), results, rights (quanli)
Cluster 7	Solution	Development, politician, autonomy (zizhi), local, solve (chuli), economy, together, masses (baixing), Hong Kong, journalists, haha, Wang Yang, people (minzhong), rights protection, history, media

(demands for democracy and reform) and meaning of the incident rather than the incident itself. No themes suggested by the clusters were related to the demonstrations by Wukan villagers and their clashes with local government or the police. Except for one theme on the actual election, the majority of the clusters are about democracy, reform and the historical significance of this event, suggesting that the solutions to the problems raised by Wukan and the guarantee of the protection of rights are democracy, reform and the achievement of local autonomy. The themes in Wukan include the demands of the protesters that are about 'democracy', 'reform', 'election', 'rights protection' and 'justice'. In addition, the Wukan discourse on Weibo is plural and has historical and contextual meanings. For example, on one theme that examines the historical meaning of Wukan, the discourse relates Wukan to what happened in Xiaogang Village in the 1980s, a symbol of China's economic reform.

These themes are also associated with the names of members of the elite, such as 'Xiong Wei', 'Xue Manzi', 'Xiao Shu' and 'Han Zhiguo', which appear in the clusters of 'democracy', 'reform', 'elites' and 'meaning', and are associated with keywords such as 'democracy', 'election', 'enlightenment', 'reform', 'change' and 'Xiaogang Village'. The name of the Guangdong provincial governor, Wang Yang, also appeared in the solution cluster. This association between elites and the discourse of democracy is prominently displayed in different phases of the incident.

The distribution of tweets over time in Wukan (Figure 3), matching the development of the incident itself, is divided into four phases: protest (before 20 December 2011), negotiation (from 20 December 2011 to 31 January 2012), election (from 1 February to 3 March 2012) and post-election (from 4 March 2012 afterwards). The themes in the protest phase are unclear, merely suggesting two focuses on the protest itself and on Weibo functionality, such as retweeting (Table 3). No keywords are relevant to democracy or election or elites at all in the top 100 keywords. When it comes to the negotiation phase, themes of 'literacy', 'election', 'democracy', 'demand' and 'justice' emerged and keywords about elites such as 'Yu Jianrong', 'Xiong Wei', 'Xue Manzi', 'Xiao Shu' and 'lawyer' started appearing in the top 100 keywords. The theme of 'literacy' was prominent throughout the last three phases. In the theme, members of the elite, such as 'Xiaoshu' and 'Xue Manzi', mobilized Web users to make donations to create a 'book fund' for Wukan villagers in order to increase their reading abilities and literacy, which was seen as crucial for achieving democracy and enlightenment. This discourse of democracy becomes stronger in the third phase of election. The theme of 'historical meaning' and new keywords of elites 'Wu Jiaxiang' and 'Han Zhiguo' appeared. The keywords of 'Wang Yang', the Guangdong governor, and 'Liu Jianfeng', a journalist, appeared in the final post-election phase. The themes in the second, third and fourth phases remain similar about democracy. And the theme of 'literacy' is also connected with the themes of 'democracy', 'election' and 'historical meaning'.

Haimen: populace-led one-way initiation of communication

By contrast, Haimen is more like a local rather than a national event. The lack of enthusiasm of elites and news organizations for the topic in contrast to the level of activity of local residents in Haimen suggests the Weibo communication about this event is led by the local population and is characterized by the initiation of communication from local residents to the outside world in one direction only.

In Haimen, local residents were the type of users who were most active, as well as those producing the messages which were mostly retweeted by other users. Only around 3% of the top 100 most active users in Haimen were members of the elites and news organizations. The messages that were most likely to be retweeted are produced by local residents (29, 29%), followed by ordinary people (19, 19%) and then elites (18, 18%). All the top 10 most active users were local residents and ordinary people (Table 4).

The themes in Haimen are from a local perspective, emphasizing keywords such as 'protest', 'pollution', 'oppose', 'town government', 'environment' and 'solution'. As illustrated in Table 5,[9] the seven clusters in Haimen reflect an emphasis on the mass incident itself: a mass incident happened in Haimen (cluster 1), its cause: a concern for possible pollution from the second power plant (cluster 2) and on-site scenes (clusters 3, 5 and 7): such as, people blocking the Shenshan highway, dialogues being sought, tear gas being used, police and armed police arriving on the scene, and 'mothers' (old female Haimennese, according to relevant news reports) appearing as a symbol of support. In addition, Weibo messages also appealed for a solution in cluster 6. The demands of protesters in Haimen were limited to 'solving' the problem and 'opposing' the establishment of the power plant. No elite names were mentioned in Haimen, except the name of a newspaper journalist who was on the scene, Li Yong, which appeared in the cluster of 'on-site scene 3'.

Table 3.   Wukan clusters in the four phases.

Clusters	Cluster themes	Keywords
Phase 1: Protest		
Cluster 1	Weibo	http, retweet, Weibo, Haha
Cluster 2	Event	China, world, attention, event, Wukan, Guangdong, Zhengfu
Phase 2: Negotiation		
Cluster 1	Literacy and democracy	Xiao Shu, one time (yici), change, get rid of (baituo), Xue Manzi, read, the more the better, support, everybody, retweet, donation, book fund, one yuan (yiyuan), Xiong Wei, enlightenment
Cluster 2	Election and Weibo	Election, they, attention, need, please, now, Weibo, one, thanks, weibo friends, together, masses (baixing), villagers, retweet, Wukan village, China, new
Cluster 3	Democracy and solution	Economy, solve, politicians, Xiaogang village, local, autonomy (zizhi), http, government, democracy
Cluster 4	Demand	Land, village head, we, people (renmin), hope, solve, work, secretary, problem, reform, society, working team, provincial, demand, news, interest, politics, Shanwei
Cluster 5	Justice	Xue Jinbo, rights protection, lawyer, law, important, event, Hong Kong, Wukan, rights, conflict, appraise, today
Cluster 6	Elite	Yu Jiarong, develop, people (minzhong)
Phase 3: Election		
Cluster 1	Literacy	Wu Jiaxiang, democracy, quality theory, precise, history book (shice), be written into (zairu), myself (benren), judgement
Cluster 2	Historical meaning 1	Basic levels, peasants, country fellows, Han Zhiguo, young people, future, influence, today, development, take place, results
Cluster 3	Democracy	Xiong Wei, enlightenment, villagers, quality, reform, China, election, democracy
Cluster 4	Election	Village committee, http, representatives, event, committee members, vote
Cluster 5	Historical meaning 2	History, people (renmin), we, attention, Xue Jinbo, retweet, country fellows (guoren), society, lawyers, land, problem, government, support, they, hope, Weibo
Phase 4: Post-election		
Cluster 1	Literacy	Enlightenment, Xiong Wei, Liu Jianfeng, library, books, boost, life
Cluster 2	Democracy	cn, http, election, democracy, China, villagers, event, support, retweet, representatives, journalists
Cluster 3	Solution	Village committee, land, secretary, village, they, share, news, solution, village officials, Zhang Jianxing
Cluster 4	Reform	Problem, reform, Wang Yang, meaning, politics
Cluster 5	Weibo	Government, society, attention, people (renmin), Wukan, we, no, please, Weibo
Cluster 6	Meaning	Experience, Wukan, hope, lawyer, Hong Kong, interests (liyi), south (nanfang)

The distribution of tweets in Haimen (Figure 3) suggests three phases in its development: rising (before 23 December 2011), declining (from 23 December 2011 to 6 January 2012) and fading out (after 7 January 2012). A detailed clustering analysis for each phase suggests that the discourse of the first two phases is about the incident itself and on-site scenes, while the discourse of the third phase is driven by mainstream media coverage of government opinion about

Table 4. The top 10 most active Weibo users in the Haimen case.

Number of tweets	Types of Weibo users
68	Local Haimen resident or someone who has personal connections to Haimen
55	Local Haimen resident or someone who has personal connections to Haimen
47	Local Haimen resident or someone who has personal connections to Haimen
46	Local Haimen resident or someone who has personal connections to Haimen
43	Local Haimen resident or someone who has personal connections to Haimen
41	Ordinary people (the Weibo profile does not include any information to reveal who this person is)
40	Local Haimen resident or someone who has personal connections to Haimen
40	Ordinary people (the Weibo profile does not include any information to reveal who this person is)
37	Local Haimen resident or someone who has personal connections to Haimen
37	Ordinary people (the Weibo profile does not include any information to reveal who this person is)

Table 5. Haimen clusters.

Clusters	Cluster themes	Keywords
Cluster 1	Event	Haimen, Shantou, Guangdong, http, cn, mass incident, happen
Cluster 2	Cause	Pollution, project, environment, power plant, second, town government, government, don't want
Cluster 3	On-site scene 1	Block, traffic, share, tear bomb, they, dialogue, gather, peasants, again, Shen(zhen)Shan(tou), protest (shiwei), masses who do not get to know the truth (buming zhenxiang de qunzhong), media, report
Cluster 4	Weibo	News, retweet, people (minzhong), we, people (renmin), mayor, Wukan, attention, one, Haimenneses, Weibo, (guanzhu)
Cluster 5	On-site scene 2	East Sea, Hong Kong, armed police, news, villagers, coal-fire, protest (kangyi), police
Cluster 6	Demand	China, demand, solve (jiejue), problem, request, today (jinri), continue, handle (chuli), serious
Cluster 7	On-site scene 3	On-site scene, develop, support, Li Yong, mothers, today (jintian), now, see, reply (huifu), haha

this incident (Table 6). In the third phase, most tweets were retweeting a link to a news report rather than posting self-generated content by Weibo users. The keywords in clusters 1, 2 and 3 are highly consistent with the news report[10] covered in the *Guangzhou Daily* on 15 January 2012. The discourse in the first two phases also mentioned 'Wukan', which shows a sort of link between these two cases in the discourse of social unrest on Weibo. Few elite names were mentioned here. Only the names of 'Wang Keqing' and 'Xu Xing' were mentioned, and this was in the context of the incident itself.

The role of Weibo

Notably, the analysis implies the importance of Weibo in publicizing the two cases. One theme common to the two incidents concerns the functionality of Weibo itself, which often appears with key words such as 'attention', 'retweet', 'share' and 'support', as suggested in the clusters.

Table 6.   Haimen clusters in the three phases.

Clusters	Cluster themes	Keywords
Phase 1: Rising		
Cluster 1	Event	Mass incident happened in Haimen town, Shantou city
Cluster 2	Event	Masses (qunzhong), Top news, share, traffic, Wang Keqing, mass incident, happen, town government, http
Cluster 3	Cause and on-site scene	Do not understand truth (buming zhengxiang de), high way, power plant, pollution, people (renmin), coal-fire, protest, demonstration, build, oppose, second, people (minzhong), report, Shen(zhen)Shan(tou), environment, aggregate, project, worry, hundreds, part
Cluster 4	Government reaction reported by mainstream media	Early stage, China energy, proof, delude, yesterday, work, morning, result in, city government, daily newspaper, value, appeal, decision city government committee
Cluster 5	Weibo	Retweet, ChaoShan, electricity plant, Haimennese, we, Weibo, see, do not want, know, pay attention to, China, hope, event, Wukan
Cluster 6	On-site scene and demand	Today, one, media, occupy, villagers, armed police, yesterday, solve, reply, thing, so, rights protection, already, Hong Kong
Cluster 7	Rumour	News, beaten to death, students, they, say, police, problem, today, this, now, angry
Phase 2: Declining		
Cluster 1	On-site scene and cause	Again, Shen(zhen)Shan(tou), throw, peasants, must, tear bomb, power plant, truth, second, recently, wisdom, dissatisfied, direct, corruption
Cluster 2	Event and cause	Do not want, power plant, town, report, protest, masses (qunzhong)
Cluster 3	On-site scene	Dialogue, high way, tear bomb, media, aggregate (juji), they
Cluster 4	Weibo	Big, purpose, cn, retweet, Guangdong, people (renmin), people (minzhong), Wukan, attention, one, government, we, http, before, Shantou, Weibo, Haimennese, event
Cluster 5	On-scene site and event	Same, continue (jixu), WK, Guangzhou, efforts, please, continue (chixu), handle (chuli), organize, opinion, my, on-site scene, serious, Yu Jianrong, come, agree, than, East
Cluster 6	Environmental concern	Science, Xu Xing, project, environment, news
Cluster 7	On-site scene	Beat, fact, women, Hong Kong, Li Yong, East sea, see, police, Anti-riot, armed police, photo, mother, news
Cluster 8	Event and outcome	Request, pollution, villagers, victory, hope, now, China, Chaoyang, Beijing, development, support, oppose, Chaoshan, shanghai, freedom, Haichao association, today, haha, reply, know
Phase 3: Fading out		
Cluster 1	Mayer's opinion reported by mainstream media	Have to arrest (feizhua buke), Zheng Renhao, some people, masses, these people, intentions unpredictable, influenced by, media, influence, can not, mayer, long talk, few people, oversea
Cluster 2	Mayer's opinion reported by mainstream media 1	Problem, expression, whether, project, China energy, response, already, continue to build, people (minzhong), journalists, recently
Cluster 3	Mayer's opinion reported by mainstream media 2	Making troubles, lightly, release, things, appeal, firmly, stress, reasonable, complete, tone, violate, light case, (provincial) people's congress, the fifth (conference)

(Continued)

Table 6. Continued.

Clusters	Cluster themes	Keywords
Cluster 4	Event	Haimen event, big, government, coal-fire, build, today, riot, electricity plant, people (renmin), Wukan, one, Weibo, we
Cluster 5	Neteast news	Neteast client end news, share, Neteast news, Haimen, happen, mass incident, cn, http
Cluster 6	Question raised	Again, a small stamp, masses who do not understand the truth?, mass incident
Cluster 7	Other mass incidents	Again, phoenix media, East, compared to the last time, this time, ten times, Xu Xing, outburst

Both cluster 1s that include keywords of the events themselves as well as 'http' and 'cn' imply that the discourse about what happened is often associated with web links.

Discussion and conclusion: national/local dynamics and the power of Weibo communication

It is clear from the analysis above that Weibo functions as a platform for protestors to express their demands and for other Internet users to communicate their views. This function has facilitated the publicizing and dissemination of information about politically sensitive social protests in locales and won the attention of the national public who resonate with local protesters across time and space. Such national attention has given 'oxygen' to social protests and helped to connect different social protests together (as manifested in the Haimen discourse that links back to the Wukan case). Local residents spelled out their demands and voiced their concerns, breaking down the control over the terms of the debate by local authorities. Local experiences shared on Weibo may be echoed by the national public that may or may not share similar experiences in their own life contexts. This is emancipatory in itself especially under the circumstances where news media are far from being independent, lacking the full capacity to facilitate what Thompson (1995) calls as 'mediated experience' and 'mediated interaction' among the national public.

Both incidents involved protests against the wrongdoing of local governments or officials, occurring nearly simultaneously in the same province. Weibo communication about the two cases, however, reveals significant differences. The length and intensity of online attention, the types of participants or the themes in discourse all signified the Haimen case as a transient populace-led local event with local demands and concerns, but revealed the Wukan case to be a long-lasting event, led by the local population as well as members of national elites, producing demands for national democracy and a critique of the current national political system in China.

In the Wukan incident, where the original event was local but influences the national debate, intense attention from elites and news organizations is crucial for keeping online discussion alive and keeping the events in the national consciousness. In this case, the communication mode was a two-way one between protesters (local residents) and outsiders. From the second stage of its development, online communication about the Wukan events became led by rightist elites from outside the village. Elites' resonance extends the scope and influence of an event at local level to a national and even international level. The discourse in this case – of democracy and reform – moved it beyond local demands. Such a discourse in fact is the discourse of liberal intellectuals, as it is highly associated with posts published by members of the elites and news organizations. They act as opinion leaders, shaping the development of the discourse and targeting political reform at the national level. In this sense, the power of Weibo lies in creating a possibility for connecting local demands with intellectuals' political demands at national level for political reform.

However, in the Haimen incident, the communication remained mostly one way from protesters (local residents) to outsiders. The communication in this case was mainly led by the local populace as they wanted to attract the attention of the whole society, while the notice paid to the events by members of the elite was short lived and weak. In this case, elites and news organizations seldom paid attention and the trend for online discussion was transient. The discourse centred mainly on local demands, requesting the local government to stop building the second coal-fired power plant and to release those who had been arrested in Haimen.

The findings suggest different levels of impacts of online communication on government legitimacy in the two cases. The Wukan discourse that is associated with national political reform and democracy brings some big and fundamental challenges to both central and local governments' legitimacy. Such demands touch the very principles underlying socio-political problems in China. While the demand for democracy threatens the legitimacy of the ruling party, the requirement to increase villagers' literacy lays the basis for a greater degree of political transparency by allowing people to see through government attempts at obscurantism. This is a forbidden zone that the Chinese central government has tried to prevent anyone from moving into since the 1989 political trauma over the Tiananmen protests. Discourses like this can have national resonance rather than be limited to locales. When the discourse began associating mass incidents with democracy and protection of human rights rather than focusing on the physical battle with the police, doubts began to be raised about the legitimacy of the ruling party as a whole. The stronger the voices for democracy are, the greater the challenge to government legitimacy is. In the process, the participation of elites and news organization as well as national attention for local events act as an important leverage, although we cannot be certain whether the participation of elites and news organizations has led to the national importance placed on any local mass incident or the severity of the local mass incident and its potential national significance has attracted the attention of elites and news organizations.

However, in the case of Haimen, there is only a critique of local government and an attempt to correct local wrongdoing. Local demands that do not correspond to the interests of distant Internet users have little revolutionary resonance. The central government appears to be separate from local governments and thus is seemingly immune from demands focused on local issues. The legitimacy of the central government can even be reinforced by punishing local governments and focusing people's anger towards local officials. Local people are willing to appeal to the central government in order to obtain justice. Through punishing local governments and correcting their wrongdoing, the central government is able not only to establish a reforming image for itself but also to reduce the social grievances of the people. Functioning as a safety valve that releases the pressure of the complaints of ordinary people, this in turn helps the solidity and maintenance of government legitimacy.

Notably, this tactic can also be seen in the third and fourth phases of the Wukan case. The voting experiment in Wukan, the support from governments of higher administrative levels and the positive involvement of Wang Yang – the party boss of the Guangdong Province – could turn the online discourse into a way of fostering an open image for the state which helps consolidate government legitimacy in China. Despite having the deceptive possibility of consolidating government legitimacy in the Wukan case, when it comes to national political reform, the village election still has some potential to undermine that legitimacy.

Communication is the power of the digital age (Castells, 2009). This study shows that the power of Weibo communication relies in the national nature of discourse surrounding particular events constructed on Weibo. The more resonance with the events the national public and intellectuals have, the bigger impact online communication has on government legitimacy in general. The deeper themes online discourse touches, the more critical and powerful online communication is. Therefore, the impact of online communication on government legitimacy in one case needs to be considered in comparison with that in another case and understood within their socio-political contexts, taking contextual dynamics, such as social tensions, into account.

Acknowledgements

The authors would like to thank the guest editor and anonymous reviewers for their valuable comments.

Notes

1. The Wukan incident refers to a series of demonstrations and petitions which villagers in Wukan, in Guangdong province, made from September to December 2011. They were unhappy principally because of seizures of village land by corrupt local officials for sale to developers without proper compensation to the villagers. In December 2011, Xue Jinbo, a village representative, died in custody two days after his arrest. His death led to a severe confrontation between Wukan villagers and local police. The Guangdong province later showed a supportive attitude towards the Wukan villagers and assigned a working team to investigate local land and election issues on 20 December 2011. In February and March 2012, Wukan villagers elected their own village government. The Haimen incident, also in Guangdong province, started with an appeal letter published on a web forum. It revealed that despite the dramatic pollution the first coal-fired electricity plant had caused there, Haimen's local government had decided to open a second plant of this kind. This letter aroused residents' fury over the local government's decision (Shangguan, 2011). A message mobilizing local residents to 'protest in front of the Town government and take collective action' was reposted by many Weibo users (Zhang, 2011). Thousands of local residents, many of whom were young people, including even teenagers, held protests from 20 to 23 December 2011.
2. Retrieved May 2, 2013, from http://www.cnnic.cn/hlwfzyj/hlwxzbg/hlwtjbg/201301/P020130122600399530412.pdf.
3. Ten of thousands of protesters clashed with police who had allegedly covered up a girl's death in the Guizhou province.
4. Censorship is identifiable in the data collection process and proved by other scholars such as Elmer (2012). For example, during some time periods, no searching results turned up because the key words were filtered and censored. However, after one or two days, we were able to have search results by using the same key words and the results were posted during the periods of time that we failed to get these results.
5. Both are computer programming languages.
6. After several tests, 100 is considered as being appropriate for detailed analysis and interpretation.
7. The types of users are judged by information published on their Weibo profiles and messages. Most of Internet users included information about their occupations and origin in their profiles. For some of them who did not reveal their background information, we judged their types by reading their message posted on Weibo.
8. Elites include cultural and economic elites such as journalists, university academics, lawyers and CEOs. No political elites such as politicians have been recognized.
9. Cluster tables are all adapted from dendrograms. Some types of keywords such as conjunctions and particles have been removed from the clusters.
10. With a title of 'Zhen Renhao, the Shantou Mayer, talked about the Haimen incident: have to arrest some people'.

References

AFP. (2011). *China struggles to tame microblogging masses*. London: The Independent.

Arquilla, J., & Ronfeldt, D. (2001). The advent of netwar (revisited). In J. Arquilla & D. Ronfeldt (Eds.), *Networks and netwars: The future of terror, crime, and militancy* (pp. 1–25). Santa Monica, CA: RAND.

Balasubramanyan, R., Lin, F., & Cohen, W. W. (2010). *Node clustering in graphs: An empirical study*. NIPS 2010 workshop on networks across disciplines in theory and applications. Vancouver, BC.

Boas, T. C. (2006). Weaving the authoritarian web: The control of internet use in nondemocratic regimes. In J. Zysman & A. Newman (Eds.), *How revolutionary was the digital revolution? National responses, market transitions, and global technology* (pp. 361–378). Stanford, CA: Stanford Business Books.

Cai, Y. (2008). Power structure and regime resilience: Contentious politics in China. *British Journal of Political Science, 38*(3), 411–432.

Castells, M. (2009). *Communication power*. Oxford: Oxford University Press.

Chen, J., Zhong, Y., Hillard, J. W., & Scheb, J. M. II (1997). Assessing political support in China: Citizens' evaluations of governmental effectiveness and legitimacy. *Journal of Contemporary China, 6*(16), 551–566.

Davidov, D., Tsur, O., & Rappoport, A. (2010). Enhanced sentiment learning using Twitter hashtags and smileys. In *COLING'10 proceedings of the 23rd international conference on computational linguistics: posters* (pp. 241–249). Association for Computational Linguistics Stroudsburg, PA, USA.

Diakopoulos, N. A., & Shamma, D. A. (2010). Characterizing debate performance via aggregated twitter sentiment. In *Proceedings of the 28th international conference on Human factors in computing systems* (pp. 1195–1198). New York, NY.

Dickson, B. J. (2004). Dilemmas of party adaptation: The CCP's strategies for survival. In P. H. Gries & S. Rosen (Eds.), *State and society in 21st-century China: Crisis, contention, and legitimation* (pp. 141–158). New York, NY: ReoutledgeCurzon.

Dong, F. (2012). Controlling the internet in China: The real story. *Convergence: The International Technologies Journal of Research into New Media, 18*(4), 403–425.

Downs, E. S., & Saunders, P. C. (1998/1999). Legitimacy and the limits of nationalism: China and the Diaoyu islands. *International Security, 23*(3), 114–146.

Elmer, K. (2012). *Battle lines in the Chinese blogosphere: Keyword control as a tactic in managing mass incidents* (The Finnish Institute of International Affairs Working Paper). Helsinki, Finland: Finnish Institute of International Affairs.

Fewsmith, J. (2008). An 'anger-venting' mass incident catches the attention of China's leadership. *The China Leadership Monitor, 26*. Retrieved July 4, 2012, from http://www.hoover.org/publications/china-leadership-monitor/article/5673

Garrett, R. K. (2006). Protest in an information society: A review of literature on social movements and new ICTs. *Information, Communication & Society, 9*(2), 202–224.

Gerlach, L. P., & Hine, V. H. (1970). *People, power, change: Movements of social transformation*. Indianapolis: Bobbs-Merrill.

Gilboy, G., & Read, B. (2008). Political and social reform in China: Alive and walking. *The Washington Quarterly, 31*(3), 143–164.

Gilley, B. (2005). Political legitimacy in Malaysia: Regime performance in the Asian context. In L. T. White (Ed.), *Legitimacy: ambiguities of political success or failure in East and Southeast Asia* (pp. 28–41). Singapore: World Scientific Publishing Co. Pvt. Ltd.

Gilley, B., & Holbig, H. (2009). The debate on party legitimacy in China: A mixed quantitative/qualitative analysis. *Journal of Contemporary China, 18*(59), 339–358.

Go, A., Bhayani, R., & Huang, L. (2009). *Twitter sentiment classification using distant supervision* (CS224N Project Report, Stanford, Technical Report). Stanford University. Retrieved July 15, 2012, from http://cs.stanford.edu/people/alecmgo/papers/TwitterDistantSupervision09.pdf

Guo, B. (2003). Political legitimacy and China's transition. *Journal of Chinese Political Science, 8*(1&2), 1–25.

Harwit, E., & Clark, D. (2001). Shaping the internet in China: Evolution of political control over network infrastructure and content. *Asian Survey, 41*(3), 377–408.

Hassid, J. (2012). Safety valve or pressure cooker? Blogs in Chinese political life. *Journal of Communication, 62,* 212–230.

He, Z. (2000). Corruption and anti-corruption in reform China. *Communist and Post-Communist Studies, 33*(2), 243–270.

Heberer, T., & Schubert, G. (2006). Political reform and regime legitimacy in contemporary China. *ASIEN, 99,* 9–28.

Holbig, H. (2006). *Ideological reform and political legitimacy in China: Challenges in the post-Jiang era* (GIGA research program: Legitimacy and efficiency of political systems). Hamburg: GIGA German Institute of Global and Area Studies and Leibniz-Institut für Globale und Regionale Studien.

Hughes, A. L., & Palen, L. (2009). Twitter adoption and use in mass convergence and emergency events. *International Journal of Emergency Management, 6*(3/4), 248–260.

Hunt, K. (2012). China tightens grip on social media with new rules. *CNN.* Retrieved on July 15, 2012, from http://edition.cnn.com/2012/05/28/world/asia/china-weibo-rules/index.html

Jansen, B. J., Zhang, M., Sobel, K., & Chowdury, A. (2009). Twitter power: Tweets as electronic word of mouth. *Journal of the American Society for Information Science and Technology, 60*(11), 2169–2188.

Jiang, M. (2010). Authoritarian deliberation on Chinese Internet. *Electronic Journal of Communication, 20,* 3–4.

Kirilenko, A. P., & Stepchenkova, S. O. (2012). Climate change discourse in mass media: Application of computer-assisted content analysis. *Journal of Environmental Studies and Sciences, 2*(2), 178–191.

Lagerkvist, J. (2010). *After the internet, before democracy: Competing norms in Chinese media and society.* Bern: Peter Lang.

Lum, T. (2006). Social unrest in China. Retrieved June 22, 2012, from http://digitalcommons.ilr.cornell.edu/crs/19/

MacKinnon, M. (2012). Chinese 'netizens' intervene where judges fail. *The Globe and Mail.* Retrieved July 1, 2012, from http://www.theglobeandmail.com/news/world/worldview/chinese-netizens-intervene-where-judges-fail/article4265793/

MacKinnon, R. (2008). Flatter world and thicker walls? Blogs, censorship and civic discourse in China. *Public Choice, 134,* 31–46.

Mendoza, M., Poblete, B., & Castillo, C. (2010). Twitter under crisis: Can we trust what we RT? In *Proceedings of the first workshop on social media analytics* (pp. 71–79). New York, NY.

Mitsztal, B. (1985). Social movement against the state: Theoretical legacy of the welfare state. In B. Misztal (Ed.), *Poland after solidarity. Social movements versus the state* (pp. 143–165). New Jersey: Transaction.

Murphy, P. (2001). Affiliation bias and expert disagreement in framing the nicotine addiction debate. *Science, Technology, & Human Values, 26*(3), 278–299.

Orcutt, M. (2012). A peek behind China's 'great firewall'. *Technology Review.* Retrieved July 15, 2013, from http://www.technologyreview.com/view/428170/a-peek-behind-chinas-great-firewall/

Pak, A., & Paroubek, P. (2010). Twitter as a corpus for sentiment analysis and opinion mining. In *Proceedings of LREC.* Retrieved July 15, 2012, from http://www.lrec-conf.org/proceedings/lrec2010/summaries/385.html

Popping, R. (2000). *Computer-assisted text analysis.* Thousand Oaks, CA: Sage.

Potter, P. B. (1994). Riding the tiger: Legitimacy and legal culture in post-Mao China. *The China Quarterly, 138,* 325–358.

Rosenfeld, M. (2001). The rule of law and the legitimacy of constitutional democracy. *Southern California Law Review, 74,* 1307–1352.

Schesser, S. D. (2006). A new domain for public speech: Opening public spaces online. *California Law Review, 94*(6), 1791–1826.

Schubert, G. (2008). One-party rule and the question of legitimacy in contemporary China: Preliminary thoughts on setting up a new research agenda. *Journal of Contemporary China, 17*(54), 191–204.

Schubert, G. (2009). Village elections, citizenship and regime legitimacy in contemporary rural China. In T. Heberer & G. Schubert (Eds.), *Regime legitimacy in contemporary China: Institutional change and stability* (pp. 55–78). New York, NY: Routledge.

Shangguan, L. (2011). Coat electricity plant project is Haimen Shantou questioned. *Southern Weekend,* December 21. Retrieved October 10, 2012, from http://www.infzm.com/content/66806

Shue, V. (2004). Legitimacy crisis in China? In P. H. Gries & S. Rosen (Eds.), *State and society in 21st-century China: Crisis, contention, and legitimation* (pp. 24–49). New York, NY: Routledge.

Stoecker, R. (2000). Cyberspace vs. face to face: Community organizing in the new millennium. In *COMM-ORG: The on-line conference on community organizing and development*. Retrieved July 15, 2012, from http://comm-org.wisc.edu/papers.htm

Thompson, J. B. (1995). *The media and modernity: A social theory of the media*. Stanford: Stanford University of Press.

Tian, Y., & Stewart, C. M. (2005). Framing the SARS crisis: A computer-assisted text analysis of CNN and BBC online news reports of SARS. *Asian Journal of Communication, 15*(3), 289–301.

Trachtman, J. (1998). Cyberspace, sovereignty, jurisdiction, and modernism. *Indiana Journal of Global Legal Studies, 5*(2), 561–581.

Van de Donk, W., Loader, B. D., Nixon, P. G., & Rucht, D. (2004). Introduction. In W. van de Donk, B. D. Loader, P. G. Nixon, & D. Rucht (Eds.), *Cyberprotest: New media, citizens, and social movements* (pp. 1–25). London: Routledge.

Wines, M., & LaFraniere, S. (2011). In baring facts of train crash, blogs Erode China censorship. *The New York Times*. Retrieved September 2, 2012, from http://www.nytimes.com/2011/07/29/world/asia/29china.html?pagewanted=all&_r=0

Wong, L. (2004). Market reforms, globalization and social justice in China. *Journal of Contemporary China, 13*(38), 151–171.

Wu, W. (2008). Measuring political debate on the Chinese internet forum. *Javnost-the Public, 15*(2), 93–110.

Xu, W. (1997). Mutual empowerment of state and peasantry: Grassroots democracy in rural China. *World Development, 25*(9), 1431–1442.

Yang, G. (2003). The co-evolution of the internet and civil society in China. *Asian Survey, 43*(3), 405–422.

Zhang, Q. (2011). Thousands protesters blocked road to protect rights in East Guangdong. *Asian Weekly (yazhou zhoukan), 26*(1), 60–65.

Zhou, X. (2009). The political blogosphere in China: A content analysis of the blogs regarding the dismissal of Shanghai leader Chen Liangyu. *New Media and Society, 11*(6), 1003–1022.

Weibo network, information diffusion and implications for collective action in China

Ronggui Huang[a] and Xiaoyi Sun[b]

[a]Department of Sociology, Fudan University; [b]Department of Public Policy, City University of Hong Kong

This study examines information diffusion and the follower network among a group of Sina Weibo users interested in homeowner associations. Using social network analysis techniques, this paper explores the network structure, the formation of follower relations and information diffusion. It reveals that micro-blogging is an important online platform because it can conveniently and inexpensively foster public online issue-networks beyond geographical boundaries. Specifically, Weibo has the potential to enable cross-province networking and communication, although geographical proximity is still at work; the trustworthiness of micro-blog users indirectly contributes to information diffusion by facilitating the formation of follower relations; and issue-specific follower networks facilitate information diffusion pertinent to the issue at stake. These findings suggest that micro-blogging services might have long-term effects on collective action by fostering issue-networks among civil society organizations or activists in different provinces.

Introduction

The Internet has long been regarded as both a public sphere and a means for mobilization (Zheng & Wu, 2005). Blogs and micro-blogs in particular provide a medium for sophisticated political expression (Esarey & Xiao, 2008; Pu & Scanlan, 2012; Xiao, 2011; Zhou, 2009). It has been argued that the primary role of China's microblogosphere is to provide a liberal-leaning space for counter-hegemony and public engagement (Tong & Lei, 2013). Still, the power of the Internet is limited by censorship (King, Pan, & Roberts, 2013; MacKinnon, 2008; Tsui, 2003), and the state is adept at using micro-blogs to its own advantage (Sullivan, in press). Perhaps a more realistic view is that the public sphere is the result of interactions between the state, the market, civil societies, and transnational actors (Hassid, 2012; Yang, 2009). For example, the secondary role of micro-blogs as a mobilization structure might hinge on the state's effort to silence collective action (King et al., 2013). Although studies of social media are increasingly gaining publication, the majority involve case studies of one or a few mass incidents, and only a few have conducted systematic quantitative investigations (Hassid, 2012). This 'incident-based' approach is inadequate for understanding the long-term political repercussions of social media (MacKinnon,

2008; Shirky, 2011) because online incidents 'may achieve a short-term effect but lose long-term credibility' (Tong & Lei, 2013, p. 306).

This paper argues that the micro-blog issue-network, defined as a network among micro-bloggers from different localities joining to advocate a specific issue, can better shed light on the long-term implications of social media for the future development of collective action and the emergence of social movements in China. For one, activism in China fails to meet the definition of a 'social movement' because it is usually localized and falls short of sustained contention, partially because of the tight control of organizational infrastructure (Stalley & Yang, 2006; Zhu & Ho, 2008). Issue-networks on micro-blogging sites can thus be seen as online extensions of and/or substitutes for organizational infrastructure in real life: they are not only a relational platform for reflexive interactions and a set of networks linking activists in a common front, but also a breeding ground for mobilization (Yip & Jiang, 2011). Second, previous studies have demonstrated that online networks and information dissemination facilitate the development of collective action (Diani, 2000; Garrido & Halavais, 2003), and that follower networks on micro-blogging sites can be turned into mobilization structures when the political conditions are ripe (Cao, Fan, & Peng, 2011; Ji, 2011).

This study takes homeowner activism as an issue area and aims to map the follower network among a group of micro-bloggers, explicate the formation of such a network, and explore the relationship between the follower network and information diffusion. Given that many of these micro-bloggers are directors/members of homeowner associations, the study of this issue network will also shed light on the inter-organizational relations between homeowner associations, which few studies have examined (Yip & Jiang, 2011). This study will analyse the micro-blog issue-network in a rigorous and systematic manner not often found in previous studies.

Homeowner collective action and the role of the Internet

China's housing reforms, privatization and marketization of housing (Wang & Murie, 1999, 2000), have resulted in a dramatic increase in homeownership (Huang, 2004). In a not-yet-mature market, however, developers and property management companies tend to encroach on the property rights of homeowners. China's weak legal system makes it difficult for homeowners to protect their rights through individual lawsuits. More and more homeowners have turned to collective action[1] to defend their rights and interests, usually through the platform of homeowner association (Read, 2008; Shi, 2008; Shi & Cai, 2006; Yip & Jiang, 2011).

Most collective action is, however, isolated and confined to specific neighbourhoods. The Property Management Ordinance (2007) sets an institutional barrier by stipulating that homeowner associations 'shall only represent and safeguard the legitimate rights and interests of all homeowners within the property management area and in property management activities'. Limiting the scale of action to the neighbourhood level is also a conscious homeowner tactic to depoliticize collective action and thus avoid a repressive government response (Zhu & Ho, 2008). Since homeowner activists encounter serious difficulty defending lawful rights and interests against powerful real-estate interest groups (Zhang, 2005), they have recently attempted to create lateral networks at the city level, in part to exchange governance experience and knowledge of policies (Interviews of homeowner association directors, July and August 2007). These initiatives can be found in almost every major city in China – Beijing,[2] Guangzhou (Yip & Jiang, 2011), Shanghai,[3] Shenyang,[4] Suzhou,[5] Suqian,[6] Xi'an[7] and Wenzhou.[8] While such lateral networks are still under the tight control of Chinese authorities, they do facilitate homeowner self-governance. The networks are not only important communication platforms for homeowner associations to share information and experience; they can also formulate codes of conduct among homeowner associations as well as provide substantial support for member associations.[9] Sometimes, they even pressure the government for favourable policies (Zhuang, 2011).

Homeowners are usually well-off, and many are middle class (Logan, Fang, & Zhang, 2010; Tomba, 2004); they thus are poised to use multiple online communication platforms in rights-defending activities (Huang & Yip, 2012). Homeowner activists have utilized homeowners' online forums (mainly BBS on soufun.com) as information disclosure and online discussion platforms (Huang, 2010). Because many homeowners' forums are public, and because online information may also be exploited by adversaries and/or local governments to counteract activists' strategies, activists prefer QQ (a popular instant messaging system in China) groups as a strategy-crafting venue to which only a handful of activists have access (Interview of a homeowner activist, 20090709). These online communication channels, however, do not change the localized nature of homeowner action. Discussions on homeowners' forums usually take place among homeowners from a single neighbourhood, and information diffusion across neighbourhoods is not common (Huang, Zhang, & Gui, 2011).

Publicly visible networking and communications between homeowner associations from different cities were not prevalent until the recent blossoming of micro-blogging services such as Sina Weibo. In this sense, these services provide homeowners a new and unique venue to advance their rights and interests. Micro-blogging offers homeowners in different provinces a low-cost way to communicate with each other. This is of great significance because activists do not have the resources to build nationwide communications networks (Interview with a Weibo user, 20130104), and the offline lateral networks described above operate only at the city level and do not include a large number of member associations. As a homeowner activist said, 'It is difficult to find someone nearby to discuss the problems I encounter, and even harder to seek professional advice from experts' (Personal correspondence, 20130104). The 'genuine identity' feature of Weibo offers entrepreneurial activists an opportunity to build a serious nationwide community around a specific issue, which is difficult to achieve on homeowners' forums because anonymity can lead to unaccountable and irrelevant postings. Furthermore, micro-blogging services are conducive to information sharing (Scanfeld, Scanfeld, & Larson, 2010; Small, 2011), and the easy integration of micro-blogging and blogging enables members of the issue-network to articulate their thoughts seriously (Personal correspondence, 20130104). Therefore, networking and communication on micro-blogging sites can function as an important complement to and extension of offline networking efforts, which may be facilitating the 'scale shift' of homeowner collective action in contemporary urban China.

Weibo: a platform of networking and information sharing

Micro-blogging services are a type of social media through which users broadcast public messages of 140 characters, known as *tweets*, to provide frequent and immediate updates on their activities, opinions, and status (Zhang & Pentina, 2012). Sina Weibo (www.weibo.com), the Chinese counterpart of Twitter, is the leading micro-blogging service in China. The number of registered users reached 300 million in February 2012.[10] On Sina Weibo, user A may choose to follow any other user B, which leads to the formation of a *follower relation*. Within the dyad, A is a follower of B and B is a friend of A. A set of follower relations and the set of Weibo users connected by these relations form a *follower network*.

Follower relations are fundamental to information dissemination on Weibo. The tweets from all users whom one follows are gathered together and displayed in a single reverse-chronological list for consumption. When a user finds an interesting tweet posted by another user and wants to share it with his/her own followers, he/she can retweet it by simply clicking the 'retweet' button. *Retweeting* has become the key mechanism for spreading information on micro-blogging services

(Suh, Hong, Pirolli, & Chi, 2010), and the *retweet network* of 'who retweets whom' can be constructed from the actual retweeting relations between a set of users.

One feature worth mentioning is that Sina Weibo encourages identity verification, either as an individual or an organization. Once the identity is verified, a symbol of '*V*' and the real identity are displayed in the profile. Verified users are perceived as more credible because only those of relatively distinguished social status are qualified for the service. For example, if a user wants to register as an educator, he/she should be at least an assistant professor in a university or a senior teacher in a top high school at the provincial level.

Previous studies on Weibo network and information diffusion

Formation of follower relations

It has already been pointed out that Weibo (because of its convenience, inexpensiveness, trustworthiness and wide geographical reach) is a new but important platform facilitating the formation of nation-wide public networks among homeowner associations. But what factors influence the formation of follower relations is an under-researched question, with only a few studies in the literature on social media (Lampe, Ellison, & Steinfield, 2007; Lewis, Kaufman, Gonzalez, Wimmer, & Christakis, 2008; Zhang & Pentina, 2012). Therefore, the authors draw on literature of social networks (Rivera, Soderstrom, & Uzzi, 2010) for guidance.[11] Extant studies suggest that actor attributes, existing relations (e.g. balancing mechanism), and proximity mechanisms contribute to the formation of social ties.[12] However, unlike social network studies that pay attention to assortative mechanisms when explaining the effects of actor attributes, this study argues that actor attributes facilitate follower relation formation because they increase the trustworthiness of the followed.

When user A follows B on Weibo, it implies that A trusts B to provide relevant information. B has the incentive to fulfil such trust because the continuation of the follower relation with A contributes to B's online social influence. This conception fits Hardin's encapsulated-interest concept of trust (Hardin, 2002). In this theory, trust and trustworthiness are linked, and it is the trustworthiness of the trusted that gives rise to trust and trust relationships (Hardin, 1996, 2002; Nannestad, 2008). Therefore, the attributes of the followed that signal trustworthiness are expected to be positively associated with the formation of follower relations.

A user's online activities provide a basis to assess his/her trustworthiness as well as the relevance of the provided information. Therefore, online activities are expected to be associated with online network size. Previous studies have demonstrated that the more time a student spends on Facebook, the larger is that student's Facebook friendship network (Lampe et al., 2007; Lewis et al., 2008). A study in China has found that time spent on Weibo significantly increases the (log of the) number of followers (Zhang & Pentina, 2012). Therefore, the authors propose:

H1a: Active micro-blogging users are more likely to form follower relations.

This study extends previous research by examining the effect of 'identity verification', a unique service provided by Sina Weibo, on follower relations. The effect of 'identity verification' on follower-relation formation has not been empirically tested. Nevertheless, previous studies have found that the public display of online social networks (Donath & Boyd, 2004), or the inclusion of many verifiable elements in a user profile, increase the reliability of the signals of that user's identify, and reduce the transaction costs of being found, thus facilitating the formation of online connections (Lampe et al., 2007). Similarly, identity verification on Weibo functions as a

signal of trustworthiness because verification requires a user to verify his/her mobile phone number and submit other supporting documents. Verified identity is not only more difficult to manipulate than other profile fields – it is also implicitly endorsed by Sina Weibo itself. In addition, a verified user usually has high social status and a good reputation, and many are professionals whose expertise is helpful for others. All these characteristics increase their chance of being followed. Therefore, it is expected that:

H1b: Verified users are more likely to be followed by other users.

Driven by a balancing mechanism, an actor has the tendency to befriend those who nominate him/her as a friend, leading to mutual friendships (Bruggeman, 2008). The same phenomenon is also found in online social networks. Wimmer and Lewis' (2010) study of Facebook friendships in the United States finds a strong and significant effect of reciprocity. A web-based experiment with randomly selected Twitter users confirms that mutuality is a significant factor in predicting users' desire to form new ties (Golder & Yardi, 2010). The Weibo system likewise facilitates mutual friendships. Whenever a user is followed, Weibo automatically sends a private message to notify him/her of the new follower, so he/she can easily inspect the profile of the new follower and decide whether to reciprocate the friendship. Therefore, it is expected that:

H1c: Reciprocity is an important predictor of follower relation formation.

Proximity mechanisms (Rivera et al., 2010), in terms of geographical distance and boundaries, might also be at work. A study in the United States has shown that Internet use facilitates participation in local communities and supports affective networks outside local communities (Stern & Dillman, 2006). A longitudinal study in Canada found that the Internet only somewhat alters the way people maintain social relations, and that distance still matters (Mok, Wellman, & Carrasco, 2010). Recent studies on the geographical properties of Twitter networks have reached a similar conclusion – that geographical distance and national boundaries influence the formation of Twitter ties, leading to a substantial proportion of ties being formed in the same metropolitan area (Takhteyev, Gruzd, & Wellman, 2012), and users tending to establish connections with others from the same continent (Java, Song, Finin, & Tseng, 2007).

Previous studies have focused on large geographical scales (nations or continents); it is less clear whether geographical proximity at the sub-national level is relevant. In fact, geographical proximity seems not only a matter of geographical distance, but also of shared interest in local issues. As a study of transnational activism points out, even global issues are rooted in local settings – the Internet cannot replace personal connections to build stable coalitions across borders (Gillana & Pickerill, 2008). Since social relations are driven by the issues at stake, it is reasonable to argue that the more local the issues, the more likely social connections are to be geographically bounded. Because homeowner action/activism is highly localized, and because socio-political contexts vary among provinces (Chung, 2008; Yip & Jiang, 2011), it is expected that:

H1d: Follower relations within the same province are more likely to be observed than pure chance.

Nevertheless, as previously suggested, micro-blogging services enable cross-province networking better than do other online communication methods. Since cross-province networking capacity is micro-blogging services' relative advantage over previous online platforms as well as offline lateral networks, it will be revealing to examine the following question:

RQ1: How prevalent are cross-province follower relations?

Follower relations and information diffusion on Weibo

Determining the channel(s) of information diffusion is crucial to understanding to what extent and how Weibo follower networks can develop into issue-based collective action. Information diffusion on micro-blogging services intertwines closely with follower relations, and follower networks can be seen as information networks (Barash & Golder, 2011) because tweets posted by user A are by default displayed on the front pages of A's followers. Moreover, information diffusion happens through retweeting when A's followers pass A's tweets to their own followers, delivering information beyond A's immediate followers (Kwak, Lee, Park, & Moon, 2010). In this study, *information diffusion* refers to retweeting, and a *retweet network* is composed of a set of users and the retweeting relations among them.[13]

As fundamental a role as follower relations play in the information diffusion process, the relationship between follower networks and retweet networks is, to a large extent, under-researched. Only a few studies have shed light on the retweeting process. A study of retweets on Twitter reveals that a tweet is more likely to be retweeted if the author is followed by many, is following many, or has been a Twitter user for a long time (Suh et al., 2010). Another study reveals that a large number of retweets only go through one- or two-hop chains (Kwak et al., 2010), which implies that if there is a correlation between the follower network and the retweet network, the correlation is modest at best. Thus, this study proposes:

H2a: Follower network positively correlates with retweet network, but the correlation coefficient is small.

Studies of the relationship between the indegree of the follower network (number of followers) and retweets result in inconclusive findings. A study of user influence on Twitter found only moderate correlation between indegree and retweets (Cha, Haddadiy, Benevenutoz, & Gummadi, 2010). The conclusion, echoed by other scholars (Kwak et al., 2010), was that indegree reveals very little about the influence of a user. On the contrary, Wu and colleagues found that the attention of ordinary Twitter users is mainly concentrated on elite users. In the process of two-step diffusion, information is first passed to intermediaries and then passed to ordinary users through those intermediaries. On average, intermediaries have more followers than do randomly sampled users (Wu, Hofman, Mason, & Watts, 2011). This implies that the number of followers might be an important determinant of information diffusion on micro-blogging services. Based on previous studies, this study hypothesizes:

H2b: The number of followers from within the studied follower network has moderate power in predicting/explaining retweets.

Previous studies have concentrated on the effect of the total number of followers (from the entire social networking site) on retweetability; they have not differentiated followers who are interested in the focal issue from those who are not. This narrow focus on total number of followers fails to reveal the relative contributions of these two types of followers to the retweetability of messages pertinent to a particular issue. In other words, extant studies implicitly conceive all followers as homogenous, which is questionable in that micro-blogging users are driven by multiple motives (Zhang & Pentina, 2012), and that flows of information are fragmented and circulated mainly within the same category of users (Wu et al., 2011). To extend our understanding of the online dynamics of social groups who share a similar concern, this research highlights the distinction between (a) the number of followers who belong to the studied follower network and (b) the number of followers from outside the network, which invites the following questions:

RQ2a: Does the number of followers from outside the studied follower network have an effect on retweetability of messages pertinent to homeowner associations?

RQ2b: If followers from both inside and outside the studied network influence retweetability, what are the relative contributions of these two types of followers?

Data and methods

This study applied social network analysis techniques to examine the proposed hypotheses and questions. Social network analysis techniques differ from those of standard statistical analysis by focusing on both actors (nodes) and relations (Bruggeman, 2008; Wasserman & Faust, 1994). Social network analysis was congruent with the foci of this study because both follower relations and information diffusion were relational. A network is a set of actors (*nodes*) connected by a set of relations (*edges*). These relations can be binary or valued – binary relations indicate the presence/absence of relations, whilst valued relations provide information about the strength of relations.

Data collection

This article focused on a group of Sina Weibo users with a shared interest in homeowner associations. The authors selected the Weibo user *yeweihui tongxun* (Homeowner Association Communication, *YWHTX* thereafter) and defined its followers as the studied group. This method clearly defined the network boundary, enabling the construction of a whole network and the application of whole network analysis techniques to explore the formation of follower relations, which would have been very difficult to untangle with ego-network data.[14] It also provided an effective way to answer questions RQ2a and RQ2b by differentiating in-group and out-group followers.

The choice of *YWHTX* was carefully considered. The authors had conducted 'virtual ethnography' (Hine, 2000) by following *YWHTX*'s status updates for about six months. Its screenname, self-description, active followers and tweets all clearly demonstrated its particular concern for homeowner associations. In fact, *YWHTX* was an individual activist who advocated homeowner associations through micro-blogs, weblogs and offline seminars. On Sina Weibo, he broadcast news about homeowner actions in various cities, acted as an intermediary between homeowners and experts, and organized discussions about salient issues of homeowner associations (Personal correspondence, 2013).

The authors also consulted researchers and homeowner activists, who all recommended *YWHTX*. It was reasonable to infer that, by and large, the followers of *YWHTX* could be seen as a concerned group for homeowner associations. Though the findings from this group might not readily be generalized to all Weibo users, they can provide preliminary conclusions and shed light on the implications of Weibo for homeowner collective action.

The authors took advantage of Weibo's open API[15] and used the Python SDK[16] to collect data. Data were collected in June and July 2012. At that time, *YWHTX* had 1840 followers. The follower relations between each pair of users were collected to construct a follower network, which was a binary-directed network with edges running from followers to the followed. In this network, *indegree*[17] was the number of followers.

The latest 100 tweets of *each Weibo user* were also collected.[18] Though not comprehensive, analysis of the latest 100 tweets was still indicative and had an advantage – it reduced the chance of retweeting relations happening prior to the formation of the studied follower network. Using these tweets, the authors were also able to construct a *retweet network* among the 1840 users. In this retweet network, nodes were users and edges were information volume (number of retweets) running from a) users who first originally posted the tweets to b) users who reposted those tweets. First, 92808 tweets retweeted from other users were selected from a total of

140,923 tweets.[19] That pool was then narrowed to 10,918 relevant tweets, which mentioned 'home-owner association', 'homeowner', 'property management', 'real estate developer', or 'property rights'.[20] Third, the original author of each tweet was traced and identified. Then, the retweet network was constructed.

Finally, Weibo users' gender, province, identity verification, total tweets, and date of account registration were also collected.

Analysis methods

In addition to descriptive statistics, an exponential random graph model was used to examine the effects of the above-mentioned factors on the formation of follower relations. In this model, the log-odds of a follower relation were modelled in an exponential form analogous to logistic regression (Goodreau, Kitts, & Morris, 2009; Hunter, Handcock, Butts, Goodreau, & Morris, 2008; Robins, Pattison, Kalish, & Lusher, 2007). The exponential random graph model was specified as follows:

$$\text{logit}(Y_{ij} = 1) = \theta_{\text{edge}} + \sum_{A} \theta_A[\delta g_A(y)],$$

where Y_{ij} was the follower relation between two distinct users of i and j, $g_A(y)$ was a network statistic dependent on the network of y, and $\delta g_A(y)$ was network statistic change when Y_{ij} was toggled from zero to one. Parameter θ_A represented the change in the log-odds that a particular follower relation was formed if the formation of this relation increased the corresponding network statistic by one, all else being equal (Goodreau, Handcock, Hunter, Butts, & Morris, 2008). When a model posited an endogenous process of relation formation, Markov-Chain Monte Carlo maximum-like-lihood estimation (MCMCMLE) was required to obtain the appropriate estimates (Hunter et al., 2008; Goodreau et al., 2009). The MCMCMLE was implemented in the R package of *ergm* (Handcock et al., 2012).

The authors also used *sna* package (Butts, 2010) to conduct QAP (quadratic assignment procedure) tests (Krackardt, 1987) to ascertain the significance level of the correlation between two networks.

Empirical findings

Description of follower network

The 1840 Weibo users were dispersed across 34 provinces.[21] Among them, 27.1% were from Beijing, 15.27% from Guangdong, and 11.2% from Shanghai. Users from these three provinces (municipalities) accounted for more than half of the studied population, a disproportionately large number, given that Internet users in these three areas were only 17.9% of all the Internet users in China (CNNIC, 2012). One explanation is that housing and property management markets are more developed and homeowner actions are more common in these three cities. A majority (71%) of these 1840 Weibo users were male. 13.2% were verified users, who were media workers, scholars and researchers, lawyers, NGO staff, homeowner association representatives, and homeowner activists (Table 1).

There were 24,737 edges in the follower network (Table 2). The average degree was 13.4 and the network density was 0.0073. Indegree and outdegree were highly correlated, and the corre-lation coefficient (0.771) was larger than that of the Twitter network (Java et al., 2007). According to the standard deviations, indegree was less dispersed than outdegree, implying that a handful of users were each followed by many. The dyadic reciprocity, which was the ratio of mutual to non-null dyads, was 0.432. The tie reciprocity, which was the proportion of reciprocated edges, was

Table 1.   Distribution of Weibo users in the follower network ($N = 1840$).

Province	Number of users (%)
Beijing	497 (27.1)
Guangdong	281 (15.27)
Shanghai	206 (11.2)
Others	856 (46.5)
Gender	Number of users (%)
Male	1306 (71.0)
Female	534 (29.0)
Identity verification	Number of users (%)
Verified	242 (13.2)
Not verified	1598 (86.8)

0.603. These two reciprocity scores were higher than (Kwak et al., 2010; Wu et al., 2011) or similar to (Java et al., 2007) that of Twitter networks. High reciprocity indicated a large number of mutual friendships.

About 27.3% (6743) of edges connected users from the same province. About 72.7% were cross-province relations, which were more prevalent than cross-country relations (25%) in Twitter networks (Takhteyev et al., 2012). It seems that as the geographical boundaries were defined on a smaller scale, cross-boundary connections became more prevalent. In all, we concluded that cross-province follower relations were quite common (RQ1).

It was obvious that intra-province relations were disproportionately concentrated in Beijing, where homeowner activism is more vibrant and politically participatory (Chung, 2008, pp. 52–57). This might imply that intra-boundary relation formation was not only constrained by geographical distance, but also driven by the social fabric in the offline world.[22]

Determinants of follower relations

The exponential random graph model simultaneously estimated the effects of user attributes,[23] proximity and network structure (Table 3). The explanatory terms included edges, the main

Table 2.   Structural characteristics of the follower network.

Property	Value
Nodes	1840
Total edges	24,737
Average degree	13.4
Density	0.0073
Degree correlation	0.771
SD of indegree	35.15
SD of outdegree	34.77
Mutuality	7462
Asymmetric dyad	9813
Reciprocity (non-null dyads/edges)	0.432/0.603
Number of cross-province edges	17994
Number of intra-province edges	6743
Edges within Beijing	3867
Edges within Guangdong	1086
Edges within Shanghai	417

Table 3.   Exponential random graph model of follower network.

	Coefficient	Standard error	Exp(coef)
Edges	−6.614**	0.018	0.0013
Network structure effect			
Reciprocity	6.102**	0.024	446.750
Proximity effect			
Same province	0.586**	0.011	1.797
Actor's attribute effect			
Identity verification of the followed	0.983**	0.014	2.672
Active in tweeting	0.333**	0.008	1.395
Male	0.201**	0.009	1.223
AIC	219,809		

Note: This model was estimated by MCMCMLE using the following settings: burn-in = 2,100,000,000, interval = 1,500,000, and MCMC sample size = 4000.
**p-value < 0.001.

attribute effect of active in tweeting,[24] main attribute effect of identity verification for indegree, province homophily, reciprocity and main attribute effect of gender.[25] Gender was included as a control variable because a study of Facebook has shown that women have more online friends (Lampe et al., 2007). However, the effects of gender are inconclusive (Lewis et al., 2008; Zhang & Pentina, 2012).

The results showed that men were more active in networking. Being male increased the log-odds of follower relation formation by 0.201. This result contradicted previous studies, which was found to be insignificant (Lewis et al., 2008; Zhang & Pentina, 2012) or negative effects (Lampe et al., 2007). This result could be explained by the issue at stake. According to the authors' field-work observations in Shanghai, members of homeowner associations were mainly male, and men generally had higher levels of interest in this particular issue. This speculation needs further investigation.

The odds of forming a follower relation involving an 'active' user, who tweeted more frequently than 'average' users, were 1.395 times the odds between two inactive users. This confirmed hypothesis *H1a*. More importantly, users with verified identities were more likely to be followed by others. The odds of verified users being followed were 2.6 times that of ordinary users, thus confirming hypothesis *H1b*. A user's 'authentic' identity enhanced the trustworthiness of the tweets he/she posted, which was especially important when his/her followers used the micro-blogging service for information seeking. In addition, identify verification on Weibo (with its rigid qualification requirements) favoured celebrities, and thus most verified users possessed high social status and professional expertise. Information from these distinguished professionals and experts (e.g. lawyers and journalists) was valuable for those who are interested in homeowner associations.

The reciprocity effect was highly significant and its magnitude was very large (coefficient = 6.102). This result implied that user A following B increased by 6.1 the log-odds of B reciprocating the follower relation and forming a mutual friendship. Thus, hypothesis *H1c* was confirmed. This network structure effect was larger than any other effect in the model, which justified the use of an exponential random graph model.

A proximity mechanism was also at work. The odds of forming a follower relation between two users from the same province were 1.797 times the odds between two users from different provinces. In other words, despite the prevalence of cross-province relations, intra-province relations were more likely observed than pure chance, which confirmed hypothesis *H1d* and was consistent with the finding in Takhteyev et al. (2012).

Table 4. QAP (product-moment) correlation between retweet network and follower network.

	Transposed follower network
Log-transformed of weighted retweet network	0.134
Dichotomized retweet network	0.132

Note: All p-values are <0.005. p-values were based on QAP tests (1000 permutations).

Retweet network structure

This section focused on tweets diffusion *within* the studied follower network. In the data set, 4439 tweets were retweeted between 2261 pairs of users. These tweets were originally tweeted by 320 users (information sources), which only accounted for 17.4% of the 1840 users in the studied network. Furthermore, most of the tweets came from a few users. Retweets originating from the top 10 most popular sources accounted for 42.5% of the total.

These tweets were retweeted by 563 users (disseminators), almost twice as many as the sources (320). The 10 most popular disseminators only retweeted 593 tweets (13.3%). This implied that the information was from a handful of users, and was disseminated to a relatively large number of users. Users who played the role of information sources were not necessarily active in retweeting. Only one of the top 10 popular sources was on the list of the most active disseminators. Tweets diffusion seemed likely to be a unidirectional process with little reciprocity, which was corroborated by low degree correlation (0.331) in the retweet network. Geographically, the majority of tweets were circulated *across* provincial borders. Analysis revealed that only 1511 (34%) tweets were reposted by users from the same province, whilst 2928 (66%) tweets were reposted by users from different provinces.[26]

Intuitively, if A followed B, it was more likely that tweets spread from B to A. To examine the correlation between the follower and the retweet networks, the follower network had to be transposed first. The edges weights of the retweet network were log-transformed because the distribution was skewed. The correlation coefficient was 0.134, and highly significant. Alternatively, the retweet network was converted into a binary network using the cutting point of 1. The resultant correlation was 0.132 and was also significant (Table 4). Thus, hypothesis *H2a* was supported.

Both correlation coefficients were small. One explanation was that tweets might travel through multiple users before reaching their destinations, but our retweet network represented the source and destination rather than the detailed diffusion paths. It was revealing to explore the lengths of geodesics[27] in the follower networks between the source and destination users. The result (Table 5) showed that 44.2% of tweets were retweeted by the followers of a source user. Another 44.9% of tweets were retweeted by the followers of followers of a source user. Only 2.3% of tweets travelled indirectly through someone outside the studied group to users in this group, which lent support to the method of defining the studied population.

Table 5. Geodesics between tweet sources and destination users in the follower network.

Geodesics	Number of tweets reposted from source and destination users (%)
1	999 (44.2%)
2	1016 (44.9%)
3	180 (8%)
4	15 (0.7%)
Infinite (no direct path)	51 (2.3%)

Follower network and retweets

The chances of tweets being retweeted varied according to the network position of their senders. Based on the 13,510 tweets relevant to homeowner associations, the authors calculated *average number of retweets* for *each* user.[28] That is,

$$Y_i = \sum_{j=1}^{m} R_{ij},$$

where Y_i is the *average number of retweets* for user i and R_{ij} is the number of times the tweet j posted by user i was retweeted. This variable roughly measured how widely a user's tweets had been circulated.

An ordinary least squares (OLS) regression was conducted to explore the determinants of retweets. The log of the *average number of retweets* was regressed on gender, identity verification, log of number of tweets per day, months since account registration, province, log of number of followers from within the studied network (indegree), and log of number of followers from outside the network.[29]

The results (Table 6) showed that tweets from those whose identity was verified seemed more likely to be retweeted (coefficient = 0.36 in model 1), but its magnitude was attenuated when the log of the indegree was included (coefficient = 0.24 in model 2), and became insignificant when the log of number of followers was included (model 3). One interpretation was that identity verification only influenced retweetability indirectly through increasing a user's number of followers.

If a user tweeted frequently, his/her tweets were *less* likely to be retweeted. Since frequency of tweet updates was mainly driven by self-expression rather than information-seeking or citizenship behaviour (Zhang & Pentina, 2012), those who frequently posted tweets might be less useful for those interested in homeowner associations, causing their messages to be less likely to be retweeted. Once the total number of followers was taken into consideration (model 3), the time since account registration had a negative effect on retweetability, which suggested that the longer someone had been a member of Weibo, the less likely his/her tweets were to be retweeted. Gender had no significant effect. Geographically, tweets posted by users from Beijing were more likely to be retweeted, and this effect was significant even when the log of indegree and the number of followers from outside the studied network were included.

The number of followers from the studied network highly correlated with the average number of retweets in the expected direction (the coefficient of log of number of indegree was 0.15 in model 2 and 0.14 in model 3). Tweets from users who had a large number of followers in the studied network were circulated more widely. When log of indegree was included, R^2 increased by 0.0915, from 0.0605 to 0.152. It suggested that the explanatory power of indegree was much stronger than all user attributes in model 1. Therefore, hypothesis *H2b* was supported.

With regard to question RQ2a, the number of followers from outside the studied network was also a contributory factor. However, its explanatory power was relatively weak, as R^2 only increased by 0.018, from 0.152 to 0.170. Regarding question RQ2b, we concluded that the number of followers interested in homeowner associations, rather than the followers from outside the studied follower network, substantially influenced how widely a tweet related to homeowner associations was circulated on Weibo.[30]

Discussion and conclusion

This study argues that Weibo should be conceived as a space for virtual organizational infrastructure building, where micro-bloggers network, exchange experience and information, and conduct reflexive interactions. In this way, Weibo both links activists into a common contentious front and serves

Table 6.   OLS regression of average number of retweets.

Independent variables	Model 1		Model 2		Model 3	
	Coefficient	S.E.	Coefficient	S.E.	Coefficient	S.E.
(Intercept)	0.60**	0.06	0.39**	0.06	0.22**	0.07
Gender (male = 1)	−0.00	0.05	−0.06	0.04	−0.07+	0.04
Verified user	0.36**	0.06	0.24**	0.06	0.11+	0.06
Months since registration	−0.00	0.00	−0.00	0.00	−0.01**	0.00
Log of number of tweets per day	−0.05+	0.03	−0.09**	0.02	−0.18**	0.03
Province: Beijing	0.18**	0.05	0.11*	0.05	0.10*	0.05
Province: Guangdong	−0.04	0.06	−0.07	0.06	−0.07	0.05
Province: Shanghai	−0.03	0.07	−0.02	0.07	−0.02	0.06
Log of indegree			0.15**	0.01	0.14**	0.01
Log of number of followers outside the studied network					0.07**	0.02
N	1012		1012		1012	
R^2	0.0605	0.152	0.17			

Notes: Dependent variable is log of average number of retweets. Only those who had tweeted prior the data collection process were included. 'Other provinces' was the reference group.
$+p < 0.10$.
$*p < 0.05$.
$**p < 0.01$.

as a breeding ground for mobilization. This conception requires scrutiny not of collective incidents, but of issue-networks, which can better shed light on Weibo's long-term implications for collective action and activism in China, in particular to whether Weibo has the potential to mitigate the afore-mentioned problem of localization and lack of networks between activists in different provinces. In addition, given the dearth of literature on this issue, the findings of this paper also contribute to the study of inter-organizational relations between homeowner associations.

This study finds that the follower network significantly correlates with the retweet network, lending support to the argument that networking on micro-blogging sites facilitates the exchange of information and reflexive interactions. Cross-province follower relations and information diffusion are prevalent on Sina Weibo (72.7% and 66%, respectively). This finding is quite interesting, given that homeowner collective action in urban China is usually confined to specific neighbourhoods (Zhu & Ho, 2008), and that neither existing offline lateral networking efforts of homeowner associations (Yip & Jiang, 2011) nor homeowner online forums (Huang et al. 2011) have the capacity to build effective cross-province organizational infrastructure. It highlights Weibo's unique feature of easy networking, not commonly found in previous online communication platforms. On the other hand, it supports the argument that micro-blogging services function as complements of and/or substitutes for offline networks by providing activists in general and homeowner activists in particular from different provinces a space to share updated information, experience and knowledge. This is of great significance, given that officially recognized offline lateral networks between activists, NGOs, and homeowner associations in particular are lacking because of the unfavourable political conditions. Even if city-level lateral networks are officially recognized by authorities, micro-blogging services still have a role to play in bridging networking efforts among various cities and/or provinces. Overall, Weibo is a valuable platform for activists to enlarge the geographic scale of their networking efforts.

Meanwhile, this study cautions against drawing sweeping conclusions – geographic proximity at the sub-national level is still at work, in that intra-province follower relations are much more likely to be formed than relations between two randomly selected users. Considering the localized nature of homeowner associations and homeowner activism, the effect of geographical proximity on follower relations implies that, even in the Web 2.0 age, collective action remains strongly influenced by provincial regulations and political contexts. Thus, whether geographical proximity at various levels plays a role in less localized issues needs further investigation. This finding also complements previous studies (Java et al., 2007; Takhteyev et al., 2012) by demonstrating that geographical proximity works on a much smaller scale than a nation or a continent.

This study also finds that circulation of tweets pertinent to the issue at stake (e.g. homeowner associations and homeowner activism in this study) is strongly influenced by the number of followers from within the issue-network, and only weakly predicted by the number of followers from outside such a network. It suggests that only when a message is congruent with the interest of the potential audience can it draw the attention of a large number of users and set viral diffusion into motion. Therefore, enlarging the issue-specific network through consensus-building and heightening the salience of the issue at stake will be primary tasks for online activists.

User attributes which provide a basis for assessing the trustworthiness of a user contribute to the formation of follower relations on Weibo. Specifically, those who tweet in a frequent manner and have their identity verified are more likely to be followed. Among the user attributes examined in this paper, identity verification exerts the strongest effect. Identity verification is also a contributory factor to information diffusion: on average, tweets posted by verified users are circulated more widely, but verified identity seems to influence diffusion only indirectly through fostering follower relations. These findings lend support to Garrett's argument that people will not indiscriminately disseminate information (Garrett, 2006). Indeed, Weibo users tend to follow and disseminate information from those who are credible, trustworthy and professional. In other words, Weibo users have the capacity to distinguish, listen to and disseminate information that is trustworthy and helpful by making good use of the signals afforded by micro-blogging services. This study contributes to the literature by highlighting the trustworthiness of content generators, whilst previous studies mainly focused on the styles of framing or the content of messages (Pu & Scanlan, 2012; Suh et al., 2010). Future studies need to assess the relative importance of these two factors.

The information processing strategy of micro-blog users and the significance of identity verification in the formation of follower relations and information diffusion present opportunities as well as dilemmas for online activists in the context of China, where the authorities actively censor social media.[31] Online activists need to be as trustworthy as possible to widen the circulation of and win support for their claims. Often, they need to disclose their identities and professional credentials, but in doing so, they expose themselves to governmental surveillance. Tight state control together with the importance of verified identity in determining one's online influence may lead to a pessimistic conclusion – that micro-blogging services may not have the power to change China's 'self-imposed censorship and de-politicized politics' (Ho, 2008) in the near future. This invites a question for future studies – how does state pressure influence information diffusion on Weibo?

The limitations of this study are related to methodological issues in using online data. Therefore, highlighting these limitations can provide implicit guidance for future studies. As one referee pointed out, the studied follower network might consist of property managers, real estate developers and/or government officials, which causes sample selection problems. The authors examined followers' self-descriptions, excluded 46 property managers and real estate developers, and then re-ran most analyses. The results were almost the same. However, it should be acknowledged that the sample selection problem was still not fully addressed because self-description is not an accurate indicator. More generally, data 'crawled' from Sina Weibo are self-reported, self-selected, and often incomplete. For example, incomplete data preclude the authors from examining other attributes of Weibo users like age, education, income, occupation and use motivations.

Researchers using online data need to evaluate its reliability, validity and representativeness. Future studies should combine online network data and traditional data sources (e.g. surveys) to present a more comprehensive picture. In the exploration of tweets diffusion, this study focused on how user attributes influence the average circulation of tweets posted by that user and did not take the content of tweets into consideration. This also invites further examination. Finally, though this study has demonstrated the presence of the network structure effect of reciprocity, it has not examined high-ordered network structures such as transitivity because of computational constraints.

Acknowledgements

This study was sponsored by Chinese National Social Science Foundation (12CSH043) and Shanghai Pujiang Program (13PJC011). The authors thank Ngai-ming Yip, Wanxin Li and the anonymous reviewers for their valuable comments and suggestions.

Notes

1. Collective action is defined as any action taken by two or more people in order to improve home-owners' conditions.
2. http://news.sohu.com/20070126/n247846747.shtml, accessed on 1 July 2012.
3. http://citynews.eastday.com/csdb/html/2011-01/13/content_35673.htm, accessed on 1 July 2012.
4. http://www.sywy.net.cn/, accessed on 1 August 2012.
5. http://wzwx.66wz.com/system/2012/05/14/103166040.shtml, accessed on 1 August 2012.
6. http://jsnews.jschina.com.cn/system/2011/12/19/012324855.shtml, accessed on 1 August 2012.
7. http://news.cnwest.com/content/2012-10/14/content_7421913.htm, accessed on 1 August 2012.
8. http://www.zj.xinhuanet.com/video/2013-01/11/c_114337566.htm, accessed on 1 August 2012.
9. http://zjnews.zjol.com.cn/05zjnews/system/2012/12/04/018990587.shtml, accessed on 1 August 2012.
10. http://news.xinhuanet.com/tech/2012-02/29/c_122769084.htm, accessed on 1 August 2012.
11. Some argue that Twitter networks are not social networks because they exhibit low reciprocity and highly skewed degree distribution (Wu et al., 2011). On the contrary, others show that levels of reciprocity are moderate or high, and that levels of reciprocity increase when confined to users from one continent (Java et al., 2007). Zhang and Pentina (2012) reviewed the previous literature on Twitter and concluded that Twitter is used to satisfy the needs of both information and social connection. As revealed in the empirical section, when indegree is confined to a group of users with shared interest, the follower network exhibits a relatively high level of reciprocity and is much closer to social networks. Therefore, the general theory of social networks can still shed some light on follower relation formation.
12. This study does not claim to exhaust all possible factors. First, 'crawling' data directly from a micro-blogging site is constrained by what exists on that site, a situation not unlike secondary data analysis. Second, teasing out the effects of actors' attributes and proximity from that of existing relationships is computationally intensive. It is extremely hard to include high-ordered network structure effects in the exponential random graph model for a network of size 1840.
13. More details on the construction of the retweet network can be found in the data and methods section.
14. An ego-network consists of ego ('focal' node) and nodes to which the ego has a direct connection. Many existing studies have explored ego-networks but cannot untangle the formation mechanisms of follower relations.
15. http://open.Weibo.com/
16. http://open.Weibo.com/wiki/SDK
17. The *indegree* of a node is the number of head endpoints of edges adjacent to that node.
18. Data collection process was constrained by the API limit, and the current study opted for a less comprehensive but feasible choice.
19. Only retweets were relevant because original tweets not retweeted by others did not contribute to the valued edges, and tweets retweeted by others were included as the retweeted of others.

20. Keywords were selected in a trial-and-error manner by examining 300 randomly-sampled tweets. They were intended to be inclusive enough to select most tweets relevant to homeowner associations and homeowner actions, whilst restrictive enough to exclude irrelevant tweets.
21. Seventy-three users did not report their locations.
22. The observed pattern might simply be the result of the research design because the influential user whom we used to define the studied follower network was located in Beijing. We could not assess which interpretation was more appropriate.
23. Exploratory analysis showed that *time since account registration* was insignificant once *reciprocity*, *geographical proximity* and *active in tweeting* were included in the model. Because the model estimation was computationally intensive, *time since account registration* was not included in the final model.
24. *Average number of tweets per day* was calculated first. It was dichotomized with the cutting point equal to the mean value. Those greater than the cutting point were coded as active in tweeting. Dichotomization had to be used to estimate the model with an average personal computer; otherwise, the computation would have been beyond the capacity of a personal computer.
25. It took about five days to obtain a final model with an average personal computer (2.3 GHz and 4G RAM).
26. Further analysis showed that tweet diffusion within a province was more likely than pure chance (p-value of QAP test < 0.001), but the correlation between the retweet network and geographical network, which was an undirected network with edges being 1 when both users were from the same province, was only 0.04.
27. The geodesic is the number of relations in the shortest possible diffusion path from one actor to another. Here, we assumed that tweet diffusion followed the most 'efficient' follower relations.
28. It was based on the *total* number of retweets contributed by users inside and outside the studied network.
29. Number of retweets, number of tweets per day and number of followers were log-transformed because their distributions were skewed.
30. The authors also used log of total number of followers as an independent variable without splitting followers into two parts. The R^2 of this alternative model is 0.113, which was lower than that in model 3.
31. http://www.bbc.com/news/technology-17313793, accessed on 1 August 2012.

References

Barash, V., & Golder, S. (2011). Twitter: Conversation, entertainment, and information, all in one network! In D. Hansen, B. Shneiderman, & M. A. Smith (Eds.), *Analyzing social media networks with NodeXL: Insights from a connected world* (pp. 143–164). Burlington, MA: Morgan Kaufmann.

Bruggeman, J. (2008). *Social networks: An introduction*. New York: Routledge.

Butts, C. (2010). *sna: Tools for social network analysis*. Retrieved from http://CRAN.R-project.org/package=sna

Cao, Y., Fan, Y., & Peng, L. (2011). Self-organization features of online collectives: The case of interests-safeguarding activity of Nanjing plane-tree event. *Journal of Nanjing University of Posts and Telecommunications (Social Science), 13*, 1–10 (in Chinese).

Cha, M., Haddadiy, H., Benevenutoz, F., & Gummadi, K. (2010). *Measuring user influence in Twitter: The million follower fallacy*. Retrieved from http://www.aaai.org/ocs/index.php/ICWSM/ICWSM10/paper/viewFile/1538/1826

Chung, Y. (2008). *Property-owning socialism in a new state-society relationship: Housing reform in urban China* (Unpublished doctoral dissertation). University of Wisconsin-Madison, Madison, Wisconsin.

CNNIC. (2012). *The 29th statistical report of the development of China's Internet.* Retrieved from www. cnnic.cn/research/bgxz/tjbg/201201/P020120118512855484817.pdf

Diani, M. (2000). Social movement networks virtual and real. *Information, Communication & Society, 3,* 386–401.

Donath, J., & Boyd, D. (2004). Public displays of connection. *BT Technology Journal, 22,* 71–82.

Esarey, A., & Xiao, Q. (2008). Political expression in the Chinese blogosphere: Below the radar. *Asian Survey, 48,* 752–772.

Garrett, K. (2006). Protest in an information society: A review of literature on social movements and new ICTs. *Information, Communication & Society, 9,* 202–224.

Garrido, M., & Halavais, A. (2003). Mapping networks of support for the Zapatista Movement: Applying social-networks analysis to study contemporary social movements. In M. McCaughey & M. Ayers (Eds.), *Cyberactivism: Online activism in theory and practice* (pp. 165–184). New York, NY: Routledge.

Gillana, K., & Pickerill, J. (2008). Transnational anti-war activism: Solidarity, diversity and the Internet in Australia, Britain and the United States after 9/11. *Australian Journal of Political Science, 43,* 59–78.

Golder, S., & Yardi, S. (2010). Structural predictors of tie formation in Twitter: Transitivity and mutuality. In *Proceedings of the Second IEEE International Conference on Social Computing* (pp. 88–95). doi:10.1109/SocialCom.2010.22

Goodreau, S., Handcock, M., Hunter, D., Butts, C., & Morris, M. (2008). A statnet tutorial. *Journal of Statistical Software, 24.* Retrieved from http://www.jstatsoft.org/

Goodreau, S., Kitts, J. & Morris, M. (2009). Birds of a feather, or friend of a friend? Using exponential random graph models to investigate adolescent social networks. *Demography, 46,* 103–125.

Handcock, M., Hunter, D., Butts, C., Goodreau, S., Krivitsky, P., & Morris, M. (2012). *Ergm: A package to fit, simulate and diagnose exponential-family models for networks.* Retrieved from http://CRAN.R-project.org/package=ergm

Hardin, R. (1996). Trustworthiness. *Ethics, 107,* 26–42.

Hardin, R. (2002). *Trust and Trustworthiness.* New York, NY: Russell Sage Foundation.

Hassid, J. (2012). Safety valve or pressure cooker? Blogs in Chinese political life. *Journal of Communication, 62,* 212–230.

Hine, C. (2000). *Virtual ethnography.* Thousand Oaks, CA: Sage.

Ho, P. (2008). Self-imposed censorship and de-politicized politics in China: Green activism or a color revolution? In P. Ho & R. L. Edmonds (Eds.), *China's embedded activism* (pp. 20–43). New York, NY: Routledge.

Huang, R. (2010). *Housing activism in Shanghai: Opportunities and constraints* (Unpublished doctoral dissertation). Department of Public and Social Administration, City University of Hong Kong, Hong Kong.

Huang, R., Zhang, T., & Gui, Y. (2011). Structure and determinants of on-line diffusion of information about contention: Empirical study of homeowner's forums. *Journalism & Communication, 2,* 89–97 (in Chinese).

Huang, R., & Yip, N. M. (2012). Internet and activism in urban China: A case study of protests in Xiamen and Panyu. *Journal of Comparative Asia Development, 11,* 201–223.

Huang, Y. (2004). The road to homeownership: A longitudinal analysis of tenure transition in Urban China (1949–93). *International Journal of Urban and Regional Research, 28,* 774–795.

Hunter, D., Handcock, M., Butts, C., Goodreau, S., & Morris, M. (2008). ergm: A package to fit, simulate and diagnose exponential-family models for networks. *Journal of Statistical Software, 4.* Retrieved from http://www.jstatsoft.org/v24/i03

Java, A., Song, X., Finin, T., & Tseng, B. (2007). Why we twitter: Understanding microblogging usage and communities. Retrieved from http://dl.acm.org/citation.cfm?id=1348556

Ji, H. (2011). Why a Weibo appeal led to collective action? – A case study of the campaign to trace China's abducted children. *Youth Journalist, 4,* 33–34 (in Chinese).

King, G., Pan, J., & Roberts, M. E. (2013). How censorship in China allows government criticism but silences collective expression. *American Political Science Review, 107,* 326–343.

Krackardt, D. (1987). QAP partialling as a test of spuriousness. *Social Networks, 9,* 171–186.

Kwak, H., Lee, C., Park, H., & Moon, S. (2010). What is twitter, a social network or a news media? Retrieved from http://dl.acm.org/citation.cfm?id=1772751

Lampe, C., Ellison, N., & Steinfield, C. (2007). A familiar Face(book): Profile elements as signals in an online social network. Retrieved from http://dl.acm.org/citation.cfm?doid=1240624.1240695

Lewis, K., Kaufman, J., Gonzalez, M., Wimmer, A., & Christakis, N. (2008). Tastes, ties, and time: A new social network dataset using Facebook.com. *Social Networks, 30,* 330–342.

Logan, J. R., Fang, Y., & Zhang, Z. (2010). The winners in China's urban housing reform. *Housing Studies*, *25*, 101–117.

MacKinnon, R. (2008). Flatter world and thicker walls? Blogs, censorship and civic discourse in China. *Public Choice*, *134*, 31–46.

Mok, D., Wellman, B., & Carrasco, J. (2010). Does distance matter in the age of the Internet? *Urban Studies*, *47*, 2747–2783.

Nannestad, P. (2008). What have we learned about generalized trust, if anything? *Annual Review of Political Science*, *11*, 413–436.

Pu, Q., & Scanlan, S. J. (2012). Communicating injustice? *Information, Communication & Society*, *15*, 572–590.

Read, B. (2008). Assessing variation in civil society organizations: China's homeowner associations in comparative perspective. *Comparative Political Studies*, *41*, 1240–1265.

Rivera, M., Soderstrom, S., & Uzzi, B. (2010). Dynamics of dyads in social networks: Assortative, relational, and proximity mechanisms. *Annual Review of Sociology*, *36*, 91–115.

Robins, G., Pattison, P., Kalish, Y., & Lusher, D. (2007). An introduction to exponential random graph (p*) models for social networks. *Social Networks*, *29*, 173–191.

Scanfeld, D., Scanfeld, V., & Larson, E. L. (2010). Dissemination of health information through social networks: Twitter and antibiotics. *American Journal of Infection Control*, *38*, 182–188.

Shi, F. (2008). Social capital at work: The dynamics and consequences of grassroots movements in urban China. *Critical Asian Studies*, *40*, 233–262.

Shi, F., & Cai, Y. (2006). Disaggregating the state: Networks and collective resistance in Shanghai. *The China Quarterly*, *186*, 314–332.

Shirky, C. (2011). The political power of social media. *Foreign Affairs*, *90*, 28–41.

Small, T. A. (2011). What the hashtag? *Information, Communication & Society*, *14*, 872–895.

Stalley, P., & Yang, D. (2006). An emerging environmental movement in China? *The China Quarterly*, *186*, 333–356.

Stern, M., & Dillman, D. (2006). Community participation, social ties, and use of the Internet. *City & Community*, *5*, 409–424.

Suh, B., Hong, L., Pirolli, P., & Chi, E. H. (2010). Want to be retweeted? Large scale analytics on factors impacting retweet in twitter network. Retrieved from http://dl.acm.org/citation.cfm?id=1907388

Sullivan, J. (in press). China's Weibo: Is faster different? *New Media & Society.* Retrieved from http://dx.doi.org/10.1177/1461444812472966

Takhteyev, Y., Gruzd, A., & Wellman, B. (2012). Geography of twitter networks. *Social Networks*, *34*, 73–81.

Tomba, L. (2004). Creating an urban middle class: Social engineering in Beijing. *The China Journal*, *51*, 1–26.

Tong, Y., & Lei, S. (2013). War of position and microblogging in China. *Journal of Contemporary China*, *22*, 292–311.

Tsui, L. (2003). The Panopticon as the antithesis of a space of freedom: Control and regulation of the Internet in China. *China Information*, *17*, 65–82.

Wang, Y., & Murie, A. (1999). Commercial housing development in urban China. *Urban Studies*, *36*, 1475–1494.

Wang, Y., & Murie, A. (2000). Social and spatial implications of housing reform in China. *International Journal of Urban and Regional Research*, *24*, 397–417.

Wasserman, S., & Faust, K. (1994). *Social network analysis: Methods and applications.* Cambridge: Cambridge University Press.

Wimmer, A., & Lewis, K. (2010). Beyond and below racial homophily: ERG models of a friendship network documented on Facebook. *American Journal of Sociology*, *116*, 583–642.

Wu, S., Hofman, J., Mason, W., & Watts, D. (2011). Who says what to whom on twitter. Retrieved from http://dl.acm.org/citation.cfm?id=1963405.1963504&coll=DL&dl=ACM&CFID= 141514187&CFTOKEN=73724690

Xiao, Q. (2011). The rise of online public opinion and its political impact. In S. L. Shirk (Ed.), *Changing media, changing China.* New York, NY: Oxford University Press.

Yang, G. (2009). *The power of the Internet in China: Citizen activism online.* New York, NY: Columbia University Press.

Yip, N., & Jiang, Y. (2011). Homeowners united: The attempt to create lateral networks of homeowners' associations in urban China. *Journal of Contemporary China*, *20*, 735–750.

Zhang, L. (2005). Beijing house owners' rights protection movement: Reason of breakout and mobilization mechanism. *Sociological Studies*, *6*, 1–39 (in Chinese).

Zhang, L., & Pentina, I. (2012). Motivations and usage patterns of Weibo. *Cyberpsychology, Behavior, and Social Networking*, *15*, 312–317.

Zheng, Y., & Wu, G. (2005). Information technology, public space, and collective action in China. *Comparative Political Studies*, *38*, 507–536.

Zhou, X. (2009). The political blogosphere in China: A content analysis of the blogs regarding the dismissal of Shanghai leader Chen Liangyu. *New Media & Society*, *11*, 1003–1022.

Zhu, J., & Ho, P. (2008). Not against the state, just protecting residents' interests: An urban movement in a Shanghai neighborhood. In P. Ho & R. L. Edmonds (Eds.), *China's embedded activism* (pp. 151–170). New York, NY: Routledge.

Zhuang, W. (2011). Beyond state-conferred rights? A case study on homeowners' confrontation in Guangzhou. *Chinese Journal of Sociology*, *3*, 88–113 (in Chinese).

Expanding civic engagement in China: *Super Girl* and entertainment-based online community

Jingsi Christina Wu

Department of Journalism, Media Studies, and Public Relations, Hofstra University

This article pursues a context-rich understanding of how digital media offer unique opportunities for citizens residing in mainland China to participate in civic engagement and organize their civic values. While the Chinese state authority keeps a heavy hand in any form of media, old or new, for use of overt political expressions, I provide empirical demonstration of the link between entertainment media experiences and the exchange on more serious civic topics. In doing so, I argue for a more expanded notion of civic engagement for political environments such as China and develop an empirical scheme that incorporates ordinary citizens' interactions with more leisure-oriented media texts. Such theoretical and empirical moves, as I point out, can contribute to a more thoughtful discussion of the Internet and civic engagement in China. Furthermore, this article pays particular attention to how the Internet provides a valuable channel for community formation among ordinary Chinese citizens outside the mainstream media, which are mostly occupied by state elites. My examination suggests that the Internet helps online discussants reach further depth in their extension from entertainment discussion to constructing serious discourses on important social issues, more so than the mainstream newspapers.

While China has been taking great strides in building its communication infrastructure and disseminating new technologies, debates about the Internet's civic influence in the country remain unresolved. For a country with a long history of repressing citizens' expressions, the Internet promises democratizing potentials. It opens up unprecedented space for ordinary citizens to reach a vast audience that is unachievable through the particularly regulated and selective mainstream media. There is less concern about the formality of one's expression and there are more channels of choice for diverse points of interest and ideological orientations. So far, much research has closely examined the Chinese citizens' use of the Internet for explicit political purposes and its implications for civic engagement. This paper instead explores how entertainment-based online communities may help expand the notion of civic engagement in China. This is an area that scholars have left understudied.

In doing so, I address discussions about how digital media offer unique opportunities for citizens residing in mainland China to practice civic engagement in informal ways and organize their civic values that can potentially find their way to the mainstream media. More specifically, I draw on public discourses surrounding one of the most popular entertainment shows in China's recent history, *Super Girl*, particularly those organized around social concerns, and examine the formation of online communities based on common entertainment experiences and how it could expand civic engagement in China. In doing so, this work speaks to the literature on the possibilities and limitations with the Internet in China, and particularly how it may help open up practices of, as well as the general understanding about, civic engagement.

Internet with Chinese characteristics

Although the dissemination of new communication technology ignites new hope, China is not immune to the drawbacks that plague the Internet as a democratic medium in other political contexts. There is a flip side to every virtue. For example, the opportunity to hide one's real-life identity behind computer screens raises concerns about misinformation or incivility (Kollock & Smith, 1996; Lee, 1996). The lack of formality leads to the easy dismissal of the Internet's capacity to host well-reasoned arguments (Weger & Aahkhus, 2003). Overall, such concerns are guided by Habermas' (1984) ideal model of public discourses, which prescribes that participants should only be persuaded by the better use of reason rather than the authority of the speaker, rely on objective factual information to support their arguments and give due respect to others' opinions. Devoid of face-to-face pressure to abide by these rules, scholars are concerned that Internet users are less motivated to be courteous, take responsibility for the information they share, or spend time organizing the logic of their arguments.

These concerns have guided the investigation of Internet in China and often led to cautious optimism in current evaluations. Weber and Jia (2007) conclude that although the Internet may open up more space for citizens on non-political issues or civic engagement in limited ways, it has not become a powerful tool for the citizenry to fundamentally challenge the state authority. Similarly, Zhou, Chan, and Peng (2008) conducted a content analysis of the discussion forum hosted by *Guangzhou Daily* and found that the venue is not mature enough for serious political discussions, judged on such standards as justification, complexity, and civility. The scholars view this finding to be extra discouraging given that their object of study is affiliated with a representative of serious media in China, which is usually associated with quality public discourses in the Habermasian sense.

Amid mixed opinions about the civic significance of this new medium in China, scholars point out that we also need to take into consideration some unique Chinese characteristics of the Internet. Liu (2011) discusses three dominant rules in China that together influence the extent to which the Internet can be used for civic purposes: market, technology, and stability. These three rules refer to three major considerations that pull the state policy on Internet in different directions. The market and technology rules highlight the medium's economic and technological contributions to the nation's prosperity, hence leading to supportive policy stimulations by the state and a fast development of the Internet in China, especially its infrastructure. However, the stability consideration has largely constrained the Internet's impact. The state's investment in the overall stability of its rule directly motivates harsh regulations and proactive interventions in its Internet policies, such as downright blocking sites that pose a threat to the state authority. The discussion of any medium in China has to be set against its notorious censorship measures.

Scholars have discussed Internet censorship in China as both forced upon the users and self-imposed. Yang (2009) discusses the former case through which the state regulates both the content and the form of expression. This regulation pushes online forums 'to implement more strict editorial interference' (Li, 2010, p. 72), therefore taking on more of offline media's rhetorical styles. The state's Internet censorship is especially obtrusive during unstable times, while Chinese netizens can be more outspoken in a less stressful climate (Lagerkvist, 2006). Wary of the social impact that can be caused by mass sentiments and magnified by the wide reach of the Internet, the state regulators actively close sites and delete online texts when they sense potential political unrest, such as during the annual convention of the National People's Congress and the '4 June' anniversary of the Tian'anmen Square protests (China's Great Firewall, 2009). During the Arab Spring movements in early 2011, the state censorship machines in China worked diligently to nip any trace of antigovernment sentiment in the bud. When citizen outcry for freedom in China was reaching its height during the movements, the social networking site LinkedIn was shut down for a day and several popular virtual private-network services were disabled (Lafraniere & Barboza, 2011).

As a result of proactive state censorship that is all too ready to crack down on online activities, Li (2010) states that the Chinese netizens have to keep searching for new channels for opinion expression and opening more private venues after previous forums were shut down. Such efforts, she worries, at smaller-scale and lower-profile venues that pose less challenge to the state authority, at the same time risk fragmenting the online opinion space and making it more leisure-oriented.

State censorship further causes self-censorship in the general society as well as among individual users. At the societal level, the state's deep involvement in the commercialization of the media sector and its collaboration with foreign investors have imposed a self-regulation by the industry (Weber & Jia, 2007). At the individual level, Yang (2003) argues that although Chinese citizens believe that the Internet gives them more freedom of speech, they tend to censor themselves for fear of state sanction. Mou, Atkin, and Fu (2011) discuss two mechanisms that encourage such a self-censorship, the 50-cent party and human flesh search engines. Chinese netizens came up with the title '50-cent party' to ridicule the 50 cents paid to state writers for each post they contribute to the praise and defense of the leadership online. Aware of such planted posts, Chinese netizens become more cynical and less engaged in serious online forums.

More menacingly, human flesh search engine refers to the Internet users' collective ability to uncover the real-life identity of targeted individuals. The concept of 'human flesh' represents a contrast to the conventional search engine, which heavily relies on the automatic machine algorithm. Instead, the social engineering of 'human flesh search' resorts to human knowledge as the foundation for collective investigations, which garnered great publicity in recent years after individual netizens pooled together bits of information from their personal knowledge networks in finding answers to common questions, especially in the disclosure of certain users' real-life identities.[1]

Although this practice capitalizes on the vast reach and easy access of the Internet in contributing to collective knowledge and creating a stronger sense of social justice among its users, the Chinese government is in a more advantageous position to implement human flesh search, thanks to the state machine's sophisticated technology and tight registration rules. While technological measures enable the state to trace online expressions to IP addresses, hence tracking down the authors behind anonymous IDs, in 2009 the state started to require online users to accompany their comments on news websites with their real names (Ansfield, 2009). The Chinese government's ability to implement the human flesh search and as a result actually punish online activists makes Chinese netizens more afraid of state retaliation, hence often practicing self-imposed censorship.

With such a restrictive nature of China's Internet in mind, scholars argue for a realistic evaluation that does not downgrade its contributions and the creative responses that Chinese Internet users display to harsh Internet control (Yang, 2009). Instead of uncritically using such ideal concepts as 'public sphere', Jiang (2010) argues that 'authoritarian deliberation' can better reveal the idiosyncratic nature of China's online public sphere. Citing Habermas' recent revision on his own public sphere theory in distinguishing between strong public and weak public, Jiang suggests that casual chat online, although only forming weak publics, can still put a check on the state, especially local authorities. Zheng (2007) echoes this mentality in suggesting that the Internet might create in China more 'political liberalization' than 'political democratization' in that although not realizing full-blown democracy, the technology at least allows the citizens to better hold the state accountable.

Such a potential is especially noticeable when the cyberspace successfully inserts its voice in the mainstream discourses on issues that the state tries to block from the public agenda (Yu, 2006, 2007). For example, in a 2011 national disaster caused by hasty construction of high-speed railway and authority oversight, the state tried desperately to cover up the scale of the damage, which included forty deaths and 192 injuries. The Chinese citizens were outraged, and took it online to press the government for answers. Such vocal protests showed the awareness among ordinary citizens about their new-found power with the new communication technology and helped them hold the government accountable. Furthermore, these efforts often have to work around diligent state censorship and adopt creative strategies, such as using different Chinese characters that share the same pronunciation as the sensitive words being censored by the government. I turn next to the ongoing discussion about an expanded notion of civic engagement that could also push further the examination about the Internet's civic significance in China. Not only can the citizens use the Internet for explicit political purposes, but we should also not overlook more informal ways of Internet use. Such uses tend to be more easily dismissed given their implicit connections to civic engagement. However, they are more firmly embedded in ordinary citizens' everyday life and can be more achievable than formal ways of civic engagement, which are extra challenging given the Chinese state's heavy policing.

Entertainment and politics: an expanded notion of civic engagement

Even before the Internet came along and became widely adopted in civil society, classic audience studies such as Ang (1985) and Radway (1991) empirically demonstrated that audiences can actively interpret popular texts based on their life situations and often incorporate such interpretations in their everyday sense-making of civic life. Other widely cited scholars such as Coleman (2006, 2007), Hermes (2005, 2006), and van Zoonen (2005) take one step further and argue for fundamental connections between audiences and publics, between popular culture and the political sphere. They propose a more expanded notion of civic engagement that would give more recognition to the political implications of entertainment audience activities. These scholars make two major revisions on a more traditional, formal conceptualization of civic engagement in highlighting: first, the affective aspect of civic engagement; second, the natural making of an everyday citizen.

To begin with, scholars argue that citizens heavily rely on their life experiences in understanding the larger society and more grand social issues, and emotions play a large part in that process. While formal notions of civic engagement treat citizens as rational-critical agents who enter serious public deliberations to form their public opinions and act on those opinions, Coleman (2007) points out that 'the language of politics exceeds the terms of instrumental rationality' and has 'symbolic, affective and aesthetic dimensions' (p. 52). These latter dimensions, largely delegitimized by traditional perspectives of civic engagement, are argued to be essential to one's everyday life. Citizens do not necessarily only gain politically relevant knowledge or form their opinions through formal political channels, but also from such popular texts as fictional television shows that can provide more experiential knowledge for the citizens' self-reflection and outreach (Hermes, 2006).

Second, and closely related to the first point, recognizing how challenging and confusing it is for ordinary citizens to keep up with developments in the formal political processes, Coleman (2007) suggests that we look at 'politics as an outcome of everyday communication rather than its structural constraint' (p. 51). In other words, civic engagement does not simply involve finding political information and taking political actions, but we should also pay attention to the making of everyday citizens through their daily communications in their natural habitats, including their home, workplace, and other social settings not specifically devoted to political purposes. The scholars point to ordinary citizens' creative use of media materials of all kinds to reflect on their life and identities, which should be recognized as alternative forms of civic engagement. For example, Coleman (2006) emphasizes in his study of *Big Brother* audience that they frequently used materials on the show to talk about real-world issues, such as sexuality, inequality, and war. Although these entertainment media experiences are usually pleasure oriented and associated with leisure, they can nonetheless provide unique opportunities for self-reflection and participation in public discourses.

Such an expanded notion of civic engagement highlights the social imagination provided by popular texts that helps the audience make sense of social norms and define their positions in the society. While these revisions seem to be less important in more developed democracies, where ordinary citizens have abundant opportunities to voice their political opinions and exercise their civic engagement in more formal manners, they serve a significant change in perspective for fully exploring the possibilities of civic engagement in China. Relatively speaking, citizens in this country are less capable of civic engagement in ways that are often taken for granted in the West, such as organizing public protests, openly criticizing the central authority, not to mention voting or engaging in other important decision-making processes. Although Yang (2009) briefly mentions that entertainment activities online are not apolitical in China, not much research has been done to develop this argument. Among the few, Tong's (2006) preliminary research of online forums on *Super Girl*, the show under study in this article, suggests that expression of democratic passion is the most familiar topic when discussing the talent show.

Even in the West, where studies that examine online activities devoted to entertainment experiences start to mushroom in recent years (Baym, 2000; Hermes, 2005; Ross, 2008), insufficient attention has been given to the political significance of this activity. Graham and Hajru (2011) premise their research on this general observation and in particular, single out the 'communicative spaces tied to reality TV' (p. 19). Through their case studies of two popular British reality show forums devoted to *Celebrity Big Brother* and *Wife Swap*, they found that discussions directly centered around the fans' entertainment experiences often connected seamlessly to their political discourses. The authors contend that the examination of entertainment and politics should not be limited to traditional notions of politics, but rather a definition more 'driven by participants' lifestyles and the personal narratives that express them' (p. 27).

This article adopts a similar perspective and provides further support of such findings in the context of China. I argue that an expanded notion of civic engagement would open up ways to examine the Internet's civic significance in China, particularly those online communities created around entertainment experiences. I urge for more research to add to a fuller understanding about connections between aesthetic attention to what happens on entertainment shows per se and broader concerns about larger civic issues and values. A guiding research question of this article is to seek whether and how expanded civic engagement occurred in the Chinese audience's discussion about a widely popular reality show, *Super Girl*. Furthermore, in exploring the unique contributions of the Internet to opening up exchanges among ordinary citizens, I compare between their online discussions and the mainstream newspaper discourses more heavily occupied by state elites.

Data and method

In this article, I examine public discourses surrounding one of the most popular entertainment shows since China entered the twenty-first century, *Super Girl*. This Western-influenced talent show shook up the national media through the weight it put on nationwide voting and ordinary contestants from all walks of life. Such a gesture appeared unprecedentedly sincere and refreshing in 2004 when the all-girl singing contest was first aired on Hunan TV, a provincial network on the forefront of marketization and entertainmentization of Chinese TV. As a result, the show ignited wide and fierce debates about its political implications. While cultural critics and scholars are still largely divided over whether the show deserves some credit for contributing to the Chinese audience's political awareness or training, it provides an excellent example for exploring the role of entertainment media in expanding civic engagement and the creation of online community in today's China.

To be sure, the Chinese government has always been wary about any potential disturbance that can be caused by the media, entertainment included. As a result, *Super Girl* started to struggle with the regulations imposed by the State Administration of Radio Film and Television after reaching its peak of success in 2005, with a state ban on nationwide voting announced in 2007 and a series of specific rules to curb audience enthusiasm about the once widely popular talent show. The show took a break in 2007 and ended production after three lackluster seasons from 2009 to 2011. Like many other stirring entertainment shows, *Super Girl* bears great political significance in building its appeals off of the life struggles of ordinary contestants and audience members. However, in heavily featuring the power of ordinary audience in fulfilling the professional pursuits of its contestants through voting, this singing contest invited wide reflections on many aspects of contemporary life in China and particularly exchanges of political imaginations. Such an unprecedented emphasis on the voting power of everyday people, which is lacking in the formal political sphere, alarmed the state. As *Super Girl* rose to its overnight popularity and quickly disappeared in China's entertainment sphere, it provided a great snippet into the intricate relationship between entertainment experiences and civic engagement in China.

Considering such a turbulent history, discourses around *Super Girl* were particularly spirited. The show garnered much public attention when Chinese producers started to more actively borrow experiences from the Western world and democratize the entertainment sphere, often unintentionally inviting reflections about democratizing the Chinese political sphere. Thanks to the attention *Super Girl* drew from the Chinese regulators and the role it played in the tightening of regulations as the twenty-first century unfolds, it provides many interesting texts for analysis. I sampled public discourses around *Super Girl* during the 2009 season, the first one after state regulators banned nationwide voting on all talent shows and a relatively more stirring season among the three that led up to its end.

The timeframe of sampling is set at July to September 2009, during the national stage of competition on the show after two months of regional auditions. Before sampling, I immersed myself in online discussions and read through threads after threads of them in search of recurring themes and patterns. This process helped guide me through a manageable subset of data randomly sampled from the boundless online discourses. For the three-month period, there were a total of 3720 discussion threads on the *Super Girl* forum operated by Hunan TV, host of the talent show. Although there were a variety of online forums dedicated to the talent show, I chose the particular site of study not primarily for its representativeness of the whole Chinese Internet. While scholarly works discussing public reactions to *Super Girl* often talk about such discourses as an amorphous whole, I adopted a case-study approach similar to that of Graham and Hajru (2011). I was particularly interested in how the audiences openly critiqued the show on its official website. To examine the online community formed here, I randomly sampled 5% of the 3720 threads and narrowed them further down to those that received more than 5 replies. As a result, I gathered a random sample of 39 discussion threads (545 posts in total).

In addition, to discuss the Internet's unique contributions in China to an expanded civic engagement, I also paid attention to the different dynamics between the mainstream and the new media. In doing so, I sampled a total of 107 articles from a variety of 36 national and local newspapers. I gathered this data from searching for the keyword 'Super Girl' on the *People's Daily* Web database, which collects some of the most widely circulated Chinese newspapers both nationally and locally, such as *Wenhui Daily, Mirror*, and *Beijing Evening News*. As a result, one may gain some perspectives into how the most read newspapers in the country differed from, or resembled for that matter, online discussions of the talent show.

Due to the limited scope of this paper, I could not fully explore all of the differences, but focused more on how online discussions potentially push the boundaries of civic engagement beyond that of serious social issues and political agendas in China. Guided by such interests, I read through these texts closely and inductively. To keep faithful to my data, I limit findings to the range of my sampled newspaper pieces and online discussions. However, during the process of data analysis, I kept up with other social discourses circulated online, in the newspapers, and in my personal network, to stay informed about recent developments and maintain a larger perspective about the research. Below I provide a detailed analysis of how reflections on entertainment experiences facilitate civic engagement in nontraditional ways.

The creation of an online community around entertainment

Through the initial reading, I find that both media spheres paid a fair amount of attention to three common themes beyond their immediate interest in developments on the show: political values, social, and cultural concerns. In general the 39 sample threads in the online sphere seemed to have a more prominent interest in 'superficial' entertainment topics than the newspapers. However, scholars argue that such interactions on the aesthetic level could help create the foundation for people's connection with each other and disclosure of their deep-seated values (Baym, 2000; Ross, 2008). Jacobs and Townsley (2011) further argue that rather than the sole pursuit of rational-critical discussion, the most important aspect for many people to participate in a public discourse is whether they can enjoy the discourse process. In that sense, the authors suggest that the media provide a foundation of intersubjectivity for small-group discussions, not just by providing objective information in the Habermasian sense, but also by creating the pleasure of discussion, the emotional feelings attached to elements of the discussion.

This function of mass sociability might be more important in the online community than the newspapers, whose dominant address form is still one-to-many. Opening its door to anyone who can have access to Internet connection and the basic skills to post online, the Internet introduces users to many anonymous others who express their opinions in a multidirectional manner. In that sense, sharing some collective entertainment experiences, which works commonly as interpersonal lubricator in face-to-face interactions, can build a social environment that resembles daily life and invites more open conversations. In contrast, the mainstream newspapers present a vastly different institutional setting in imposing on its reporters strict editing, set formats of composition, and editorial guidance. Although the Communist Party has loosened its requirement of the mainstream media to serve as tools of state propaganda, widely circulated newspapers still have to weather strict state control and have less space for free and open exchanges among ordinary citizens.

With this difference in mind, it is probably not surprising that the online sphere went into further depth in their discussions of each theme than the newspapers. And the lower threat posed by entertainment than that of explicit political exchanges further expands the alternative space for civic engagement on the Internet, which is certainly not free from state monitoring. My findings of the extension from aesthetic interest in the talent show to more serious discourses about civic concerns support the argument that we need to take entertainment more seriously for expanding civic engagement, particularly in states where traditional forms of engagement are more limited. Furthermore, whereas it may appear unsurprising to many that the Internet hosts more diverse and open civic exchanges than the mainstream newspapers for reasons discussed above, it is nonetheless worth noting that this new medium bears great potential in pushing open the boundaries of civic engagement.

Such findings speak to concerns that the Internet simply provides a new space where ordinary citizens find new ways of distracting themselves from more serious civic issues and simply indulging themselves in pointless entertainment. Instead, I find that not only do such entertainment materials inspire expression of political values, but the Internet users tend to reach further depth into the foundational values that define a political system or culture, such as fairness, the power of the masses, and freedom of expression. While such discourses threaten to be more sensitive elsewhere in China's media environment, the newspaper contributors stayed clear of them by turning to the technical aspects of selection and democratic operation. To elaborate on such connections and differences, I focus on the discourses organized around social concerns next.

Super Girl producers failed the social responsibilities of a cultural institution

According to the 2012 Pew Research Center's Global Attitudes survey, the ever-enlarging wealth gap in China has become a pressing social issue (Pew Research Center, 2012). The lack of social mobility and corruption often go hand-in-hand as contributors to the public's prevalent 'group mentality of resentment' towards the rich (Wang & Yang, 2011). The Pew survey specifically found out that about eight in ten of its respondents agree with the sentiment that 'the rich just get richer while the poor get poorer', with 45% completely agreeing with this gloomy assessment. More concerning is the lack of hope in hard work as leading to one's rise in the society. One in three disagrees with the statement 'most people can succeed if they are willing to work hard'. At the same time, the Chinese express great concern about the ethics of public officials and business people. Half of the respondents view corrupt officials as a very big problem, and 32% do so about corrupt business people, both up from 11 percentage points since 2008. While ordinary citizens are getting disheartened by the observation that public officials and business people help each other get astoundingly richer and more powerful, they gradually become more cynical about their own fair chance of social mobility. Such a widespread cynicism comes out of the public's discussion about *Super Girl* as well. In other words, watching the show does not merely provide entertainment, but also an outlet for expressing grave social concerns.

Both the mainstream newspapers and the online discussions in my data devoted their attention to two types of manipulation, one blatant on the show, staged by producers to shore up viewing rates; the other more secretive beyond the show, wielded by the rich and powerful to promote their special interests. Such discussions of manipulation went beyond entertainment gossiping but reflected a strong moral anxiety about this phenomenon. They showcased how entertainment talk could help expand the boundary of civic engagement and how the two media spheres reached this expansion differently. In my sampled data, the newspaper articles were more concerned about how manipulation behind the contests failed the social responsibilities of a cultural agency. In comparison, the online sphere went deeper in the discussion of certain hidden values that served as a foundation for the newspaper pieces, such as inequality and ordinary Chinese's resentment towards the rich. With manipulation on the show, people expressed their concern about social regression towards the pursuit of transient attention, away from genuine spiritual and artistic aspirations. The newspaper articles appeared to be more concerned about this social implication than that of the manipulation beyond the show. The following excerpt from *Wenhui Daily* discussed the repercussions of an over-emphasis on hyping the sensational aspects of the show[2]:

It (manipulation) seems all to make sense: the TV network can gain viewing rates; the judges will get public exposure; and the audience has had fun with all the drama. Everyone takes what s/he wants. But wait – how about the contestants who are supposed to be at the front and center? They are fully devoted to singing and wait in respect for the judges' comments. Although they may not have the wild dream to make it to the end, they certainly can expect each step to draw them closer to their dreams. For talent shows, given that they adopt the name of singing contests, shouldn't the judges and the show respect music and respect the music dreams of the contestants, as a basic bottom line? Based on the behavior of many judges, the bottom line has been broken. The result of this is that those 'stars from the masses' emerging out of talent shows are drifting farther and farther from their music dreams – either they are entangled in disputes over breaking their contracts, or they are only making do in those copycat TV dramas or copycat TV dramas adapted from copycat TV dramas. (*Wenhui Daily*, 21 August 2009)

According to the author, while different parties eventually benefited from manipulation over the drama and conflicts on the show, it was extremely unfair for the contestants that were pursuing their music dreams through these outlets. An over-emphasis on personal dramas or controversies among the judges and the contestants would draw attention away from the talent of the contestants or the improvement of their talent. As a result, the stars that made a name from being on the show could only enjoy their fame for fifteen minutes, unable to build a long-lasting career.

The chief critique reflected in the newspaper coverage of this phenomenon was that manipulating progress on the show to gain short-term attention from the audience failed the social responsibilities of cultural institutions, when they are supposed to guide the public towards quality music and performance. Rather than simply gossiping about 'publicity stunts', the newspaper pieces composed an overarching thesis about today's Chinese society and voiced a genuine concern that society is drifting away from valuing true talents, most disturbingly by such cultural institutions as TV networks. Some critics mourned this phenomenon as a giant waste of public resources and bad influence on the younger generation. A reporter from *Mirror* cited Jin Zhaojun, secretary of the national Golden Bell Cup Popular Music Contest committee, in voicing the following critiques:

Jin has expressed in a few public occasions his antipathy towards the fact that the *Super Girl* contestant Zeng Yike sings out of tune. Yesterday during his interview with me, he clarified that he was not targeting this particular contestant, but the enablers behind her. According to him, there is not much to blame the grassroots talent shows for entertaining the masses. They also have a lot of good experiences to learn from. But some talent shows went too far. Then he threw out an opinion that '(I)t is a crime to promote tone-deafness' and answered the reporter's question with a question: 'Television is a public resource. Isn't this (the promotion of tone-deafness) fooling people with their own taxes?' (*Mirror*, 31 July 2009)

In this case, as in many others that solely focused on the producers and judges as the manipulative villains, the specific contestant in question was not faulted. Rather, Jin criticized the producers and the judges for blindly promoting Zeng Yike, a most controversial contestant in the 2009 season who often sang out of tune but kept progressing on the show, and wasting public resources with their misleading judgments. Loosely translated into *the Legal Paper* from its Chinese title, the fact that a newspaper like the *Mirror* that usually reports on legal issues and crimes picked up such a story suggests that for some people the blatant promotion of tone-deafness on a talent show is a serious issue. It is not simply a problem of bad taste. Indeed, Jin used a heavy accusation 'crime' to call for more general social concern about the show using taxpayers' money to fool them.

With the last point, it was no longer one or few cultural critics against a show promoting bad taste. It was no longer an aesthetic debate about whether contestant A or B is a better singer. Critics like Jin were mobilizing the general society to take a moral stance against cultural institutions that 'went too far' and wasted public resources. Otherwise, public institutions will keep drifting away from their cultural responsibilities and suppressing their social conscience in the pursuit of commercial interests. In comparison to the online sphere, the mainstream newspapers represented a more conservative voice from the state-owned and elite media perspective, in enthusiastically criticizing the television industry for losing their souls amid the commercialization craze.

The rich and powerful are manipulative, evil people: venting about the lack of social mobility in contemporary China

Discussions revolving around producer manipulations demonstrate how people can extend from entertainment topics to important civic concerns, hence expanding the boundary of traditional civic engagement. Furthermore, both media spheres also linked discussions about manipulation beyond the show to recently formed social stereotypes and sentiments about the rich and the powerful in China. The controversial progress made by certain contestants was not only attributed to producers staging sensations, but also to stealthy forces beyond the show promoting special interests. In the latter scenario, there seemed to be a mysterious tie between a person's incomprehensible success and his/her family background, which reveals a deep-seated cynicism about one's own lack of chance at social mobility. Again, in the case of Zeng Yike, the story that her father was a big tobacco company boss was immediately accepted and spread as the primary explanation for her success on the show and the enthusiastic support she received from certain judges. As conspiracy theories spiraled out of control to make sense of Zeng's success on the show, journalists made extra efforts to verify such rumors. In doing so, they relied on an implicit assumption that the rich and powerful are bad people or how easy it is to corrupt authority figures like the judges. The following piece by *Dahe Daily* represents such an effort:

> A contestant who spoke under the condition of anonymity told such an 'anecdote' to the reporter: Once during rehearsal, judge Gao Xiaosong was very unhappy (with Zeng's performance) and asked her bluntly 'how many chords she knows', which made her very embarrassed. But when it came to the actual contest, almost all of the judges, including Gao, were 'one-sidedly' supporting Zeng. Such evidence seemingly suggests that Zeng has a pretty 'solid background' ... Yesterday, when the reporter asked Dachunzi (an eliminated contestant) whether such rumors are true, she did not answer me. She only described Zeng in her eyes: 'We lived next door to each other's dorm room (during the contests), so we ran into each other quite often. I also met her parents. Her Dad helped wash her socks and her Mom mopped the floor. They both look very ordinary. Zeng is also a very nice person, like a little sister. In the beginning of the contests, she still looked quite unfashionable. It was later that she started to look a little different. I feel that the Internet may have demonized her. She is not that horrific in person. In fact, she is only 19 and may have been ruined by this'. (*Dahe Daily*, 8 July 2009)

This investigation primarily resorted to Zeng Yike's peer contestants to reveal how she was like 'backstage'. The assumption was that there might be other explanations for certain judges' support of her, given how hard it was to justify that support. It certainly did not serve Zeng's interests for the reporter to find out that even her most vocal supporter on the show evaluated her skills differently off the stage. The reporter then implied that maybe it was Zeng's 'solid background' that pressured or corrupted certain judges into supporting her. Its closest counterpart in English being 'background', *beijing* is a frequently used term in Chinese to refer to someone's social status and often appears in the context of 'family background'. 'Someone has background' usually suggests that the person is backed by strong social capital that is often derived from financial power or governmental connections. This reference reflects a strong anxiety in today's society about the intimate relationship between the rich and the powerful.

This piece of reporting was published in early July of 2009, at a time when Zeng was still progressing closer and closer to the national throne with great momentum. This was also a time when reporters and Internet users were digging out all kinds of evidence that fueled the speculation that Zeng was from a rich family and her father had bought a position for her on the show. The second contestant interviewed in this piece (Dachunzi) described Zeng and her family in a very 'ordinary' light, suggesting that her family background may not be as complicated as people suspected. However, the reporter highlighted the fact that the contestant avoided verifying the rumors about Zeng's actual family background. The undertone of this observation was that the rumors might still be true, although Zeng and her parents could be very nice and low-key in person, defying common stereotypes about the rich in China.

Similar to this discussion, the mainstream media's attention to controversy around contestants like Zeng largely fed off the public's distrust towards the authority in granting ordinary people a fair chance at success. It appeared much easier to explain away someone's questionable progress on the show with rich people corrupting the integrity of a talent show than the judges' unique tastes. In this sense, public discourses did not artificially distinguish between competition on a talent show and that 'in real life'. The former merely provided an object of social commentary and exchanges about wide-reaching life experiences and public mentalities. The investment in contestants' personal background reflected a weakened sense of social justice in the general society. This sentiment was shared in the cyberspace, in addition to which the online discussants also more explicitly discussed the connection between the audience's cynicism towards the show and that in the broader social sphere.

Many online posts painstakingly studied the process of competition on TV and pointed to evidence of manipulation. Below is an excerpt of a long post that handpicked all the traces that the show producers were protecting one particular contestant, Li Xiaoyun, during the contest that generated the final 3 on the show.[3]

> Everyone can see that the first round is singing while dancing, which is doubtlessly the weak spot for Li Xiaoyun. Therefore, she went on the temporary PK stage[4] after the first round … However, Huang Ying went through the PK challenge three times. She lost all three challenges, which sent her to the final PK stage. The key myth is here, please note. Li Xiaoyun did not do too well in one song, the result of which for her was that she successfully made it to the next round. Huang Ying also did not do too well in one song, the result of which for her was that she was sent to the final PK stage. Have you ever thought about the possibility of switching the first round and the second round? The one who would have been sent to the final PK stage must have been Li Xiaoyun, but not Huang Ying. (*Kuailetingge*, 2 September 2009)

The author then listed other evidence from the same contest that the arrangements seemed to all have worked to the advantage of Li. Without nationwide voting in the 2009 season, the producers came up with a variety of ways to sift through the contestants, including an overwhelming number of rounds of competition on a single night that often ended up confusing the audience and creating abundant space for conspiracy theories. The way the author laid out the analysis is like doing detective work, noting how each and every step of the contest 'happened' to help Li out. However, it could also be argued that chance had played a big role with or without the producers' manipulation. Lacking direct evidence that the producers had designed the order of competition with that intention in mind, the author emphasized a few times that s/he was merely speculating. Indeed, this was the tone of much of the discourses circulated among the newspapers and in the online community about manipulation. Most of them were just speculations, which nevertheless did not stop people from taking a moral stance against the show.

But why are the rich necessarily bad? A more explicit discussion in the online sphere

Sharing a strong sense of moral concern with the newspapers, the online data went deeper in the discussion of some hidden values that served as a foundation for certain newspaper pieces, such as the general grievance held by the Chinese towards the rich and the powerful. Although the newspaper reporters showed great interest in uncovering certain contestants' personal background and its connection to their progress on the show, they did not spend much time discussing the reasons for doing so (however evident it may seem) and the social implications of such a phenomenon. Below are two representative posts in a chain of discussion that shed light on the connection between the game on the show and that beyond the show:

> #6: This dark drama could have lasted this long, thanks to the skillful maneuvers by her family, in addition to the two clowns, Shen Lihui and He Jiong.[5] Of course, this trick is very pale, nothing beyond power, money, or sexual appeal. We are only not sure which tool exactly was used by her family. The sure thing is that they must have used one. (*Shishiqiushi*, 8 July 2009)

> #15: With her fake voice and a rich family, she made it to the national 10. Which eliminated singer is not better than her? How would you feel if you were better than her yet lost to her? How would the super girls who have left feel about losing to her? The darker background a super girl has, the more supportive those big entertainment companies are for her. You are not qualified to operate an entertainment company. Please sign her if she is really good. (*II*, 8 July 2009)

Here, unlike the newspaper coverage, the online discussants did not shy away from connecting the dots. Instead of dancing around the premise on which Zeng's family background mattered, the viewers online more incisively connected this concern to the power of one's social capital in today's China. Furthermore, they were more explicit about the sources of social capital, be it political, economic, or sexual favors. The viewers buying into the story of manipulation here took a much stronger moral stance on the socially powerful in scolding everyone involved in the 'dark drama' and mourning the consequences shouldered by contestants from ordinary families. They even challenged the judges to sign Zeng Yike into their own companies if they saw that much potential in her. The mainstream newspapers were reserved about making such blatant claims. Perhaps the reporters were simply relying on prevalent social sentiments or they were afraid to make such accusations without sure evidence. Nevertheless, whereas the reporters were occupied with verifying the rumors about Zeng's family background, online discussions more explicitly expressed their repulsion about manipulation waged by the socially powerful.

Like the newspaper coverage, online discussion of social concerns was not one-sided. Not every post discussing this topic accused Zeng of having a rich family or her family having manipulated development on the show. However, absent in the mainstream newspapers was a deeper discussion of the connection between being rich and being manipulative. The newspapers only hinted at such a connection, whereas certain online posts more deeply explored this implicit assumption underlying some newspaper pieces. Here is a post that intended to look at the connection constructively against China's recent history:

> I don't think it is a big deal even if she is (from a rich family). Rich people do not all use dirty tricks behind the scene.

> The Chinese have a very serious hatred for the rich, which may be due to two reasons: one, except the generation born after the 90s, most Chinese have experienced or have some knowledge about the 'big-pot' era. All of a sudden, gaps in the material life have become so distinct that people cannot fully accept it yet. If they cannot make themselves richer, and they cannot make others less rich, they can find a certain way to vent and seek balance. Second, the quality of most Chinese is still not

very high, flaunting their money excessively when certain people make it, which gradually makes people form the opinion that a rich guy equals half a bad man. (*Wenxingzhongxin*, 10 July 2009)

First, the author addressed the sentiment that ordinary Chinese have a strong hatred towards the rich people, which the newspaper coverage did not address upfront. This post also spelled out sources of the hatred – a suddenly enlarged gap of wealth that still keeps going and sensational scandals caused by the new rich flaunting their wealth in public and abusing their power through connections with public officials (Richburg, 2011; Xinhua News, 2011). During the 'big-pot' era from the 1950s to the late 1970s amid China's 'Big March' movement towards a socialist prosperity, the ideal was that everyone should share the same amount of material wealth no matter what kind of labour or how much labour they put in. Then came the 'Opening and Reform' era since the late 1970s when people were encouraged to accumulate as much personal wealth as they could with their own skills or efforts.

State stimulations enabled and further encouraged the gap in people's material life, which has been enlarging to an astonishing extent. At the same time, corruption has also been getting out of control, as the rich would gang up with local officials for further economic gains and social power. Amid China's exponential economic development as a nation, the rich become richer and the powerful become more powerful. Therefore, the author of the above post suggested that accusing the rich of manipulation is at least a way for the Chinese to vent about their daily cruel struggles in contrast to the privileges enjoyed by the rich. In addition, like the previous online posts, *Wenxingzhongxin* here pointed out that it does not help that certain rich people flaunt their wealth and social power in ways that do not benefit the general society, if not doing damage to it.

These are the premises on which the newspaper reporters carried out investigations of certain contestants' family background and their personal characters. These considerations justified why it was necessary to do such investigations but seldom got specified in the newspaper coverage. Having laid out such reasons, the author of the post suggested that the rich or powerful do not always manipulate behind the scene, even when they are expected to do so. Although it was rare to find such defenses for the rich, the online discussions provided deeper analysis than the mainstream newspapers.

Overall, both media spaces expanded the boundary of civic engagement in that discussions about developments on *Super Girl* reached into broader and more serious concerns that will affect the civil society and the state. Through a closer examination of the narrative structure in developing these themes, I argue that the Internet provides a valuable space for ordinary Chinese not only to reach out but also to express their deeper values that may be more heavily censored elsewhere in the country's public sphere.

Discussion

Amid the country's reform and developments, China's Internet presents its unique trajectory and boundaries. This may be an ironic phenomenon as conceptually the digital media are supposed to connect one globally. On the one hand, the Internet is an integral part of China's investment in technological advancement and contributes immensely to its economic development. On the other hand, boasting one of the greatest firewalls, the state isolates its netizens from the rest of the world with its tight grip on political and cultural uses of the digital media. If the evaluation of the Internet's civic significance remains inconclusive elsewhere, one may never be able to close the chapter on China.

Weger and Aahkhus (2003) argue that simply dismissing the democratic potential of online discussion due to conflicting evidence is like seeing the glass half empty. Although they also identify major features of Internet chat rooms that are problematic for supporting rational-critical discussions, the authors view the chance of being exposed to diverse opinions and building social connection as the most significant contributions of the Internet. In addition to these two aspects, my analysis of online discussions revealed some unique features of Internet use in China that deserve recognition.

Although the Internet in China suffers from such universal issues as incivility and informality based on an ideal model of rational-critical public deliberations, and such unique local challenges as censorship, online discussants bonded over their leisure activities, reached into the discussion of deep values, and very importantly, contributed oftentimes to discourses with greater depth on important social concerns than the mainstream media. The nature of my data being about entertainment probably stirred their imagination and protected them from strict state censorship that is more focused on explicit political expressions. As researchers still primarily follow the normative agenda set by Habermas' ideal type, much academic work on the digital media misses the lively dynamic of such everyday exchanges and the potential of apolitical conversations to expand civic engagement, especially in authoritarian regimes.

This research shows the contribution of a more qualitatively organic perspective and an expanded vision in examining the civic significance of the Internet. In providing specific examples and developing a detailed case around these examples, one would risk the methodological loophole of cherry-picking. However, on the one hand, such observations are backed by examination into discourses beyond the specific sample collected for this paper. On the other hand, even within the random sample, I pointed out that the majority of online discussions did not make the jump from entertainment conversations to more serious civic discourses. Indeed, I argue that such a connection built on common interests in entertainment experiences served a foundation for the discussants to form a sense of community and comfort to open up and reach further depth in their discussions. Scholars should devote more attention and develop more in-depth research based on the fact that once in a while such discourses did reach further to weave collective reflections on more serious social concerns.

In researching public discourses about *Super Girl*, I found that 'net pals' constituted the most frequently mentioned source among the newspapers. While 'the net pals' were oftentimes used interchangeably with 'the audience', 'the fans', or 'ordinary citizens' by reporters, the Internet seemed to have provided a space where they turned for evidence of audience receptions. The Internet further provided a space from which the reporters could cite controversial opinions or stories without themselves being held accountable for those ideas.

As a visible reflection of public opinions, the Internet helped Chinese users channel their voices in the mainstream media space as the show producers, judges, and other public figures were often pressed to respond to online opinions. However, reporters still tended to use online opinions in such a way that treated them more as a fodder for discussion or point of entry in their reports than an invitation to open and reciprocal conversations. This reflects the general strategic use of cyberspace by reporters to serve their coverage angles without themselves running into trouble for statements that would challenge the authority. It is remarkable nonetheless that the Chinese netizens have carved their own communication space where they can carry out independent exchanges of opinion that are drawing significant attention from the mainstream media. Future research should further explore this interaction between the two opinion spaces.

In this paper, I primarily focus on how discourses around entertainment texts online may contribute to the expansion of civic engagement in China, and what is unique about Internet use here compared to the mainstream media. Due to limited space, I could not fully explore the multidirectional interactions between the mainstream media and cyberspace. Future research could take a closer look at how the mainstream news coverage influences online interactions and vice versa. This can further pinpoint how Internet users in China channel their new found voice into the mainstream public sphere and interact with the latter through untraditional ways of civic engagement. More research could also expand the snapshot provided in this paper by examining different types of data, for example, other shows, magazine texts, television coverage, and other Internet sites. We could benefit from more comprehensive discourse analyses that examine data on a greater scale.

While many exciting research materials are being produced on a daily basis, we need to recognize the significance of apolitical discussions among ordinary citizens and immerse ourselves in their actual exchanges. The Chinese state continues to exercise strict gate-keeping and prioritize the opinions of state elites channeled through the mainstream media, whereas the Internet provides an empowering platform for ordinary citizens to gather and participate in apolitical discussions. Although such discussions bear little political relevance on the surface, they create the basis for bonding, forming political imagination, and organizing voices of social concern. Collectively and gradually, they help expand civic engagement in China and may push back for increased presence in more formal discourse spaces.

Notes

1. One of the earliest and most publicized cases in China was in 2006 when a woman posted a series of pictures online in which she abused kittens with her high heels and tapped into online groups who are into such graphics. However, it also offended many other online users who are advocates of animal rights. With individual contributions of knowledge about details in the pictures, such as the appearance of the woman and the background setting of the pictures, the netizens were able to uncover her offline identity in 6 days and shared such information both online and with the police, which led to wider criticism of her behaviour.
2. All excerpts in this article were directly translated from Chinese into English as closely as possible by the author.
3. All examples of online posts come from the 39 discussion threads sampled for this study.
4. 'PK' is borrowed from video game language, meaning two contestants on the bottom of the contest would face off in one last round, after which the winning contestant would continue on the show while the losing one left. The *Super Girl* temporary PK stage is where contestants on the bottom waited before all rounds of competition were completed and the two with lowest scores went through the PK round.
5. Shen is a judge on the show, while He is one of the hosts.

References

Ang, I. (1985). *Watching Dallas: Soap opera and the melodramatic identification*. London: Routledge.

Ansfield, J. (2009, September 6). China web sites seeking users' names. *The New York Times*, p. A4.

Baym, N. (2000). *Tune in, log on: Soaps, fandom, and online community*. Thousand Oaks, CA: Sage.

China's Great Firewall. (2009, August 17). *The Washington Post*, p. Editorial.

Coleman, S. (2006). How the other votes: *Big Brother* viewers and the 2005 British general election campaign. *International Journal of Cultural Studies, 9*, 457–479.

Coleman, S. (2007). Mediated politics and everyday life. *International Journal of Communication, 1*, 49–60.

Graham, T., & Hajru, A. (2011). Reality TV as a trigger of everyday political talk in the net-based public sphere. *European Journal of Communication, 26*, 18–32.

Habermas, J. (1984). *The theory of communicative action*. Boston, MA: Beacon Press.

Hermes, J. (2005). *Re-reading popular culture*. Malden, MA: Blackwell.

Hermes, J. (2006). Hidden debates: Rethinking the relationship between popular culture and the public sphere. *Javnost/The Public, 13*, 27–44.

Jacobs, R., & Townsley, E. (2011). *The space of opinion: Media intellectuals and the public sphere.* New York, NY: Oxford University Press.

Jiang, M. (2010). Authoritarian deliberation on Chinese Internet. *Electronic Journal of Communication, 20.* Retrieved from http://www.cios.org/www/ejc/v20n34toc.htm

Kollock, P., & Smith, M. (1996). Managing the virtual commons: Cooperation and conflict in computer communities. In S. C. Herring (Ed.), *Computer-mediated communication: Linguistic, social and cross-cultural perspectives* (pp. 109–128). Philadelphia, PA: John Benjamins.

Lafraniere, S., & Barboza, D. (2011, March 21). China tightens censorship of electronic communications. *The New York Times*, p. A4.

Lagerkvist, J. (2006). *The Internet in China: Unlocking and containing the public sphere.* Lund: Lund University Press.

Lee, G. (1996). Addressing anonymous messages in cyberspace. *Journal of Computer-Mediated Communication, 2.* Retrieved from http://jcmc.indiana.edu/vol2/issue1/

Li, S. (2010). The online public space and popular ethos in China. *Media, Culture & Society, 32*, 63–83.

Liu, S. (2011). Structuration of information control in China. *Cultural Sociology, 5*, 323–339.

Mou, Y., Atkin, D., & Fu, H. (2011). Predicting political discussion in a censored virtual environment. *Political Communication, 28*, 341–356.

Pew Research Center. (2012). *Growing concerns in China about inequality, corruption.* Retrieved October 16, 2012, from http://www.pewglobal.org

Radway, J. (1991). *Reading the romance: Women, patriarchy, and popular literature.* Chapel Hill, NC: University of North Carolina Press.

Richburg, K. (2011, August 21). China's nouveaux riches. *The Washington Post*, p. A12.

Ross, S. (2008). *Beyond the box: Television and the Internet.* Malden, MA: Blackwell.

Tong, F. (2006, June). *Discourse of fandom in the cyberworld: A Chinese entertainment show and its empowered constituency.* Paper presented at the International Communication Association Conference, Dresden, Germany.

Wang, J., & Yang, Y. (2011). *Annual report on social mentality of China.* China: Social Sciences Academic Press.

Weber, I., & Jia, L. (2007). Internet and self-regulation in China: The cultural logic of controlled commodification. *Media Culture Society, 29*, 772–789.

Weger, H., & Aahkhus, M. (2003). Arguing in Internet chat rooms: Argumentative adaptations to chat room design and some consequences for public deliberation at a distance. *Argumentation & Advocacy, 40*, 23–38.

Xinhua News. (2011). *Son of Chinese general gets one-year confinement for attacking a couple.* Retrieved from http://news.xinhuanet.com/english2010/china/2011–09/15/c_131141173.htm

Yang, G. (2003). The coevolution of the Internet and civil society in China. *Asian Survey, 43*, 405–422.

Yang, G. (2009). *The power of Internet in China: Citizen activism online.* New York, NY: Columbia University Press.

Yu, H. (2006). From active audience to media citizenship: The case of post-Mao China. *Social Semiotics, 16*, 303–326.

Yu, H. (2007). Talking, linking, clicking: The politics of AIDS and SARS in urban China. *Positions, 15*, 35–63.

Zheng, Y. (2007). *Technological empowerment: The Internet, state, and society in China.* Stanford, CA: Stanford University Press.

Zhou, X., Chan, Y., & Peng, Z. (2008). Deliberativeness of online political discussion: A content analysis of the Guangzhou daily website. *Journalism Studies, 9*, 759–770.

van Zoonen, L. (2005). *Entertaining the citizen: When politics and popular culture converge.* Lanham, MD: Rowman and Littlefield.

Regional variation in Chinese internet filtering

Joss Wright

Oxford Internet Institute, University of Oxford

Internet filtering in China is a pervasive and well-reported phenomenon and, as arguably the most extensive filtering regime in the world today, has been studied by a number of authors. Existing studies, however, have considered both the filtering infrastructure and the nation itself as largely homogeneous in this respect. This article investigates variation in filtering across China through direct access to internet services across the country. This is achieved through use of the Domain Name Service (DNS), which provides a mapping between human-readable names and machine-routable internet addresses, and is thus a critical component of internet-based communications. Manipulation of DNS is a common mechanism used by states and institutions to hamper access to internet services that have been deemed undesirable. Our experiments support the hypothesis that, despite typically being considered a monolithic entity, the Chinese filtering approach is better understood as a decentralized and semi-privatized operation in which low-level filtering decisions are left to local authorities and organizations. This article provides a first step in understanding how filtering affects populations at a fine-grained level, and moves towards a more subtle understanding of internet filtering than those based on the broad criterion of nationality. The techniques employed in this work, while here applied to geographic criteria, provide an approach by which filtering can be analysed according to a range of social, economic and political factors in order to more fully understand the role that internet filtering plays in China, and around the world.

1. Introduction

For over two and a half billion people, the internet has become a central tool for communication, interaction and access to information. The volume of data travelling over the internet and the number of individuals that rely on it make the internet a powerful tool for controlling the flow of information to society.

A significant and increasing number of nations participate in some form of internet filtering or censorship (Deibert, Palfrey, Rohozinski, & Zittrain, 2008). Whilst these policies can be open and transparent, at least to a limited extent, their nature tends towards secrecy. Due to the power that internet filtering provides over individuals and society, it is crucial to understand how, why, and to what extent filtering occurs around the world.

Several groups have investigated internet filtering, most notably Deibert et al. (2008) and Herdict (2012). To a large extent, however, these groups have focused on national-level filtering; studying the targets of filtering and the approaches taken by states as a whole.

National-level filtering, however, is a necessarily abstracted description. Many states have national filtering policies but it is false to assume that the implementations of these policies need be consistent between regions, networks, or even individual computers. To understand filtering and its role in a globally networked world, it is necessary to explore connectivity at a more geographically and organizationally fine-grained level.

To this end, this article investigates regional variation in internet filtering. Specifically, it considers censorship occurring in China and the apparent variance of this censorship between cities. Filtering varies in its targets, its application, and its effects. These factors reveal the technical infrastructures that underlie filtering and their limitations. More importantly, these factors provide insight into the organizational structures and political decisions that drive the instantiation of filtering as experienced by Chinese citizens.

Key to this work is the hypothesis that Chinese state internet censorship operates through a system of *centrally coordinated local implementation;* that the application of filtering policies is decentralized, to varying degrees, amongst actors such as internet service providers. While certain filtering decisions are replicated strictly across the entire nation, other policies are more or less open to interpretation by local operators.

This article focuses on the case of China for a number of reasons. First, China's 'Golden Shield Project' (金盾工程, jīndùn gōngchéng) or 'Great Firewall', represents arguably the largest and most technologically advanced filtering mechanism in use today. The system operates over a total population of roughly 1.3 billion citizens and an internet population estimated at 513 million users as of 2011 (CNNIC, 2012), making the total number of Chinese internet users comparable to the entire population of the European Union.

Second, the Chinese state implements a strict and dynamic filtering policy in which globally popular websites, keywords, and services are commonly blocked. These blockages occur both over the long-term and in response to political events. At a national scale, economies must be made in the mechanisms of filtering in order to limit computational and human resources to a manageable level, which may be reflected in the effects of filtering on users. Finally, China presents a geographically and culturally diverse subject of study. These factors, amongst others, combine to make China illustrative of the possibilities of broad-scale and thorough internet filtering.

The central finding of this article is that filtering varies widely across China, strongly suggesting that the specific implementation of filtering policies is deferred to local-level organizations. Despite this, nationwide patterns of specific filtering behaviour are clearly apparent, reflecting the existence of detailed filtering decisions that can be imposed on local organizations. A secondary outcome is that certain of these behaviours strongly imply that the censorship mechanism is employed not only to block access to websites, but also to track attempted connections to blocked resources.

This work proceeds as follows: Section 2 details existing work that has studied the theory and praxis of filtering around the world, and in the case of China particularly. Section 3 examines approaches to mapping filtering and censorship, the limitations of existing methods, and ethical concerns in researching internet censorship. Section 4 presents the experimental and methodological approach followed in this work. Section 5 examines the results of the experiments, with further discussion and analysis in Section 6. Finally, Section 7 summarizes the findings of the experiments and proposes avenues for future work.

2. Existing work

A number of studies and ongoing projects investigate both global internet censorship and the specific case of China. Perhaps the most comprehensive study of global internet filtering has been presented by Deibert et al. (2008). This work is notable both for its scope and its focus on the sociological as well as technical aspects of filtering, examining the nature of filtered topics and the levels of state transparency in the filtering process. The methodology in Deibert et al., however, takes a national view of internet filtering without considering variations within a state.

The Herdict (2012) project relies on users in filtered regions to report blocked websites. These reports are aggregated and summaries on a per-country basis. Herdict provides a web-based tool that presents users with potentially blocked websites for their region, allowing them to confirm reported blocking.

Morozov (2011) studies the effects of online surveillance and censorship on internet-based activism as a means for political change. This work presents a pessimistic view of the potential of the internet to effect such changes and explores the various ways in which political actors take advantage of the internet to manipulate and stifle debate. Morozov argues that the balance of power is typically weighted significantly towards existing state-level actors and that internet-based activism, through organization via social media or more direct social disobedience, is a largely ineffective application of the effort of activists.

MacKinnon (2012) presents a more positive view of the power of individuals to act collectively online to negotiate and demand changes in access to information and services. MacKinnon surveys the state of global information control and the responses of individuals to that control. The focus of the work is largely, but by no means entirely, on the actions of corporations as providers of services, and the broad-scale decisions made with or without government collaboration. MacKinnon argues that corporations should consider, and be held accountable for, the ramifications of their business decisions. This echoes arguments made in a less adversarial setting by Pariser (2011) who explores the algorithmic filtering employed by corporations to customize content for users. This behaviour leads, according to Pariser, to a 'filter bubble' that restricts the opinions and informations available to users by obscuring viewpoints that disagree with their own. Both Pariser and MacKinnon assume the power and efficacy of the internet as a major source of information for individuals in contrast to the more pessimistic view of Morozov.

In direct relation to the theme of collective action, King, Pan, and Roberts (2012) develop a theoretical framework for understanding the state-level motivations of internet filtering in China through empirical analysis of patterns of censorship in popular Chinese blogging platorms. King et al. argue that content is directly removed by the Chinese authorities when it is deemed to have violated unwritten rules of conduct. By studying the nature of removed posts and how quickly authority responds to particular topics of discussion, King et al. argue that Chinese censorship is not, as typically assumed, focused on preventing state critique of the Chinese Communist Party, but is instead predicated on preventing discourse that leads to collective action; reducing the *collective action potential* of the society, while still allowing critique of the state. This theory has interesting implications for the potential, as investigated in this work, for regional variation in censorship to be adapted for regions with different social or economic makeup.

The use of the internet in China is examined in detail by Yang (2009), who highlights its rôle as a force for activism and dialogue for Chinese citizens. Most interestingly, Yang claims that, while the central government is intolerant towards speech that aims to criticize the state as a whole, it is far more lenient with criticism of local-level government and officials. This viewis again a driver for the regional variation in filtering investigated here.

There have been several technical studies of the means employed to filter and surveil internet connections. A useful overview of the technical scope of filtering technologies was presented by Murdoch and Anderson (2008) who organize internet filtering according to four major categories with varying degrees of complexity and efficacy. These approaches, in particular Domain Name Service (DNS) filtering which is key to this work, are discussed in greater detail in Appendix 2.

A seminal study of one major approach employed by the Chinese national firewall was presented by Clayton, Murdoch, and Watson (2006), who identified the specific mechanisms by which the firewall instructed both ends of a communication to abandon their connection when objectionable content was detected. Clayton et al. proposed that by ignoring this instruction, a TCP RST ('reset'), Chinese filtering could effectively be ignored by appropriately modified systems.

A study of the targets of Chinese filtering was carried out by Crandall, Zinn, Byrd, Barr, and East (2007). This work made use of direct requests to identify blocked keywords, along with an approach based on latent semantic analysis to identify previously unknown keywords related to known topics of interest. The analysis not only identified a broad range of topics and keywords that fell within the scope of Chinese state filtering, but also that topics may be blocked for differing amounts of time according to their perceived severity. Importantly, this work also revealed that the Great Firewall filters communications within China, rather than simply on the interface between China and other countries. China's 'firewall' is concerned both with control of information within the country and with information flowing across its borders.

Xu, Morley Mao, and Alex Halderman (2011) look more directly at the infrastructure of filtering in China by examining precisely where filtering actions occur, and how these actions interact with the networks of neighbouring countries. Xu et al. identify particular *border routers* – hardware devices placed on the border between China and its neighbours – where filtering physically takes place. These results identify, at a relatively coarse-grained level, which major internet organizations within China are responsible for hosting the majority of the filtering infrastructure.

The work of Xu et al. suggests that the infrastructure of filtering is relatively well dispersed across China in both geographic and organizational senses, with some level of concentration in Guangdong. Xe et al.'s study supports the view, argued in this work, of a distributed and partially decentralized filtering infrastructure in China.

3. Mapping filtering

To understand regional variations in network behaviour it is necessary to take measurements from multiple locatoins within a target region. Several existing projects involve an aspect of mapping, either at a logical or a geographical level. The Herdict (2012) project allows users to report apparently blocked websites via a browser plugin. These reports are used to present both a global map of filtered sites and a per-country breakdown of those most commonly reported. The Alkasir project (Al-Saqaf, 2008) combines user-based reporting of blocked content with an anti-censorship tool that attempts to penetrate such filtering. A relatively new project at the time of writing, the Open Observatory of Network Interference, seeks to develop and deploy an open network of monitoring tools managed by volunteer operators that would allow for active monitoring of global filtering (Filastò, & Appelbaum, 2012).

Perhaps the most internationally well-known technology to bypass internet filtering is the Tor network (Dingledine, Mathewson, & Syverson, 2004) that allows users to divert their connections through a global network of volunteer-run anonymising proxy servers. Whilst originally designed to preserve the connection-level privacy of users, the Tor network is a highly effective tool for bypassing national filtering and invests significant resources in supporting this use. Similar tools include Psiphon (Psiphon Inc., 2012) as well as numerous Virtual Private Network (VPN) servers that allow users to evade national filters. Each of these services works by re-routing connections through different countries than that in which the user is located. This technique allows users to experience the internet as if their connection originated in the final country on their route. A user from Saudi Arabia, where censorship is common, is therefore able to route their connection through the United States at the cost of a slight loss in connection speed. This allows the user to avoid their nation's local filters, gaining any filtering or surveillance imposed by the United States or the provider of the proxy.

These examples suggest two major possibilities for studying internet filtering. The first is to ask users in a given country to report their experience, as exemplified by the Herdict project; the second is to make use of a service such as Tor or a VPN to experience filtering directly. Both of these approaches have limitations when applied to a large-scale measurement of filtered networks. User-centred approaches such as Herdict cannot easily target their results; if there is no population of users in a given region of interest then no results can be obtained. It is also difficult to produce results on demand in response to real-world developments such as an election or natural disaster that might have an effect on filtering policies. For proxy-based approaches, there is no way to conduct an experiment in a region of interest where no proxies exist, although those regions that do hold proxies can be queried on demand.

One advantage of systems such as Tor, Psiphon, and VPNs is that they allow a researcher to control traffic directly. Sites of interest and even specific traffic patterns can be sent, and their effects examined. This allows a much more detailed examination of the technical behaviour of a given network. The approach taken by Herdict, in contrast, cannot reproduce this level of sophistication. In the absence of a large network of experienced and technically capable users, user-level reporting reveals only that a site is unavailable without reference to the conditions that cause the unavailability.[1]

Two major points of interest must be considered to map filtering at a fine-grained level. The first of these is the precise geographical location of a particular computer. Means to determine the originating country of an IP address are relatively well known, and location to the level of a city can be obtained with some accuracy. Recent results from Wang, Burgener, Flores, Kuzmanovic, and Huang (2011) have proposed mechanisms that achieve a median accuracy of 690 metres, albeit within the United States. In many cases, it is also possible to determine the organization that has been allocated a particular IP address to the level of an ISP or major company. This approach is partially explored by Xu et al. (2011). This information can be used to build up a much more detailed view of filtering.

The second point of interest is to study, in detail, the technical nature of the filtering that is imposed on a given connection in a given location. While work has been conducted into specific methods, as in the work of Clayton et al. (2006), most large-scale projects focus more on the existence of filtering rather than the details of its implementation.

4.   Experimental approach

The work described here aims to discover and map variations in internet filtering between geographical regions of China and to determine the nature of the filtering that occurs. The goal of this investigation is to gain insight into the nature of filtering decisions both in terms of centralization and control and in the devolution of filtering to local-level actors.

The chosen approach is data-driven, focusing on obtaining geographically diverse data regarding filtering experienced by Chinese internet users. The internet's DNS provides a rich and accessible source of such data. DNS has a number of attractive features for technical reasons, but also avoids the legal and ethical concerns that are detailed in Section 3.1.

Due to their crucial role in resolving human-readable resource names to IP addresses, DNS servers provide a level of coverage that is difficult to match with other direct sources of data. DNS servers are also often openly accessible, meaning that there is no technical or legal restriction in making requests to these remote systems.

DNS servers are typically run either by internet service providers for the benefit of their customers or by large organizations that manage their own large-scale networks. The results returned by a given DNS server therefore typically reflect one view of the internet as experienced by a reasonably large class of users.

DNS servers function, at an extremely simple level, as a simple database of mappings between domains[2] and IP address. Requesting information regarding a given domain therefore does not cause any direct access to potentially sensitive resources on behalf of a third party,[3] as would be the case for the proxy services mentioned in earlier discussions. Importantly, this avoids involving any third parties, willing or otherwise, in experiments. These factors make DNS an ideal source of legally, ethically, and technically sound data regarding an important aspect of China's internet censorship.

To obtain a useful sample for investigating DNS censorship across China, a list of DNS servers was retrieved from the Asia Pacific Network Information Centre (APNIC), the Regional Internet Registry responsible for allocating IP addresses and Autonomous System numbers across the Asia Pacific region. The APNIC maintains a WHOIS database that stores information regarding registered domain names in their region, including the DNS servers that are considered authoritative for given domains. A list of 278 DNS servers located in China was retrieved from the APNIC WHOIS database, of which 187 were found to be available and responsive to remote queries.

The freely available MaxMind GeoIP database (MaxMind Inc., 2012) was employed to resolve IP addresses to their city of operation, allowing geolocation of almost all DNS servers in the test set. It is worth noting, as will be discussed later, that this does not represent the location of the users of that service; these users make DNS requests from their own network connections and could potentially be located in almost any geographical location. In practice, all users can safely be assumed to be within China.

A list of potentially filtered domain names was obtained from the Herdict (2012) project's website. As the Herdict project receives reports regarding filtered websites from crowdsourced reporting, sorted according to country, this provides a useful source of data for potentially blocked domain names. An alternative approach, which is perhaps less efficient, but potentially more revealing, would be to employ a list of the most commonly visited websites worldwide via the Alexa rankings (Alexa, 2012).

The Herdict project lists the most frequently reported blocked websites for each country, each list comprising the top 80 reported domains. In addition to these, five popular Chinese websites were included in the test set that, presumably, would not be blocked in mainland China. A full list of tested domains is given in Appendix 1.

Each potentially blocked domain name was requested from each DNS server retrieved from the APNIC WHOIS database. The results were recorded and analysed according to the nature of the DNS response received in each case.

To determine whether results were accurate, an equivalent query was conducted on a self-managed DNS server located in a country that does not perform extensive internet filtering.[4] The results of the remote query were compared heuristically[5] with the local result, and any differences were were noted.

The sequence of requests was repeated six times at one-hour intervals to minimize genuine network errors. The results from the different experimental sets were combined in such a way that timeouts, which could represent genuinely poor connectivity, were eliminated unless they were seen to be consistent across all result sets.

4.1 *DNS response types*

The categorization presented in Appendix 2 identifies four major filtering techniques, of which manipulation of DNS results is only one. It is important to distinguish intentional DNS 'poisoning' from genuine network errors or misconfigured servers. The key responses of a DNS server to queries, for the purposes of the current work, are discussed here.

4.1.1   *Invalid server errors*

On receiving a given query, a DNS server may respond with an indication that it is not, in fact, a DNS server. In this case, the requesting party will not receive a mapping from the requested name to an IP address, and so cannot connect to the requested machine. Such a response could also indicate that the server was genuinely not a DNS server. If this behaviour is consistent for all requests, then this could be the result of a genuine misconfiguration. In other cases, this may denote censorship.

4.1.2   *Timeout errors*

A simpler behaviour, and one that is harder to categorize unambiguously as censorship, is for a DNS server to accept requests, but not to respond in any way at all for blocked domains. The requesting party will eventually exceed a given time threshold and abandon the query. This again prevents a client from learning the IP address of the requested domain. Such behaviour could again be ascribed to a genuine network error in some cases.

A secondary effect of this behaviour is that the requesting party does not receive an immediate response to its request. This can cause internet requests to blocked sites to pause until a timeout threshold is reached, slowing down the end user's connection.

4.1.3   *Unknown domain errors*

The simplest form of direct DNS censorship is for the DNS server to deny the existence of the requested domain, causing the requesting party to receive an error. For known existing domains, this response is easily identifiable as malicious behaviour on the part of the server.

4.1.4   *Misleading results*

A more subtle approach to censorship is for requests for blocked websites to generate a valid DNS response, providing the client with an IP address for the requested hostname, but to provide false information in the form of an incorrect IP address.

This approach has several implications. One potential outcome is that the requesting party may be directed to a host that logs all attempts to access banned websites. This allows requests for blocked content to be logged from a central location when misdirected users connect to incorrect destinations. As can be seen in Section 5, the use of misdirection to suspicious IP addresses is clearly observed in the case of China.

4.1.5   *Genuine results*

A final possibility is that a DNS server returns the correct IP address that corresponds to the requested hostname. While this particular piece of information may be accurate, censorship may, of course, occur through other means.

4.2   *Ethical considerations*

By their nature, the majority of filtering detection mechanisms attempt to access filtered content in order to detect whether or not that content can be accessed. Filtered content typically occurs in the form of websites or IP addresses that are believed to be subject to blocking, although it may also be specific keywords or network traffic patterns. It is possible, however, that sufficiently high-volume requests for banned content such as those caused by some automated detection methods may risk further unwelcome scrutiny.

A user is, in general, unlikely to face repercussions for seeming to attempt access to blocked content. The scale of internet use, even in smaller countries with low internet penetration rates, is simply too high for there to be significant policing of users who request filtered material. In the vast majority of cases, it is likely that such attempts may not be logged at all. As will be discussed in Section 6, however, there is evidence that DNS requests for blocked services may be logged in the case of China.

Deliberate misuse of a network service for the purposes of detecting internet filtering may be illegal in many jurisdictions, and such misuse without the consent of users or system operators is clearly unethical. Even when using openly available and general purpose services, however, there are serious considerations when attempting to access blocked content via a third party.

Volunteers who participate in censorship research of this nature by running a filtering detection tool must do so having been fully informed as to the nature of the tool and the potential risks involved. From this perspective, there is a significant added burden on researchers to state to the participant, who may not have a significant level of technical expertise, the nature of the tool's operation and the incurred risks. With the lack of knowledge regarding the precise nature of filtering, surveillance, and enforcement in countries of interest, there are significant barriers to performing ethically sound broad research into online censorship. These issues are discussed in greater detail by Wright, de Souza, and Brown (2011).

5. Results

The experiments conducted in this work provide evidence that China's approach to national filtering relies on loosely coordinated filtering based on instructions and guidelines from central sources, that are implemented more or less strictly – a system of *centrally coordinated local implementation* rather than a uniform and centrally controlled nationwide infrastructure.

The results presented here support this hypothesis by showing patterns in the variance of filtering across China. Whereas certain domains are blocked almost uniformly by all servers, others are blocked according to different methods or may be left unblocked. Furthermore, in several cases, specific blocking decisions are replicated across geographically and organizationally distinct networks, strongly implying that centralized guidance had been given in these cases.

The results of querying DNS servers across China for reportedly banned domain name are presented below, along with a number of identified trends in the responses. A number of particularly unusual observed behaviours are also highlighted and explored. This section first presents broad trends identified in filtering behaviour across the country. This is followed by the treatment of particular blocked domains, highlighting countrywide consistency in some cases and variations in others. Finally, revealing behaviours related to specific DNS servers are presented.

5.1 *Broad trends*

Experiments were conducted on 187 DNS servers across China; 178 of these servers answered at least one query with a valid, but not necessarily truthful, IP address. Of the responding servers, 79 answered at least one query with a response that appeared to be accurate, meaning that 99 servers returned only some form of invalid results for the requested domains.

A small number of servers were clearly either misconfigured, or deliberately providing invalid results to requests. Five servers consistently timed out on DNS requests, despite an allowance for an artificially long timeout period of 60 seconds. One server consistently produced an invalid nameserver error, despite apparently accepting DNS requests.

5.1.1 *Widespread DNS poisoning*

The experiments provide evidence of widespread manipulation of DNS results, occurring in all the forms discussed in the previous section. Interestingly, individual DNS servers do not, in general, display consistent blocking behaviour across all domains. Instead, a server may return an incorrect IP address for one domain, claim that a second domain does not exist, and refuse to respond to requests for a third domain.

This may reflect filtering on any given server being continually updated in response to changing conditions. As new domains or topics are added to the list then the behaviour of the server is itself updated, possibly by different operators choosing different methods of filtering. It also appears that, as discussed in detail later, certain domains are redirected to centrally specified IP addresses, and thus cannot be claimed to be non-existent. Other domains that are not specifically redirected may be blocked as the local operator sees fit.

Figure 1 demonstrates the 10 most widely misdirected domains observed in experiments. These domains were thus almost universally blocked across China at the DNS level. In addition to this overwhelming majority of misleading results for each domain, other servers were likely either to time out or to claim not to be a valid name server for this result.

The fact that these domains are universally blocked with only minor variance in implementation provides strong evidence that operators are given specific instructions regarding these domains. An alternative explanation is that requests for these domains are manipulated, while in transit as they pass across the border routers of China. While this cannot be entirely ruled out, the variations that do exist weigh against such a centralized and, presumably, homogeneous approach.

Figure 2 lists the 10 domains that are most often claimed not to exist by the tested DNS servers. Claiming a domain as non-existent is far less common than returning an inaccurate IP

Domain	No Domain	No Answer	No Nameserver	Timeout	True IP	False IP
www.backchina.com	0	0	13	7	5	162
www.ntdtv.com	0	0	23	7	0	157
www.open.com.hk	0	1	20	7	3	156
www.torproject.org	0	2	24	7	1	153
www.tibet.net	0	2	22	7	3	153
www.peacehall.com	0	1	20	7	6	153
www.6park.com	0	0	26	7	2	152
www.hotspotshield.com	0	1	29	7	2	148
www.boxun.com	0	1	29	7	2	148
wezhiyong.org	0	1	33	7	2	144

Figure 1. Ten most misdirected domains from experiments, showing DNS error result counts for each domain.

Domain	No domain	No answer	No nameserver	Timeout	True IP	False IP
www.ahrchk.net	4	17	64	40	60	2
killerjo.net	4	17	65	37	62	2
www.x365x.com	3	17	65	41	59	2
www.websitepulse.com	3	18	65	36	63	2
www.voanews.com	3	17	64	38	63	2
www.tumblr.com	3	17	64	38	37	28
www.steves-digicams.com	3	17	65	36	64	2
www.scribd.com	3	17	65	36	38	28
www.pinyinannotator.com	3	18	67	36	61	2
www.newgrounds.com	3	16	64	36	66	2

Figure 2.   Ten domains most often claimed non-existent.

address result. Note also that the domains listed in Figure 2 receive large numbers of timed-out requests, as well as both accurate and inaccurate IP responses.

These results show that approaches to DNS poisoning favour misdirection over claims of non-existence. Allowing a request to timeout by not responding, as opposed to generating an error, is also common.

As has been suggested, these results support the hypothesis that the potential for surveillance is evident for requests to access blocked domains. By returning inaccurate responses, users' computers are directed to attempt connections to incorrect computers; such connections can be observed. By contrast, when a domain is claimed non-existent, no further observable actions takes place on the part of the user.

5.1.2   *Timeout responses*

The prevalence of timeouts could be explained by filtering occurring at other points in the network rather than at the DNS servers themselves. This could represent requests for certain domains not being allowed to pass across the borders of the Chinese network, but instead being silently dropped by intermediary routers either before or after reaching the server in question.

To understand this, it is useful to comment on the underlying *transport* of the DNS protocol. DNS typically makes use of a simple and efficient underlying internet transport protocol known as UDP, in contrast to the widely used TCP protocol employed by the majority of common internet services such as the World Wide Web.[6] UDP has the advantage of higher speeds and lower transmission overheads than TCP, but does not provide reliable data delivery, nor does it implicitly confirm the success of data transfers. It is, therefore, the case that, if DNS requests for particular domains were blocked or dropped in the network, it would be difficult to detect this fact; the result would be observed simply as a timeout.

Another alternative is that when the DNS servers in question receive a request for a blocked domain, they simply ignore the request. From the experiments detailed here, it is difficult to verify either of these claims with certainty. Filtering of DNS traffic in transit to block requests would be more complex and costly, however, and would likely result in a more homogeneous and extensive pattern of timeouts than were observed. The lack of correlation between servers on geographically close networks also suggests that network-level filtering is unlikely to explain this behaviour. The argument for filtering at the server level, or some combination of both arguments, therefore appears most likely.

5.1.3   Common misleading IP addresses

In those experiments for which DNS servers returned an IP address that did not correspond to the requested domain, the observed IP address was typically drawn from a comparatively small pool of possible responses amongst all servers; misleading IP addresses were neither random nor returned on a per-server basis.

The experiments detailed here made requests for 85 domains to 187 DNS servers, resulting in a total of 15,895 requests in total. Of these requests, 6658 gave a response that pointed to an IP address, 2258 of which were judged to be misleading. These 2258 misleading results each pointed to 1 of only 84 IP addresses, showing significant correlation between misleading IP addresses returned by DNS servers across the country.

Two possible explanations exist for this result. The first is that a centralized list exists that provides IP-specific DNS poisoning instructions for DNS server operators to implement. The second possibility, as above, is that the observed DNS responses were manipulated in transit. Again, there is insufficient evidence to choose between these explanations with any certainty, but the lack of exact replication of results implies that server-level filtering is most likely. Investigation of these two possibilities through an analysis of the routes taken by DNS requests is an intriguing subject for future work.

5.2   Domain statistics

The results of requests for the same domain to different servers reveal disparities between the behaviour of servers operated by different organizations. Despite a level of variation across the servers tested, there were striking similarities between servers that were both geographically and logically separated, strongly suggesting that centralized policies were being implemented to varying degrees. In some cases, for well-known blocked domains, there was a strong correlation in blocking behaviour. For others there was a much greater degree of variation. The results in this section detail notable correlations that support this decentralized but coordinated view of filtering.

5.2.1   Purposeful misdirection of torproject.org

The Tor Project produce a number of tools that aim to provide anonymous and untraceable internet communications, as well as to bypass censorship. Both the tool and the project website are commonly blocked in countries with extensive internet censorship, and are engaged in an ongoing filtering arms race with the operators of the Great Firewall.

On querying servers for the Tor Project's website, www.torproject.org, a set of consistent misdirections was found in DNS server responses from multiple organizations and geographical locations; a total of 29 responses redirected Tor Project traffic to a unique alternative domain. The subject of this misdirection was http://www.thepetclubfl.net, a pet grooming service in Florida. On contacting the administrator of this site, it was confirmed that the site has for some time been experiencing a previously unexplained large volume of Chinese traffic. This confirms that these particular redirections do not appear to undergo subsequent blocking within China. The possible purpose of these redirections is explored in Section 6 (Figure 3).

DNS Server	Location
122.102.0.10	China, Chaoyang
159.226.8.6	China, Beijing
162.105.129.27	China, Beijing
182.50.116.252	(Unknown)
202.102.224.94	China, Henan
202.115.32.39	China, Chengdu
202.127.12.8	China, Nanjing
202.99.216.75	China, Xian
202.99.96.126	China, Tianjin
211.161.46.86	China, Beijing
221.13.28.234	China, Guiyang
221.7.92.99	China, Chongqing
59.63.158.124	China, Beijing

Figure 3.   Example torproject.org requests resolving to alternative domain thepetclubfl.net.

The redirected domains is, of course, not in any discernible way linked to the Tor Project. The number of results from disparate servers all pointing to the same domain strongly imply some broader connection, either through direct instructions implemented by local servers or, potentially, through sharing of block lists between multiple organizations.

It should also be noted that this redirection was not the only set of consistent redirections noted for the Tor Project. The owner of a second domain similarly receiving traffic destined for the Tor Project has requested the author not to publicize their domain. While this request has been respected, the domain in question is a particularly interesting case as the redirections occur not simply to a single domain name, but to a number of similarly named domains with different suffixes, such as <domain>.com, <domain>.net, and <domain>.org.ez-site.net.

These results present the intriguing possibility that the redirection in question is in response to instructions from a third party, but have been misinterpreted by local operators. Each clearly redirects Tor Project traffic to a similar domain name, but the top-level domains vary.

5.2.2   *Poisoning of uncensored domains*

In addition to the list of 80 domains obtained from the Herdict project, the experiments incorporated domain names for five popular Chinese internet services with the intention that these would be unfiltered. Surprisingly, in several cases results appeared to show misleading results for a number of these domains. This could be due to misconfiguration of DNS servers, deliberately invalid results returned due to the request originating outside of China, or some other cause.

An illustrative example is that of renren.com, a popular Chinese social network. Invalid IP addresses were returned for this service in at least two cases, as shown in Figure 4. These servers are located in different cities, and are apparently operated by separate companies; they are both logically and physically distinct. Both servers, however, return the same list of misleading IP addresses, none of which appear to belong to servers of renren.com.

On directly querying the IP addresses in question, several appeared to be running unconfigured web server software. It is not known what, if any, the significance of these addresses may be.

Server	Location	Remote Result
202.95.0.10	China, Beijing	renren.com. 900 IN A 123.125.38.2
		renren.com. 900 IN A 123.125.38.3
		renren.com. 900 IN A 123.125.38.239
		renren.com. 900 IN A 123.125.38.240
		renren.com. 900 IN A 123.125.38.241
121.101.208.41	China, Chaoyang	renren.com. 900 IN A 123.125.38.2
		renren.com. 900 IN A 123.125.38.3
		renren.com. 900 IN A 123.125.38.239
		renren.com. 900 IN A 123.125.38.240
		renren.com. 900 IN A 123.125.38.241

Figure 4.   Inaccurate results for renren.com. Distinct servers show identical incorrect results.

5.3   *Server statistics*

In contrast to the results of domain queries between different servers across China, there are also a number of important features to be observed in the behaviour of individual servers as they respond to queries for multiple domains. The results in this section show unusual patterns of behaviour for individual servers that seem to reflect specific instructions implemented on those servers.

5.3.1   *Misleading results*

The majority of servers queried returned a variety of result types, with varying degrees of misleading results. A small number, however, demonstrated an unusually extreme range of negative responses and are thus demonstrative examples of the invalid responses given.

5.3.2   *DNS server 113.11.192.25*

This server is apparently located in Beijing. Over the course of 85 domain name requests, this server responded with 'no answer' a total of 68 times. This included the five presumably unfiltered services, including Baidu and RenRen, and may indicate discrimination against requests located outside of China. This discrimination could occur either on the server itself, or through interception of the traffic whilst *en route.*

A further 13 requests resulted in the return of a valid IP address. On examination, none of these IP addresses were found to be associated with the requested domain. The list of domains and associated IP addresses can be found in Figure 5.

The nature of the IP addresses in question are of interest. There is no discernible pattern in these results; they point to seemingly random hosts corresponding to domains and organizations that do not appear connected with each other or with the originally requested domain. Certain blocked domains, however, point to the same IP addresses even though those IP addresses are not related to the domain in question. As can be seen from Figure 5, both YouTube and Facebook redirect to the same IP address, as do peacehall.com and wujie.net, and backchina.com, boxun. com and open.com.hk. It is possible that this represents misleading results that were entered

Domain	Returned IP
www.hotspotshield.com	8.7.198.45
www.tibet.net	159.106.121.75
www.boxun.com	46.82.174.68
wezhiyong.org	8.7.198.45
www.backchina.com	46.82.174.68
www.ntdtv.com	8.7.198.45
www.peacehall.com	59.24.3.173
www.youtube.com	203.98.7.65
www.facebook.com	203.98.7.65
twitter.com	159.106.121.75
www.wujie.net	59.24.3.173
www.6park.com	159.106.121.75
www.open.com.hk	46.82.174.68

Figure 5.   Misleading IP addresses from a Beijing-based DNS server.

into the server at the same time, although this would not necessarily justify the use of identical IP addresses. Another interpretation could be that these represent different 'classes' of blocked domain that fall under different categories of possible surveillance. Without further evidence of surveillance practices in the Chinese filtering infrastructure, however, these explanations cannot be more than speculation.

The remaining four domains requested from this server resulted in a claim that no such domain existed.

5.3.3   *DNS server 202.99.224.203*

This server is apparently located in Baotou. Of 85 domains, the majority of results were to claim that the server was not valid for returning DNS requests. In total, requests for 14 domains resulted in one or more IP addresses being reported, none of which led to the appropriate servers.

It was once more observed that although invalid IP addresses were returned, these were not purely random but instead were consistent with each domain, and were drawn from a small pool of IP addresses that were used multiple times for different domains.

The poor results from these two DNS servers implies that a normal user would find them impossible to use as a main DNS server. The misleading results for known blocked websites, however, suggests a specific purpose. One explanation is that these servers exist as a primary DNS server for users, intercepting those requests that are to blocked websites while refusing to respond to requests for others. In the case that the servers do not reply, users' connections could be configured to fall back to a secondary server that provides unfiltered results. As most end user network connections are configured to use a primary and secondary DNS server for reasons of reliability, this could be a simple and efficient way to implement filtering over multiple servers.

As with other misdirected domains, however, these servers again choose to use fixed and specific IP addresses drawn from a small pool.

5.3.4 *Localhost redirection*

An interesting choice of address to return when providing inaccurate IP addresses is to point the request back to the computer from which it originated. This can be achieved through use of the reserved IP address 127.0.0.1, which has the DNS designation of 'localhost'.

Local redirection has the advantage of not requiring a genuine IP address to be selected from the internet, which can lead to unpredictable behaviour. It also minimizes traffic passing over the internet, as any further requests made to this connection remain on the user's computer without travelling over the general internet.

Despite this, the use of redirection to the localhost was not particularly widespread amongst the queried servers. Of the 187 servers queried, only six servers returned results pointing to the localhost, of which four consistently returned the localhost for any DNS query. This could represent either a misconfigured DNS server, or a blanket policy for unauthorized or non-Chinese requests.

Two servers, however, with addresses 202.99.224.200 and 202.99.224.223 returned 127.0.0.1 for the majority of requests, but also resulted in an invalid nameserver error for seven domains. In a further 13 cases, an IP response was given that, again, appears random, resolving to Azerbaijani-, Irish-, US-, Italian-, and New Zealand-based hosts.

The lack of redirection to the 127.0.0.1 address, as with the lack of non-existent domain errors, results in a connection attempt to the misleading IP address when a blocked domain is requested. It would be more efficient, in terms of network usage, for such attempts not to occur. This lends further support to the view that such network traffic may be subject to monitoring or surveillance. As such surveillance will not have an easily measurable effect on connections, however, this remains pure speculation.

5.4 *Geographical distribution*

Figure 6 presents an overview of the variations in filtering observed across the various cities covered by these experiments. Darker grey markers represent a greater percentage of misleading DNS responses compared to accurate responses. As results were obtained for potentially many servers within a given city, the median average percentage of all results observed for all servers in the city is represented. To indicate cities with a greater number of DNS servers, markers are log-scaled according to the number of servers tested, ranging from a single server in cities such as Dongguang and Harbin, to 72 servers in Beijing.

No overall pattern of filtering is apparent in the results for different cities or regions; there is clear heterogeneity across the country. This supports the core hypothesis of this work, supported by Xu et al. (2011), that high-level controls over filtering are relatively loose in many cases. Whilst the subjects of blocking may be specified to a greater or lesser extent, the technical details are decided at the local rather than regional or national level.

5.5 *Experimental limitations*

There are a number of limitations to the experimental methodology employed in this work. The first and most obvious is that the experiments relied on a restricted list of DNS servers obtained from the APNIC WHOIS database. While the set of servers used provided a reasonable coverage of China geographically, with a notable bias towards the East of the country due to the higher

Figure 6.   DNS queries across China showing median percentage of misleading results for queried domains, with darker points representing a higher percentage of misleading results. Circle size represents the relative number of servers queried in each city.

density of population and development, there was a great disparity between the number of servers observed in each city. This figure ranged from 72 servers in Beijing, to only one server in several of the smaller cities. While this will, to some extent, reflect the realities of DNS server placement in China, it appears insufficient for a genuine analysis of the relative experience of internet users.

A more fundamental limitation is that DNS servers are not necessarily, or usually, located in the same geographical area as a user. A DNS server is typically operated and managed by an ISP, and made available to its users automatically. It is therefore likely that a given ISP's customers, who may be widely dispersed, all use the same DNS server. As such, the results presented here arguably represent *organizational* variation, rather than geographical.

Further, the results in this article represent a snapshot taken in the middle of 2012, and as such cannot reflect changing patterns of censorship. Given the automated nature of these tests, however, and the relatively short time required to conduct them, the gathering of time-series data is a relatively small step, and has the potential to reveal useful patterns of censorship over time, which would be of significant value in observing the relationship between real-world events and the extent to which these dictate or affect filtering policy.

The final major limitation to this work is that it provides a purely technical view of one form of filtering occurring in China. These results provide a window into the limitations imposed on users' internet connections, but can provide little data with respect to the effects of censorship on users' browsing behaviour, social attitudes to various forms of content, choice of forums, modes and means of communication, and access to news sources. The experiments detailed here, therefore, provide a partial understanding of the wider phenomenon of internet censorship in China.

6.   Discussion

The power of the internet as a tool for freedom of expression and communication has been widely recognized (MacKinnon, 2012; Yang, 2009), even though some doubt its efficacy at achieving genuine political or social change (Morozov, 2011). What is clear in the case of China, through these experiments and others, is that the Chinese state is willing to expend significant resources in maintaining a level of active control over the flow of information across its national networks.

An interesting result in this respect is that there is a clear lack of *overt* filtering, which might be expected in the form of non-existent domain results. Instead, across the majority of servers investigated, misleading IP addresses were provided in response to queries. The practical results of these misdirections, from the perspective of a user, are varied. In some cases, an alternative webpage may be displayed, as in the case of the Tor Project and its redirection to a pet grooming service in Florida; in other cases, where the misdirection does not point to a valid web server, an error message will be displayed to the user. To a large extent, however, there is no explicit statement of filtering such as is seen in many other states that censor the internet.

A possible explanation for this behaviour is that when a DNS response results in an invalid domain, the user's computer immediately terminates the connection – it has no valid address to reach. By providing an alternative address, the firewall ensures that the user's computer will make *some* connection. If, as the experimental results show, this connection is to a computer located outside China, it can be guaranteed that the user's connection will pass across the *border routers* of China, where a significant level of filtering is believed to occur (Xu et al., 2011).

This behaviour strongly supports the hypothesis that the purpose of such misdirection is to ensure that users who attempt to connect to banned services make observable connections through known routers. It has been established in the course of this research that, at least in the known examples, that connections to the falsely reported IP addresses do complete successfully. This behaviour allows for surveillance and monitoring of users attempting to reach censored information, even if such monitoring need not be actively taking place.

The focus of the experiments conducted in this work is on the regional variation in filtering to support the hypothesis that filtering implementation is devolved to local organizations based on central policies. As clearly demonstrated in Figure 1, there is a wide diversity of filtering across China, although no overall geographical patterns have been identified in the broad-scale filtering results. The extent and variance in filtering, however, demonstrates significant involvement of local actors in making the low-level filtering decisions, even if these reflect broadly stated guidelines such as requests to block particular topics or websites.

The patterns of filtering identified in these experiments are most interesting in terms of correlations across the country that demonstrate coordination. These experiments, however, also demonstrate a clear capability for differentiated filtering to occur on demand in different locations. An important avenue of future work in this area is to identify the development of filtering decisions over time and to observe the rapidity of response as filtering decisions pass from central government policy to regional implementation.

7.   Conclusions

The work presented here has proposed that it is, in general, false to consider internet filtering as a homogeneous phenomenon across a country, and that the practicalities of implementing a filtering regime are likely to result in geographical and organizational differentiation between the filtering experienced by users. This results in a necessary decentralization of the practice of filtering, reflected in varying but correlated patterns of blocking that reflect centralized policy – a policy of *centrally coordinated decentralized implementation*. The experiments conducted in the course of this work support this hypothesis

– filtering varies widely from region to region, but certain patterns and signatures are clearly expressed in the experimental results. The study of these correlations and differences are of great interest in understanding both the technologies and the motivations behind filtering, and suggest various mechanisms that could be employed to gain this understanding.

In response to the technical and ethical challenges of censorship research, these experiments represent a nationwide remote survey of the apparent filtering experienced by Chinese internet users, with specific reference to blocking attempts that occur through the DNS. These experiments have revealed widespread poisoning of DNS results, including invalid server responses, valid domains claimed to be non-existent, and the return of IP addresses that do not correspond to the requested domain.

Analysis of these results has revealed a number of trends in this filtering, most notably the prevalence of misleading responses for domains over claims that domains do not exist. The extent of filtering varies geographically, but frequent correlations in misleading IP addresses returned in response to requests for blocked domains by different servers imply top-down involvement in local filtering in addition to any national-scale manipulation of data as it passes across the internet.

The filtering experienced through DNS manipulation reflects a clear preference for misdirection rather than direct blocking; it is possible that this is partially due to a desire to soften filtering by making it appear more akin to a network error than overt restriction. As suggested by the consistent misdirection to given IP addresses for certain domains, and the subsequent evidence that these connections are not themselves blocked, there is reason to believe that a level of surveillance operates in addition to more direct blocking.

The experience of internet filtering in China lends support to a limited form of Morozov's argument (Morozov, 2011) that the potential for activism via the internet is severely challenged by the capabilities that it provides to entrenched holders of power. The scope and extent of filtering apparent from these experiments, and the low levels of filtering seen in some regions, suggests that an ongoing fine balance is being struck between the desire to filter and the need to allow certain freedoms. This aligns with the technical data presented by Crandall et al. (2007), and the theoretical developments of King et al. (2012), that demonstrate varying responses to different classes of censored topic in response to political circumstances.

It is clear from these experiments that the infrastructure of filtering in China is complex, and is managed and operated by multiple geographically and organizationally differentiated actors communicating imperfectly with each other. Centralized decision-making is evident in some cases, where in others it is local. Whilst the architecture of this filtering system aims to control the flow of information both within the country and across its borders, it provides potentially deep insight into the policies of China's decision-makers, and the actions and responses of its citizens.

Notes

1. The Herdict project does allow a user to express their opinion as to the cause of the blocking, but in the absence of direct experimentation this data has significant limitations.
2. Strictly speaking, DNS servers return the IP for a particular *hostname*, many of which may exist under a given domain name. For the purposes of this article, the two may be considered functionally equivalent as request were not made for multiple hosts within a single domain.
3. For completeness, it should be mentioned that DNS servers function in a hierarchy, and may request information for unknown domain names from more authoritative servers. This normal function of the service would not, however, implicate any third party, and would in fact be directly traceable to the computer used in our experiments.
4. In the case of the experiments detailed here, this was the UK. Whilst the UK certainly does engage in national-scale internet filtering, it does not, in general, involve this particular form of DNS manipulation, and care was taken that such filtering would not affect the results of these experiments.

5. Specifically, the first two-dotted quads of the IP addresses returned by the remote and the local DNS server were compared. If these differed, the response was marked as incorrect. Large internet services often make use of dedicated content distribution networks that employ a wider range of IP addresses. Experimental results were manually examined to detect any such networks, and any domains that resolved to these networks were assumed to be accurate responses. This automated approach does risk introducing both false positives and false negatives with respect to the existence of misleading DNS results, but this risk is relatively small and should not unduly skew the overall results.

6. DNS can, in fact, make use of TCP as a transport. The use of UDP, however, represents the overwhelming majority of DNS requests for reasons of speed and efficiency.

References

Alexa. (2012). Alexa Ranking: Top 1,000,000 sites. Retrieved January 15, 2013, from http://s3.amazonaws.com/alexa-static/top-1m.csv.zip

Al-Saqaf, W. (2008). Alkasir for mapping and circumventing cyber-censorship. Retrieved August 8, 2012, from http://www.alkasir.com/

Clayton, R., Murdoch, S. J., & Watson, R. N. M. (2006). Ignoring the great firewall of China. In *6th workshop on privacy enhancing technologies*. Cambridge: Springer.

CNNIC. (2012). China internet network information center homepage. Retrieved August 31, 2012, from http://www.cnnic.cn

Crandall, J. R., Zinn, D., Byrd, M., Barr, E., & East, R. (2007, October). *ConceptDoppler: A weather tracker for internet censorship*. Proceedings of the 14th ACM conference on computer and communications security (CCS), Alexandria, VA.

Deibert, R. J., Palfrey, J. G., Rohozinski, R., & Zittrain, J. (2008). *Access denied: The practice and policy of global internet filtering (information revolution and global politics)*. Cambridge, MA: MIT Press.

Dingledine, R., Mathewson, N., & Syverson, P. (2004). *Tor: The second-generation onion router*. Proceedings of the 13th USENIX security symposium, Toronto, Canada.

Filastò, A., & Appelbaum, J. (2012, August). *OONI: Open observatory of network interference*. 2nd USENIX workshop on free and open communications on the internet (FOCI), Bellevue, WA.

Herdict. (2012). The Herdict project. Retrieved August 8, 2012, from http://www.herdict.org/

King, G., Pan, J., & Roberts, M. (2012). How censorship in China allows government criticism but silences collective expression. *American Political Science Review, 107*(02), 326–343.

MacKinnon, R. (2012). *Consent of the networked: The world-wide struggle for internet freedom*. New York, NY: Basic Books.

MaxMind Inc. (2012). MaxMind GeoIP City database. Retrieved August 8, 2012, from http://www.maxmind.com/app/city

Morozov, E. (2011). *The net delusion: The dark side of internet freedom*. New York, NY: PublicAffairs.

Murdoch, S., & Anderson, R. (2008). Tools and technology of internet filtering. In R. Deibert (Ed.), *Access denied: The practice and policy of global internet filtering (information revolution and global politics series)* (2nd ed., pp. 57–72). Cambridge, MA: MIT Press.

Pariser, E. (2011). *The filter bubble: What the internet is hiding from you*. New York, NY: Penguin Press.

Psiphon Inc. (2012). The Psiphon project. Retrieved August 8, 2012, from http://www.psiphon.ca/

Wang, Y., Burgener, D., Flores, M., Kuzmanovic, A., & Huang, C. (2011). Towards street-level client independent IP geolocation. In *Proceedings of the 8th USENIX symposium on networked systems design and implementation*. USENIX Association, Boston, MA.

Wright, J., de Souza, T., & Brown, I. (2011). *Fine-grained censorship mapping: Information sources, legality and ethics*. 1st USENIX workshop on free and open communications on the internet (FOCI'11) (USENIX Security Symposium), San Francisco.

Xu, X., Morley Mao, Z., & Alex Halderman, J. (2011). Internet censorship in China: Where does the filtering occur? In *Proceedings of the 12th passive and active measurement conference (PAM)* (pp. 133–142). Vienna: Springer.

Yang, G. (2009). *The power of the internet in China: Citizen activism online*. New York, NY: Columbia University Press.

Appendix 1. Tested domain names

A1.1 Potentially blocked

Top 80 reported blocked domains for China retrieved from the Herdict project

www.torproject.org	wikileaks.com	flickr.com
www.google.com	www.backchina.com	t.co
mail.live.com	huffingtonpost.com	www.livejournal.com
www.blogger.com	www.ntdtv.com	www.twitzap.com
dropbox.com	www.rthk.org.hk	killerjo.net
www.wretch.cc	www.abuoluowang.com	www.paltalk.com
vimeo.com	www.voanews.com	www.pinyinannotator.com
www.scribd.com	www.wenxuecity.com	www.python.org
anchorfree.com	www.dw-world.de	www.midwest-itc.org
developer.android.com	zh.wikipedia.org	www.cafepress.com
www.gmail.com	www.danwei.org	tar.weatherson.org
www.demonoid.com	news.bbc.co.uk	secure.wikimedia.org
www.bing.com	www.peacehall.com	theviennawilsons.net
thepiratebay.org	www.youtube.com	www.gamebase.com.tw
piratebay.org	www.facebook.com	www.newgrounds.com
www.hotspotshield.com	twitter.com	angrychineseblogger.blog-city.com
www.box.net	www.wujie.net	www.open.com.hk
mail.google.com	www.6park.com	bbs.sina.com
chinagfw.org	www.steves-digicams.com	www.mitbbs.com
blogspot.com	www.hotmail.com	www.parantezbaz.com
wikileaks.org	www.x365x.com	www.aixin119.com
www.tibet.net	www.wenku.com	english.rti.org.tw
www.boxun.com	picasaweb.google.com	www.ahrchk.net
www.bbc.co.uk	www.camfrog.com	mashable.com
wezhiyong.org	www.tumblr.com	www.siqo.com
www.bullogger.com	www.foursquare.com	www.websitepulse.com
www.rfa.org	www.imdb.com	

A1.2 Unfiltered reference domains

The following domains represent popular Chinese services that were anticipated not to be blocked within China, used as a test of the results returned by queried DNS servers

baidu.com	qq.com	caixin.com
renren.com	chinaview.cn	

Appendix 2. Filtering techniques

Murdoch and Anderson (2008) categorize internet filtering approaches into four major families, largely according to the means by which traffic to be filtered is *recognized*, rather than the specific mechanism of blocking. These four categories, along with a fifth hybrid category, are discussed here.

A2.1 TCP/IP Header filtering

IP, the internet protocol, is the fundamental standard that largely determines the format and mechanisms by which computers are identified and located on the internet, and by which traffic passes from network to network. Fundamental to IP is the encoding of data into a series of discrete IP *packets,* which contain information such as the numerical address of the sending computer and the recipient, and the content of the data itself. Filtering may occur through inspection of the *header* of an IP packet, which details the packet's destination.

In terms of filtering, therefore, packets may be filtered according to lists of banned destination IP addresses. This method is simple and effective, but difficult to maintain due to the potential for services to change, or to have multiple, IP addresses. This approach may also incur significant collateral damage in the case of services that share IP addresses, causing multiple innocent services to be blocked along with the desired target.

A2.2 TCP/IP content filtering

Rather than inspecting the header of packets, a filter may search the *content,* or *body*, of packets for banned terms. This presents a far more flexible approach to filtering, allowing packets to be blocked only if they include banned keywords or the traffic signatures of particular applications. This approach is also known as *deep packet inspection*, and is known to be employed to some extent by the Chinese national firewall. Deep packet inspection can be partially defeated by using encrypted connections, which obfuscate the data stored in the body of the packets, however filters may choose simply to block all encrypted connections in response, or to block traffic according to identifying traffic signatures that can occur even in encrypted protocols. The most significant limitation of this approach is that inspection of traffic content comes at a significant computational cost.

A2.3 DNS poisoning

The Domain Name Service, or DNS, maps human-readable names, such as bbc.co.uk, to numerical IP addresses usable by computers for routing data, such as 212.58.241.131. The DNS is thus critical for most user-focused services such as the web. By altering DNS responses, returning either empty or false results, a filter can simply and cheaply block or redirect requests. This mechanism is simple to employ and maintain, but limits filters to entire websites, and can be relatively easy to bypass for technical users. DNS manipulation, or *poisoning,* is often employed as a first approach to web-based filtering, due to its low resource requirements and in spite of its ease of bypass; it has been noted that states typically being with DNS filtering before graduating to more sophisticated filtering techniques over time (Deibert et al., 2008).

A2.4 HTTP proxy filtering

A more sophisticated approach to filtering, to reduce resource requirements whilst maintaining flexibility, is to pass all internet traffic through an intermediary *proxy server* that fetches and, typically, caches information for users. This is a common internet service that can be used to speed up internet connections and reduce traffic. A suitably enabled proxy can, however, employ sophisticated filtering on certain destinations, whilst leaving other connections alone. This approach can, by ignoring the majority of traffic, be efficient on a national scale while still allowing for detailed filtering similar to TCP/IP content filtering.

A2.5 Other approaches

Various other means can be taken to regulate content on the internet. States can request that websites are removed from the internet, either by taking down their servers or by removing their names from the global DNS records. A state may also choose not to block a connection entirely, but to slow any connection to that site to unusable levels. It is also common for some nations to force the takedown of posts on internet forums and social media websites in order to control debate; this is extremely common in the case of China and the Sina Weibo microblogging service (King et al., 2012). At a less technical level, legal and social constraints can be imposed to make access to certain services illegal or socially unacceptable.

Index